To Pete,
Life is short. Do two
fun things everyday!
Jack Livingston

A Lot Like Fun — Only Different

Chris jumping from a covered bridge into the Battenkill River - 1998

Jack Livingston

NFB Publishing
Buffalo, New York

For Mar, who is the best listener I know.

Acknowledgments

I am indebted to the following people for their contributions to this book:

To Rick Ohler, for looking over every word I wrote. You gave me enough rope to hang myself, and when I did, you'd cut me down, and give me your suggestions. Your seemingly carefree style could never disguise the passionate desire to help me make this book the best it could be.

To my first readers, Barb Taylor and Bob Herrmann, for your encouragement that helped me believe my words were worth reading. To Steve Eoannou and Vicki Rohl, for your advice and many suggestions. And especially to Shaylyn Livingston, for insisting I needed to see what Chris thought about all of this. Your idea made the last chapter the best chapter.

To Chris's family and friends, especially Brent Kelley, Jennifer Kelley, Diane Damon, Paul Sugnet, Dave Norton, Mike Lazickas, Mac McCready, Peter Diebolt, Thad Rice, Shai Ben-Dor, and Shaohai Yu for patiently answering my questions about those things I needed help remembering and for those things I came to understand about my friend Chris, for the first time.

To more than I can practically list, for graciously allowing me to use photographs of you. And to those that provided pictures: Jennifer, for that wonderful picture from Singapore, Diane Damon for the picture of Sandra Lee, Alex Sowyrda for the picture of the brew crew at the Five Cow Sugar Shanty, and to Paul Sugnet, Bill Shanahan, and Dave Norton, who provided pictures from so many years ago on the mighty Battenkill. The pictures added so much to each chapter.

To Mar for never tiring of listening to me talk about my ideas for the book and gently giving me your opinions and suggestions. I listened to all of them and acted on most.

Never be so focused on what you're looking for that you overlook the thing you actually find.

Ann Patchette, *State of Wonder*

Contents

When Jack Livingston announced a few years ago, "Hey, I'm working on a book about Chris Kelley—about all of our adventures before he got sick and how we're still hanging together," I didn't even let him finish his sentence before I said I was all-in. As a writing teacher and freelance editor, all manner of potential editing projects, from novels to poetry to memoir, come my way, but this project excited me more than any I can remember. It was such a damn good idea, a noble idea, a heartwarming idea, to chronicle a genuine friendship that was enduring even in the face of Pick's Disease, a progressive form of dementia that began attacking Chris's brain in his mid-50s.

I knew it would be a daunting task for Jack—for any writer. On one hand he would have to tell the story truthfully enough that it would make engaging reading and perhaps, be helpful to others in the same situation. But he would also have to use discretion, holding Chris and his family lovingly and supportively in his heart at the same time.

When you read *A Lot Like Fun—Only Different*, you will see that Jack has succeeded on both counts. As the title suggests, there's plenty of fun, oh yes. With Chris as their leader, Jack and a colorful cast of characters—great friends from as far back as high school—embark on grand—if occasionally ill-advised—hiking, biking, skiing, boating adventures, some of which end in uproarious mishaps and all of which are celebrated with "a couple-tree beers."

Jack tackles the "different," as well. He describes the harsh realities of losing a great friend, bit by bit, to dementia. He shows how a strong family and loyal friends can take a difficult situation and make the best of it.

It might sound like a contradiction in terms to say that a book with fun in the title is a labor of love. But that's just what it is. You won't find a writer who labors harder than Jack Livingston. We spent many mornings in several coffee shops going over every word, sentence, paragraph and chapter of *A Lot Like Fun — Only Different* to fine tune the writing and to make sure Jack had been fair, forthcoming and entertaining, as well. And love? You'll discover the love Jack has for his friend on every page, as he gives Chris the voice the disease has taken from him.

A Lot Like Fun — Only Different, is a testimony to a friendship that has spanned five decades. So far.

Thad Rice, the Geek, Chris, Wally, me, and Caz at our camp-ground on the shores of the Battenkill River - 2002

Is That All You Got?

IT HAD SOUNDED LIKE *fun*, but that's how Chris described everything when he enlisted us for another adventure. What he meant, of course, was *a lot like fun—only different*. Fun was far from my thoughts on that day in 2002, with the wind howling on the Battenkill River, threatening to pluck our canoes from the water and smash them against boulders the retreating glaciers had so carelessly left in their wake. I'm not ashamed to tell you, I was scared. He'd done it again. How did Chris talk me into these things?

Five of us paddled furiously against the wind, attempting to pierce the choppy waves of the boiling river. We aimed two canoes and a kayak toward shore, but the storm repelled our efforts, playing with our battle-scarred vessels, cupping us in one hand and dropping us into the other. A surge of water pushed us laterally in the irregular troughs. If we breached, we'd be screwed. Chris was in the stern of one canoe, or as he would have corrected me, "Jeeesus, Jack, it's the back," ruddering his paddle deep in the sawtooth waters while Wally, in the bow (front), pulled for shore. The Geek and I struggled to stay afloat, yelling over the wind that sounded like a freight train whooshing past. Chris laughed—I braced for catastrophe.

He yelled at Caz paddling in his kayak, "Caz, what the *fuck* are you doing?"

Caz was doing it all wrong. Of course he was. I suppose in Chris's mind none of us got it right very often, but somehow we had all made it to this point, queued up as human sacrifices to the wind and river gods.

"Geek, this thing is going to flip!" I hollered, envisioning myself bobbing in the river like a sodden cork, sliding beneath the surface, smashing my head against algae-covered rocks, and guzzling a mouthful of the Battenkill. Drowning. *I hate when that happens.*

"The bridge! Get under the bridge!" I pleaded with the Geek.

"I know! I'm trying!"

21

Despite Caz *doing it all wrong*, he'd gained on us. Maybe it was the Geek and I who were *doing it all wrong*. We crashed through the waves toward the small bridge fifty yards downriver. As we got closer, the bridge acted like a funnel, channeling the fierce winds toward us. I yelled to the Geek, but the wind snatched my words and hurled them in the river. I imagined our campsite a few miles downstream; gear tossed helter-skelter and tents hanging from the trees like shredded kites.

We banged into the bridge footer, and I sunk my fingernails into the eroding concrete like a grappling hook. Extending an arm, I prepared to come alongside Chris and Wally, but the river had other ideas, spinning us out of control like a 1976 AMC Pacer on an icy Western New York road. We collided into their canoe, an angry fist slamming into an empty 55 gallon drum. As we tipped, inches from submerging below the roiling waters, Chris clamped onto our canoe with his gnarled claw of a hand, righting it.

"Wally, pull forward. Fuck the paddle," yelled Chris.

Caz came alongside us and like a flotilla of hinged percussion instruments we clanged to the off-beat in the turgid river, shivering in temperatures that had dropped twenty degrees in ten minutes. In the distance, jagged lightning stabbed the mountains, followed by muffled thunder.

"Did you see that?" I yelled.

No one answered. And then it started. The rain, like pins pricking our skin.

"I'm getting out. I don't want to get fucking electrocuted in a canoe." I stood up. The canoe rose in the waves as if a giant hand pushed the bow from beneath. And the wind, sensing my vulnerability, shoved me hard, sending me sprawling. I smashed my elbow against the thwart behind my seat. "Fuck!" I knelt in the canoe with one hand on the gunwale and the other hanging in front of my face, a ridiculously poor shield from the raindrops pummeling my face and bare chest. The torrent came at us sideways, thrown at us, rather than raining down from above.

"Wally, put your paddle against that rock. Geek, grab that. Not that. *That!* Caz, are you getting out or what?" Chris barked commands like a drill sergeant. We followed his directions; what did we have to lose? It's not like Chris ever suggested something that would cause us bodily harm. *Sure.*

Overhead, the sky dripped with dark clouds, and the wind continued its tuneless caterwauling. I looked to the heavens, knowing I wouldn't see a wicked witch pedaling a bike with a wicker basket on the back as spinning houses crashed to earth. That's movie stuff. Still, I looked again just to make sure nothing was coming at us.

Chris and the Geek pulled our canoe from the water, flipping it upside down. The paddles, our beer, and my backpack dumped onto the inclined riverbank.

"The beer! Jack, grab the beer!" Chris yelled like his wallet was about to slide through a sewer grate. "And the paddles."

Shivering in the numbing wind, I grabbed the paddles while rain sheeted across my glasses rendering them useless.

"The beer, Jack! Grab the fucking beer!"

Yeah, Chris. I know. I get it. I'll grab the beer.

We huddled together on the banks of the Battenkill, shirtless, arms across our chests, losing our core heat to the wind gods, freezing our asses off.

Chris loved it. He stood, arms spread wide, smiling, daring the gods to have their way with him. "Is that all you got?!" he hollered.

The wind dug deeper, exhaling a furious burst. Chris wavered slightly, still smiling, his feet firmly planted. And he challenged them one more time, "Is that all you got?!"

The gods tried their best to defeat us, but failed. Chris laughed. We all laughed.

The next day we read in the local paper: "TORNADO TOUCHES DOWN IN BATTENKILL RIVER NEAR CENTER FALLS"

Me and Chris at Hunter's Creek Park - 2017

My Friend Chris

I'VE SPENT THE better part of 45 years watching my friend Chris come at life full speed, with hard-nosed obstinance, without regard for authority, convention, or concerns for his safety. He could be fractious, rebellious, unruly, contrary, contumacious, defiant, indomitable, insubordinate, intractable, opposing, radical, refractory, and uncontrollable. But understand, Chris had his reasons. I believe he was like this because so many times "things" got in the way of what he wanted to do. Things that he considered to be "bullshit." Recalcitrant is the word that best described this aspect of his personality. It's almost as if the word had been coined especially for Chris. I could tell you he was stubborn, but to do so would be selling him short. No, Chris was thoroughly recalcitrant.

Not to say I would've spoken such a word in his presence. He would have chewed it up and spit it back in my face, "Recalcitrant? Jeeesus, Jack! What the fuck is that?!" Then he'd stretch its syllables like it was a sentence all by itself, "Re-cal-ci-trant," and if I had explained to him what it meant, he would've tormented me with examples of recalcitrance, punctuating each instance with, "Re-cal-ci-trant, Jack."

We've been great friends, but Chris scared me, especially when we were younger. It wasn't that he was evil, but at times he appeared like the shape-shifting clown in Stephen King's *It* looking at me from a raging storm drain, daring me to join him. "It's going to be great, Jack!" So for most of my high school days, while Chris was skipping school; pounding twelve packs on school nights; pogeying down Main Street at 50mph; organizing a group to set fire to the totem pole of rival Iroquois Central; embracing full-contact bowling, golf, anything; and smoke bombing the high school, I avoided him, fearing serious injury, trouble with my parents, school suspension, or arrest.

At some point in my mid-thirties, Chris and I reconnected. He seized upon my thirst for adventure, tests of endurance, camaraderie, and "doing two fun things in one day." Surely enough time had passed since his single-brain-cell thinking days of high school. We had families by then, for God's sake. Chris said it would be great, and I believed him.

I wasn't prepared for what was to come.

I'd be lying if I told you he goaded me into riding the rim-bending trails of our 24-hour mountain bike races, snowshoeing to the top of mountains in howling windstorms, joining "Hockey Night in Colden" knowing full well there'd be injuries, and all sorts of other things that endeared me to him. I went willingly. There were no velvet ropes that limited entrance to Chris's world. I just had to say, "Sure, I'll do that with you."

There was no instruction, no guidance, no manual for what you should bring along; he left that all up to you. At times, it was as if I had agreed to ride a mechanical bull and suddenly was on a real live bucking bronco. I'd brag to friends, who watched from a safe distance, "Look at me, look what I'm doing." I'd show off for another second before the "bronco" would throw its hindquarters in the air, sending me sprawling to turf peppered with horseshit and human guts that hadn't been raked clear from the last rider. Like a fool, I'd wait my turn for another ride. Why did I do it? Because Chris was cool, it made me feel cool, and I craved the adventure.

It didn't matter what it was we were doing. He'd frequently remind us, "You're doing it all wrong," or get frustrated if, in his opinion, we weren't moving fast enough. But he'd always manage to sprinkle in a bit of praise and motivation. "Nice riding, Jack," and "You know, there's cold beer waiting."

Not everybody got this about Chris, but it wouldn't be because he treated them any differently. A jalapeño is a jalapeno; some people can handle the heat, some can't. I liked the taste, and so it was that Chris and I became the best of friends. I counted on him to conjure up "epic" expeditions for me—for all of us. And at the end of every adventure, we'd catch our breath, inventory our wounds, crack open a "couple tree" beers, and Chris would instruct us, "Beers up, beers in," and remind us that, "Life is short."

Our days rarely ended with a tidy click of closure when we finished telling our stories from the past; no, it was more like trying to sit on an overstuffed suitcase. Eventually, we'd realize we had other things to do that day, or in Chris's case, we'd run out of beer. At that point we'd sit on our suitcase of memories until we got it closed and secured the whole mess with a bungee cord. We liked telling our stories; it bonded us. And we liked making people laugh, the ones who had wished they'd been there.

Chris led me to places I might not have experienced, unlocking things that couldn't be opened with keys or codes. For him, it was about pushing the limits and trying to get others to join him. While doing just that I discovered amazing places and formed an unbreakable friendship.

Why do I tell you this? Why have I spent the last two years writing about the unforgettable times we've shared? You see, my friend Chris is dying. His hands drumming *rat-ta-tat-tat-rat-ta-tat-tat* on his well-worn blue jeans, his incessant pacing down a path of invisible stepping stones in his hallway, his one-word answers to my questions signal the fading of a friend. Chris has Pick's disease, a rare type of dementia..

Pick's doesn't make the headlines like the big killers: cancer, HIV/AIDS, diabetes. Even COPD has been getting some love from the major drug companies. There aren't any commercials showing those afflicted with Pick's strolling hand-in-hand with their loved ones along a sandy beach, smiling, knowing they've staved off a deadly disease. Pick's doesn't have a cure.

Western New Yorkers will recognize the name Ted Darling, former "Voice of the Buffalo Sabres." His performance began to suffer and his behavior became erratic, causing some people to think he had an alcohol problem. In October 1991, Darling was diagnosed with the disease and was placed on medical leave for a month. He returned to call six more games before being relieved of his duties. He was brought back, however, as a studio analyst for games in the 1992-93 season before announcing his retirement. After a five-year battle with Pick's, he died on December 19, 1996, at the age of 61.

Pick's disease affects parts of the brain that control emotions, behavior, personality, and language. It's also known as frontotemporal dementia (FTD) or frontotemporal lobar degeneration (FTLD). A healthy brain uses a transport system to help move around the nutrients it needs. This system is made up of proteins that act like railroad tracks guiding nutrients where they need to go. And the proteins that keep the tracks straight are called tau proteins. Chris's tau proteins aren't working the way they should. His abnormal clumps of tau proteins, called Pick bodies, are derailing his transport system's railroad tracks. Chris's tracks are no longer straight, and the nutrients in his brain can't get where they need to go, causing irreversible brain damage. Those afflicted with Pick's are susceptible to abrupt mood changes, compulsive and/or inappropriate behavior, disinterest in routine activities, repetitive behavior, deteriorating social skills, and less than adequate personal hygiene. Chris hit the "jackpot." He's had all of these symptoms, at one time or another.

If Chris was reading these words, he'd remind me, "Jeeesus, Jack, nobody wants to read about any of this bullshit. Tell 'em our stories."

And I'd tell him, "I know, I know, I'm getting to that, just be patient." By now I should know better. Chris patient? *Sure.*

So out of respect for him I'll let you look up the details about Pick's, but I'll give you a primer on its ability to chip away at the brain with the subtlety of a pickaxe. Back when Chris was still able to form multi-word sentences he would have explained, like he did so often, "It's a lot like fun—only different." And then he'd bellow the laugh we had come to know so well. It was a laugh with the heartiness of a savory beef stew and as discriminating as a wrecking ball in the Corning Museum of Glass. That was before. Before it turned into a laugh that would get him in trouble. Who laughs at the sight of an armed security guard at an airport? Who laughs at a New York State Trooper who has pulled you over for speeding? Who laughs when he hears that a lifelong friend has had some serious health trouble? Who laughs at the fat man running? Okay, maybe that one, but geez, be a little discreet about it. It was just Chris being Chris, we would say, shrugging it off. If we had known then what we know now, maybe we would have reacted differently, and understood that his behavior was a symptom of something more serious than a momentary lapse of judgment. Maybe we could have been quicker to respond with empathy, and tried to help as we do now. Today his laugh is still there, but it's different, a pre-programmed laugh track on an endless loop.

Unfortunately, this isn't *Tuesdays with Morrie.* I can't sit with Chris and have a friendly conversation while he feeds me sage wisdom on how to live the rest of my life, learning from mistakes, and making good choices that will have a lasting impact on those we love. No, that isn't possible. Over the past year it's been more like *Weekend at Bernie's*. Chris is with us, walking, pacing, in the room, but more like a prop in our life. That's not to say you won't find these pages scattered with pearls of his wisdom; you just might have to take a closer look, a deeper dive. Chris has spent a lifetime smearing, jamming, shoving, cramming, and when all else failed using his charming penchant for insolence to grace all of us, his friends, with his opinions about everything. If we got off track he'd trip us, grab us by the neck, pin us to the ground, and hold us down until we took his medicine.

My collection of stories, from a lifetime of friendship, ping around my head needing a place to land, to escape. They're like that old video game, Breakout. Remember that one? That little square of white hitting those colored rectangles. Slow at first, and then picking up speed as more and more rectangles were obliterated. The time I spend with Chris now helps me capture these memories. I smile and laugh as I remember these times, but it also makes me sad. It makes all of us, his friends and his family, get in touch with just how fragile life can be. One second you're conquering a tornado on the Battenkill, or riding down a rocky ridge on a mountain bike, the next you need someone to change your diaper.

I won't be offended if you say, *thanks for the info, but I think maybe I'll just read something a bit more uplifting, or if I want to be completely terrified, I'll grab myself one of them Steve King books. At least I'll know the scary clown isn't real, it's just a story.* To those who might cry out, "Hey, you've got it wrong, man. Why didn't you write about the time Chris and I ..." Well I'm sorry, I know some of you have your own Chris stories, but maybe you should "Write your own damn book!"[1] I need to tell you, Chris isn't an easy subject. He's a bacon-wrapped enigma in a sugar-coated conundrum. Some things aren't meant to be completely understood. It's not that I think I have it all figured out just because I'm the guy that wrote "the book." It's only now that I try to make sense of those times with Chris.

---

[1] These aren't my words. I've heard them often while writing about my friend Chris. I've asked my friend, Rick Ohler, on frequent occasions, "What about Wally's stories?", or "What about all the times with his family?", or "What if I've left out someone important, or I screwed up a critical detail?" To this Rick would reply, without hesitation, "Let them write their own damn book." Thanks for keeping me focused, Rick. I know Chris appreciates it.

You may wonder if I've blended some ragged edged fiction into the very true tale of my friend Chris. Take my word on this. If I had, you wouldn't be able to separate fact from fiction.

So here are my Chris stories, almost three dozen of them, told to the best of my ability to reconstruct them. The stories are not in chronological order, but rather, in the order they came to me while on our current hikes and after visits with Chris's friends and family. I'm grateful for the help I've received from those who understand that there will be no more stories, so we need to keep the ones we have. I'll do my best to put on a smiling face as I tell them, to have one last laugh, a laugh that will remain. But my smile will be a mask; I miss my friend. These few pages are what I can give him in gratitude for his friendship. You were right, Chris; life *is* short. And now, we can't do all those things we used to do and it makes me remember them more, it makes me wish we could go back to those days; one more ride, one more snowshoe expedition, one more "Beers up, beers in," and one more wild ride down the Battenkill.

Janelle and Chris at Chestnut Ridge Park - 2019

The Go-To

High school friends and family have been pitching in to do things with Chris, giving his wife Jennifer a break. We help out because he's our friend, our brother, our uncle, our dad; he's Chris. I suppose some might feel obligated to help, but I hike with Chris because it's what we have always done—spent time with each other doing normal things, crazy dangerous things, stuff that I would've never attempted, or even considered, if not for him.

Spending time with Chris these days isn't exciting like it used to be, but I still look forward to our outings. They give me compassion for his unusual behavior: laughing at smiling strangers, refusal to cut his long girly fingernails, and locking himself in the bathroom, to name a few. In the moment I might laugh or smile, but later I think about it and I'm sad enough to cry. I haven't yet, maybe a bit of the watery eyes. I think he'd be okay with my emotions. Back in the days when Chris was speaking in complete sentences, he'd get emotional over our friendship.

Chris would tell us, "Jack, you and the Geek, and me ... I don't know what I'd do without you guys ... you guys are ..."

"Yeah, Chris, we know. Now knock it off," we'd tell him and laugh. Hard-assed Chris was who we were comfortable with, not reflective Chris.

Before COVID-19 impacted our routine I made an attempt to spend time with him every week. When the weather is warm, we've hiked and when the weather is cold we've hiked. We've even got out snowshoeing despite him staring at the smallest fissure in the ice or a narrow stream crossing like he's Evel Knievel preparing to jump the Snake River Canyon. And then when we were done with that day's trek, he'll stand by the car looking at me.

"What?" I'll ask him.

He'll look into the sky searching for something before settling his vacant stare on me.

"Are you going to take off your snowshoes, or what?"

"Nooo."

"Did you need help? Do you want me to take them off?"

"Yes," he'll chuckle.

"What the hell, Chris?"

The first time that happened, I'd figured he was busting my balls, but he just smiled. Now, I know he's not, so I dutifully kneel before him, releasing the straps on his snowshoes and helping him step out of the bindings.

THE NEWS about Chris hit all of us hard. His nephew, Alex, told me first, "Oh, by the way, did you hear? Chris has this frontal lobe thing. There's no cure. He's got like two to ten years." *Well that explains a few things. Thanks for the info.* Yes, things have changed. No longer do I receive Chris's calls to join his hair raising, hell raising, eyebrow raising adventures testing us against the elements of nature. Now it's our turn. These days *we're* the ones taking *Chris* on an adventure.

It's not like it came as a shock. There were signs; we just didn't realize what they were trying to tell us. In particular, Chris had developed a penchant for repetitive storytelling. Those stories went beyond remembering our fun times, reliving them over a "couple tree" beers and a pizza in the barroom at Wallenwein's. He began to repeat everything, as if by doing so he was tightening his grip on the remaining fragments of his memory.

"Yeah, Chris. We know. You told us."

There was no stopping the stories. Telling him that we'd heard all of it just yesterday was like trying to stop a tractor trailer barreling down the I90 with a roadblock of Boston cream pies.

It was his son-in-law, Dan Glover, who I'd first heard call them "go-to" stories, I suppose a kind of mnemonic for Chris. In some cases there were go-to stories that were meant to be private; still he'd blast it right out there for everyone to hear. He must have told me a couple dozen times about my daughter, Janelle. "You know, Jack. I know you had problems with her when she was a teenager, but she's a peach."

"Chris?" I'd nod in the direction of Janelle, widening my eyes in the hopes that he'd understand my daughter was right next to us and that I'd rather she not hear what I may, or may not have discussed a decade ago regarding the trials and tribulations of raising a teenager. He'd blow through those Boston cream pies, not picking up my non-verbal cue, laughing the great big laugh, the fun laugh, and his shoulders would rise and fall as he grabbed me around my neck with his brawny hands.

And then he'd proceed full steam ahead with the go-to.

"I remember that time at the gym. There was a guy. He'd passed out and your daughter Janelle went right over to him. She got down on the floor to help the guy while everyone else stood around doing nothing." He'd punctuate the tragedy with a laugh, as if the whole scene was an episode from a TV sitcom. And then he'd bellow, "The guy was huge!" He'd laugh stretching his arms like the wings of a condor, ending the go-to with a smile, telling me, "She's a peach, Jack—a real peach."

There used to be more to the story. The details of Chris's go-tos have faded like the once crisp VHS tape of a long ago family reunion. To say they'd fallen through the cracks of his brain would seem cliché, even a bit insensitive (not that Chris would care). But I didn't think of it like that. He was our mighty oak. It was autumn, approaching winter, and our oak that had once held its leaves tightly, couldn't hold them any longer. Chris's leaves are falling. Every day more fall. Some fall at his feet, and others, sensing a greater purpose, are scattered by the winds.

But there are stories to tell. Life is short; let's get started with The Carrot Finger.

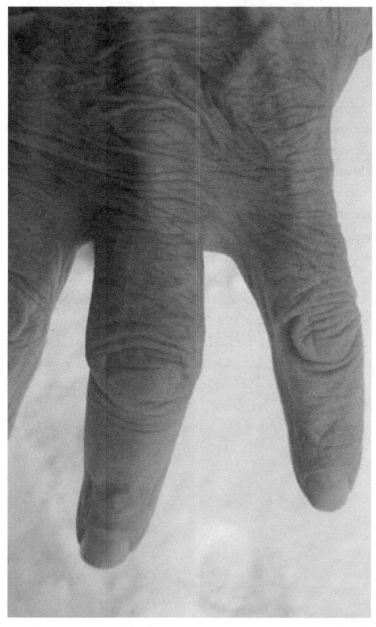

Chris's Carrot Finger - 2019

The Carrot Finger

I T'S A WARM Saturday morning in the middle of September and the parking lot bustles with the routine maneuvers of dog walkers and people "getting in their steps." A speedy dork walker in pastel pink yoga pants flashes in front of me; it's not a good look, and I rubberneck like I might look at a car accident on the other side of the highway. I turn my attention back to the Newton Road entrance of Chestnut Ridge Park. Chris's driving days are over, so it's the Geek's van I'm keeping a watch for.

We hike with Chris because among other things, he's always been so much more interested in what's going on outside as compared to the restrictive walls of inside. Chris had reminded us often, "The fat-assed Buffalonians love the great indoors." *Hey, hey! Chris, that's our city and our neighbors you're talking about. You might be kind of right, but do you have to say fat-assed?* And so it was, we spent most of our time together outdoors.

Perhaps that was one of the reasons, for most of his adult life, he despised going to church. The stained-glass windows with pictures of long haired women and men wrapped in colorful robes, adorned with yellow halos would have screened his view of the outside. Chris probably would have interpreted Jesus, with his arms spread wide, as an invitation for him to come out and play. Of course if those stained-glass windows had been cranked open, Chris would have found the means to wedge his way outside; just like he did in his senior year of high school. Skipping classes 60 times! It takes a pretty smart guy to miss 60 days of school, in one year, and still graduate something like number 212 out of 260; or maybe the powers that were, had concluded that it was best to heave the live hand grenade named Chris Kelley off school grounds, before it exploded.

THE GEEK was running late. It couldn't be Chris, he was always on time; it had to be the Geek. He's diligent about his penchant for tardiness. I won't say anything about it today like I would've in the past.

A few years ago I might have jabbed them, "You guys are late!"

Chris's eyes would bulge, "Don't look at me!" and he'd snap his head in the direction of the Geek like a hammer pounding a nail. "Geek *had* to say goodbye to Cindy!" he'd castigate the Geek for the mortal sin he had committed. *Really Geek, come on, did you have to kiss your wife goodbye. There are incidents that await our instigation.* And so it would go. We'd laugh and get on with that day's adventure, taking it to the edge and when we were done, drink a "couple tree" beers. Regarding the inevitable incidents, Chris had this expression, however figurative or facetious, but a mantra nonetheless: "Everything's funny, unless there's spinal damage." You need to understand the stuff Chris did lent itself to physical calamity. During our adventures, we'd experienced punctured lungs, mountaintop hernias, cracked bike helmets, fractured collar bones, cleaved lips, and of course the hilarious intestinal nightmare, giardia. And always, Chris managed to laugh. Spinal damage is where things became serious; on this point we were in agreement.

Understand that "It's funny as long as there's no spinal damage," was a catchphrase we used, nothing more. But Chris found laughter watching us struggle, feeling pain, catapulting our way through a gruesome fall, mashing our faces, pulling a "hammy," or knocking back a shot of 58 proof Ratzeputz schnapps during "Hockey Night." Conversely, if Chris witnessed the less fortunate struggle, he'd laugh, maybe even make fun of them, but then he'd be the first at their side to help out, albeit in his jagged-edged way. He'd provide an able hand, doing it his way, dousing the moment with a heaping tablespoon of uplifting levity. Making sure they understood they had been doing it all wrong.

Chris is now a creature of habits: same trail, same cereal for breakfast, same clothes, same tapping beat on his pant legs, same bathroom break halfway through our hike near the creek, same steps around the island countertop in his kitchen. And he sleeps a lot.

So I wait. I don't mind.

I see them on Newton Road before they pull into the parking lot. I know it's them, not because I can see their faces through the windshield, or because I know the make and model of Geek's van. I don't even remember the color—maybe it's kind of gray. I know it's them because of the bike rack. It's pink.

It was many years ago when I first saw it. While I silently wondered why the Geek had just acquired a pink bike rack, Chris opened the topic for discussion, squalling, "A *pink* bike rack?!"

"Yeah, Chris, it's breast cancer awareness," the Geek defended his purchase. Chris laughed.

Good for you Geek, it takes a real man to buy a pink bike rack.

Later that day, the Geek explained, "I didn't realize I'd bought a pink one until I got it home and unpacked the box. I thought I'd be a real heel taking it back to the store for a gray one." *That's okay Geek; you're still a good guy.* Pink things seem to find their way to him. On a recent ski trip out west we found a pink flip flop in a snowy parking lot (I have no idea) and a pink binky in the same lot the following day. He hung them off the rear wiper of our rented van for the rest of the trip. When we turned in the van he plucked them off the wiper and stuffed them in his luggage. He added these trinkets to the pink bike rack. *Which is kind of nice.*

He pulls up next to me and I push the button for my passenger window. "Hey, Geek."

"Hey, Jack."

"Too bad you guys just missed the pink yoga pants."

Chris twists in his seat so he can get a better look at me and I see his smirky smile. He doesn't ask me how I'm doing, or even shout, "What's up!" He just laughs as if I have egg on my face, or mustard on my shirt, or a big zit on my nose, or maybe I'm just a funny guy to look at.

"Good morning, Mr. Kelley." Lately, for some unknown reason I've taken to calling Chris by his last name.

Still, he has no words for me.

We drive to the trailhead and park. Chris stares at me through the passenger window. Is he waiting for something? I stand by my door as he looks at me with that tight lipped goofy smile, like he swallowed a canary. *What's he waiting for? Geez Louise, are we now at a point where we have to open the door for him?* And then I get it. *He's waiting for me.* He doesn't say anything, but I'm sure he's thinking, close your fucking door, idiot, so I can get out. The cars are parked too close together to get our doors open at the same time. I close my door quickly before he has a chance to ram Geek's van door into mine. The Geek probably wouldn't care—but I would. Chris would think a dent in my door was hilarious. It'd be nothing as legendary as the rear window of Thad Rice's SUV exploding into a million glass prisms when an errant bocce ball fell from the heavens. I'll get to that later.

Chris waits for me. There will be no car door smashing today. No exploding windows. I shake his hand, pulling him into me for a hug. "This one isn't from me, it's from Mar." I hope he remembers my wife. If he does I'm sure he'd rather have a kiss from her, but a hug is all he's getting. I give him one more hug from me. He breaks free from our embrace and before I can pull out my bug spray he's stomping down the trail.

I look at the Geek, "Alrighty then, I guess we're ready to go." We follow Chris. He's moving fast.

I think of the hand I'd just shaken. I could close my eyes, shake a thousand hands, and would know which one was Chris's, unless, of course, it was his brother Brent's, whom I've recently gotten to know better on our Tuesday hikes with Chris. Apparently, it's a Kelley thing, the strong wrinkled hands, like grabbing a piece of 80-grit sandpaper, but prune-y as if they'd been in a swimming pool all afternoon.

If Chris had told me once, he'd told me seventeen times, "You know, Jack. When I was doing roofing, I'd hang my hands out the window of the van in the middle of winter while we were driving to the job. No gloves. My hands were freezing!"

"Why? Why didn't you wear gloves?" I could have proceeded with further questioning, but I felt two whys adequately addressed the absurdity of the situation.

Chris would explain, "So when I was working they'd feel warm. You know, compared to how they felt hanging out the window in the cold at 60 mph."

Sure Chris, whatever you say. It kind of made sense. A lot of what Chris said and did, kind of made sense. But of course it kind of *didn't* make sense, either.

And what hand wouldn't be complete without a middle finger shaped like a carrot? It was a carrot that had appeared to have struggled while growing in hardpan soil. Surprisingly, Chris didn't use his middle finger like you might think. That wasn't his way. Despite its hideously disproportionate appearance, it served him well, not holding him back from anything he did, although hand modeling was categorically off the table, except maybe for the Burpee Seed catalogue.

I don't want to get ahead of the story. But I'll let you know the carrot finger was only a mild misfortune in comparison to a long line of calamities that had befallen Chris as a youngster. For instance, there was the time when Chris was only in kindergarten and was abducted, along with his two brothers, by his father, Paul Nimon. Paul's girlfriend was an accomplice, joining the ride across the country with her three sons. Six young boys with two irresponsible adults settled in Elko, Nevada, living out of a motel. After a month of "detective" work, his mother and his Uncle John, whose one arm was punctuated with a hook for a hand, retrieved them as if it had all been a long vacation.

There was the time when Chris was in high school and the father he knew best, his step-father, Bud Kelley, died suddenly from a heart attack. He was only 55.

And then there was the smoke bomb incident in our senior year of high school that resulted in the entire center of learning sitting outside on a warm day in June for most of third and fourth periods while the EAFD cleared the building. Unfortunately, it also resulted in Chris having discussions with the cops.

So in comparison, the carrot finger wasn't a big deal. Despite it all, he'd done all right for himself and his family. Chris, like the carrot finger, is misshapen and rough on the outside, not a thing of beauty, but at the same time, something to admire. The carrot finger is filled with metal pins, swollen at the knuckle, bent and tapered like a carrot. Was he born with that grotesque thing? Was he transformed into a hideous beast, until love would find him? No, as always, there was an incident.

Chris had had quite a few jobs, especially toward the end of his working career. We thought he'd lost the jobs because he was just pissing people off, people that didn't have a tolerance for his brazen impertinence, who weren't hardened to his ways like we were. Maybe it was the disease. The job he held the longest, the one so well-suited to his devil-don't-give-a-fuck attitude, was as a salesman for Derrick Corporation, an international company headquartered in Buffalo, N.Y., best known for mining equipment. In that capacity, he either chose to, or was encouraged to entertain a wide variety of people from foreign countries.

That's how we got to know the guy he called Sam the Chinaman, who worked with Chris. We were probably told his last name, but it was easier to remember Sam and it was plain to see he was Chinese. He wasn't offended by our politically incorrect means of identification. After all, how were we supposed to know if we were talking about Chris's nephew Sam Sowyrda, or Sam from China? Chris would invite Sam the Chinaman to parties and he was one of the few that stuck it out, mountain biking with us on numerous occasions.

"Chris. I don't see trail. Where is trail?" Sam the Chinaman would question in a soft panic filled voice.

"There is no fucking trail, Sam. Ride faster and you won't need a trail, just follow us."

Despite Chris's instructions, we temporarily lost Sam, twice, once in Ellicott-ville and another time in Hunter's Creek Park. Fortunately, we found him, so Sam would endure more rides with us. Looking back, maybe he was trying to escape.

One time we asked, "Hey, Chris. Why isn't Sam riding with us today?"

"There was an incident," he laughed. "He's at a defensive driving class."

"What's that all about?"

He explained with another laugh, "Sam was at the airport picking up my secretary. He forgot to put his car in park and it rolled into another car in front of him. A guy was putting his luggage in the trunk and Sam's car squashed him against his rear bumper."

I wondered who mandated the defensive driving class, but didn't ask. Of course, none of this was Chris's fault, or was it? Incidents. So many incidents. They swirled about him like the 67 moons of Jupiter. As a result, perhaps, somewhere in the world a man walks with a limp.

THE CARROT finger incident happened on Halloween night. Chris was bowling with the Russians. That sounds like a reality TV show, one that certainly would be more entertaining than *Keeping up with the Kardashians*. Chris was frustrated with the ball return thing-a-ma-jig. The balls were jammed, a clog in the pipes, so to speak, preventing the sixteen pounders from coming back. I'm sure Chris was quite polite about the situation, as always, telling the proprietor of the lanes, "Ah sir, we are having some form of difficulty. You see, we are having a jolly good time bowling at your fine establishment, but there seems to be a mechanical difficulty with our bowling balls being returned in a timely manner. Would you be so kind as to take a look at what is causing the malfunction?"

No.

It probably went something like this. "What the fuck! Get out of the way Kasporov, let me take a look at that. Whoever designed this fucking thing was an idiot." Chris submerged his arm into the throat of the ball return gizmo, like a plumber trying to unclog a pipe filled with hair, using his arm as the snake in the bowling alley's main drain. Not a good idea. *Sure Chris, just stick your arm right in there and pull those bad boys free. What could possibly go wrong?*

Chris plunged for bowling balls without success, or so it seemed. Finally, the clog burst as he brought his arm out and put his hand on the ball that had made its way into the bowling ball rest stop. Smash! Sixteen pounds of smooth poly-urethane made solid contact with Chris's finger. That didn't hurt much. It was when that ball smashed into the ball on the other side of Chris's finger that sent the scene into hysterics. Blood spurted from his finger like the old Monty Python skit, "Sam Peckinpah's Salad Days." Look it up on YouTube and you'll get the picture. A fun watch, indeed (make sure young children are out of the room).

The Russians watched as Chris was whisked to the MAC Center in Orchard Park by his friend and co-worker, Steve Valleen. His wife, Jennifer, met him there in the late hours. Recently, I asked her about that night.

"The doctors told me, 'There's nothing we can do for him here.' His finger was completely mashed. The next day I drove him to Buffalo General Hospital. He was in a lot of pain. After many hours in the operating room the surgeon came out and told me, 'It's not my best work.'"

"Didn't they insert pins in his finger?"

"Yes, and his whole arm was wrapped to the elbow. He was supposed to keep it immobilized."

I thought about that, knowing it would've taken more than a smashed finger to immobilize my friend Chris. I remembered when he first showed me the swollen knuckle on his right hand. It had healed quite a bit by that time, but it still looked horrible. "How long was he out of work?" I asked Jennifer.

"He had me drive him to Derrick the next day. The Russians were still in town."

Understandable, they had come a long way. I imagined Chris laughing that next morning at the office, retelling the story of his smashed finger—what I would later describe as the carrot finger. What a jolly good time it was.

The Geek, Caz, John Cimperman, me, Alex Sowydra, Sam Sowydra, and Chris at Holiday Valley - 2008

Barreling Down the 219

THE GEEK AND I talk while Chris walks; he's thirty yards ahead of us. He'd always been the one setting the pace. Our fearless leader, in some cases taking us to the escarpments of disaster. He'd hang there, tempting us to follow, and then pull up short at the cliffs of life, looking back at us, smiling, and then, of course, the big laugh. How predictable. We'd fall for it every time.

The Geek joins our hikes as often as he can. The outside world knows him as Dave Norton. Long ago, his father had sanded the splintery edges off Nadratowski (their name from the homeland), ensuring that all the Norton children (there are nine) would be able to spell their last name while still in grade school. The Geek earned his nickname in high school. He's a tall guy, 6' 4", maybe an inch taller when he was shooting hoops for the East Aurora Blue Devils, and back then there wasn't much meat on his bones. I believe it was our friend Brian Barton along with one of the Hansen brothers, Bob I think, that locked on to the lyrics of Freddie Blassie's song titled, "Pencil Neck Geek":

> *You see if you take a pencil that won't hold lead*
> *Looks like a pipe cleaner attached to a head*
> *Add a buggy whip body with a brain that leaks*
> *You got yourself a grit eatin', pencil neck geek*

They thought they aptly described Dave's physique and started calling him Pencil Neck Geek. Over time, it was shortened for expediency, as in, "Hey Geek, how many sausages do you want?" The Geek has kept his frame lean despite a legendary appetite. He's also kept the nickname. It takes a pretty good guy, comfortable in his own skin, to revel in being called the Geek for over 45 years. Everyone loves the Geek.

It's been a while since I've seen him; Chris was the glue that held us together, but now, things are different. So we have some catching up to do; I talk about my granddaughter in pre-school and the Geek tells me about his daughters' plans after college.

Every so often I holler, "Chris, how ya doin'?"

Sometimes he'll say, "Good," and sometimes he doesn't answer.

"You need a break?"

"Nooo."

He stops anyway, staring at us with bug eyes, scratching his wasp nest of a beard, before turning, and hoofing back down the trail. *Is he messing with us? I wish.* I'd give anything for him to blurt, "Jaaack, I don't need a fucking break. Okay!" He used to regularly emphasize his point by stretching his words like a sour note on an out of tune trumpet. "Jaaack, we're going to the Sugar Shanty. Maaaple Pooorter, Jaaack," or, "We're snowshoeing tomorrow, Jaaack. Seven a.m. It's going to be greaaat." Always pushing us. "Life is short, Jack."

Chris scurries up a hill. I look at the Geek and nod in the direction of the short incline. "Impressive."

"Nice work, Chris!" yells the Geek.

Chris gets to the top and stops; he searches the treetops. What does he see up there? I wish there were answers in the treetops, a miracle cure, a case of Labatt Blue.

"You okay?"

"Yeah," he answers, exhaling like you might after gulping a cold drink.

It's refreshing to see a little more jump in his step.

Life has slowed down quite a bit for Chris in the last year. He no longer speeds down the trails on his mountain bike, and no longer drives; gone are his days bombing down the highway in his blue-gray Mazda6. I wondered how that came about, thinking Chris wouldn't have given up his car keys easily, but Jen told me, "At that point he didn't care. I just told him he was done driving and that was it. He surrendered his driver's license and now has a license for ID purposes only." That was probably about three years ago; quite a bit has changed since then. It was for the best. No longer would Chris have driving incidents, like the time his car may, or may not have been driven over a snowbank and off the road. He abandoned his car like a shopping cart with a wobbly wheel and proceeded the rest of the way home on foot. What happened when Chris got there wasn't good. It's my understanding the local authorities were involved and most likely the air was filled with belligerence. One thing was certain—there had been an "incident." Whatever it was, it wasn't good.

Driving with Chris was always an adventure, like the time we were in Cattaraugus County and came upon a road south of Ellicottville named Brewers Cross. What were they thinking? Chris took this as a sign.

"Geek! Brewers Cross! Pull over, we gotta have a beer."

Back in Chris's speeding days he'd throw caution to the swirling tornado—to the snow covered roads—to the State Troopers in the median, and to me asking, "Chris, what's that thumping sound?" When we were all together on one of our road trips, I'd try my best not to say anything about his driving. That would only make things worse. If you told Chris to slow down, he'd go faster. If you asked Chris how many more miles to go on the trail, he'd take a *shortcut,* adding five miles. If you told Chris to turn down the music, he'd turn it up.

I THINK it was the second to last Liverfest in Ellicottville, our annual celebration where we ate and paid tribute to an underappreciated "delicacy"—the chicken liver. The year was 2011 when I thought our day was done, but Chris had other ideas, turning up the music to a new level.

"38, Jack!"

Spinal Tap had its 11, we had 38.

"No, Chris. Party's over. Turn off the fucking music."

"We're puttin' it on 38! 38 Jack!"

Neil Young's "Cinnamon Girl" penetrated the second floor bedrooms. Most of us figured, by 2:30 a.m. and being in our mid-50s, it was time to get some rest.

Not Chris.

Someone yelled, "Turn off the fucking music."

It was me.

There, I'd done it now. 38 would turn into 48. The music was lowered for a minute and then it came back—louder. I put a pillow over my head, resigning myself to a sleepless night.

YEARS AGO, Chris had become my skiing go-to on trips to Holiday Valley. It was pretty simple setting up plans with Chris; he was like a light switch, ON or OFF, no embroidered excuses or expanded theories of our evolution. It was yes, or no.

"You want to go skiing tomorrow at Holiday?" I'd ask.

"What time?"

"How about we meet at the park-n-ride (off Boston State Road) at 7:30 (a.m.)? Is that good for you?"

"7:30."

I couldn't tell if he'd posed a question, or confirmed the meeting time.

"So you're good for tomorrow?"

"Yeah, you said 7:30, didn't you?!" he bellowed.

Yes, I supposed I did.

"See you tomorrow."

I'd tell Mar I was skiing with Chris and she'd tell me, "Be careful."

And I remember the time my younger daughter Shay asked, before she knew Chris like she does now, "Dad, is he the guy that walked to the top of Kissing Bridge in his ski boots?"

And I'd say, "Yeah, that was Chris."

And Shay would ask, "Why'd he do that, Dad?"

And then I tried to explain to a little girl in elementary school about the "principle of things" and why Chris decided not to ski that day. The fine folks at KB told him he couldn't use his pre-purchased ski-pass; there were certain restrictions on the days you could use them. Chris politely told the young lady who had the misfortune of working the ticket counter that day, "This is bullshit!"

It was a waste of my breath trying to convince Chris that he should just buy a pass for the day since he was already there. Still, I told him, "You're wasting a good day," and to not let a little thing like some confusion about a ski pass ruin the whole day. But it wasn't a little thing to Chris.

He reminded me, "This is bullshit!" as I put a finger to my lips and nodded in Shay's direction.

Chris didn't end up buying a pass that day; and since he had conveniently parked at the top of the slopes and skied down Holly to meet us at the bottom, he needed to get back to the top.

I told him, "Just ride the chairlift. They never check passes."

Chris would have none of that. True to his principles, he hoisted his skis and poles onto his shoulder and proceeded to climb the 550 vertical feet of Rooster Run, jabbing his ski boots into the incline like he was walking up a broken escalator. Shay and I watched him from the Holly lift, passing over him three or four times, before he was gone from our sight.

Yeah, Shay, I remember.

Years later, perhaps scarred by the whole incident, Chris couldn't bring himself to spend money on a ski pass. *Sure, that was it; he was scarred by the incident.* We'd have to go to the main chalet at Holiday Valley, where through some connections he always finagled a freebie. And no worries if we were skiing at Holimont; there were freebies there for both of us. So what if my guest pass would advise anyone looking closely that my name was Jane Rademacher.

There was the time a friend of mine, Tom Degaul, met us at the park-n-ride with a few of his buddies. I risked an intergalactic collision of worlds by introducing other circles of friends to Chris. And so I proceeded, as always, during such interactions, under code yellow (significant risk).

I introduced Tom to Chris and took a step back as is prudent when lighting any incendiary devices. They shook hands. Mike Lazickas was there, too. We call him Caz, short for his middle name, Casimir. It sounds way cooler than Mike. I figured Caz could provide some counterbalance to anything Chris might say or do. Also, he had his van.

Caz grew up with a passel of brothers and sisters who were impacted by a broken household. It's not something he talks about much so I won't either. What I have come to understand more recently is that as a result of these difficult times he found a bond with Chris. They became good friends, and like Chris, he had an advanced capacity for mischief; it came to both of them quite naturally. In Caz's case it got him suspended in his senior year from the East Aurora Blue Devils football team. A silly thing really, when compared to what he may, or may not have contributed to The Smoke Bomb incident. Caught smoking a cigarette. Sure it was against school rules, but in my opinion, the punishment didn't fit the crime. It was the team's loss. Caz eventually found his wife, Mary (or maybe she found him), and went from carefree bachelor to father of five in a span of a couple years.

Mary introduced him to two daughters from a previous marriage, married Caz, promptly gave birth to twins, Matt (now also called Caz) and Val, and a year later Elise. His freedoms evaporated like a cactus dewdrop in the desert, which wasn't entirely a bad thing. During this period, Mary became the Caz whisperer, taming the wild right out of him, and making him the kind and gentle soul he is today.

Having a van was a curse. It meant you always got stuck with the driving. We jammed our ski equipment in the back and fit ourselves wherever there was room. Four of us bounced in coach-section while Caz drove and Chris claimed shotgun. We were on our way to Holiday Valley. The tires, better suited for the racing slicks of a dragster, fishtailed down the 219.

RECENTLY, I ran into Tom at Spot Coffee in Hamburg. Seeing me with my head staring at my laptop, tapping away at the keyboard, he laughed and said, "It looks like you're working on something serious."

"Yeah, kind of," I answered. "It's about my buddy, Chris. You skied with us a couple of times, remember?"

"Oh, yeah, I remember!" Tom said enthusiastically with a big smile. "Didn't you tell me he's got Alzheimer's?" His smile fades.

"Yeah, Pick's disease, actually," I clarified.

"That too bad man. How's he doing?"

"He's doing okay." I showed him a recent picture of Chris.

"He looks good, man!"

"Yeah, we're still getting out there, hiking most weeks."

Tom turned to his wife, Kim. "This guy, Chris, was unbelievable. Alpha male, he was like Superman."

I let Tom continue, smiling as he told his wife about Chris. It's cool when people know you're friends with Superman.

"He was insane, man. And what was the name of the other guy with the van?"

"Caz."

"Yeah, I was just talking about that time when we had to get out of his van, all of us, and push it up Holiday Valley Road." Tom gleefully recounted the episode for Kim's benefit. "Kim, it was crazy. We were all in this guy's van, the tires were spinning and we all had hopped out and pushed. And when we got to the top, we jumped in the side door while it was still moving." He laughed. "It was crazy, man. What was it that your other friend said when we busted on him about his tires?"

"The tires were a bit marginal."

"Oh, yeah, that's right, hilarious."

It really wasn't much of a story, but Tom remembered it. That's the way it was with most things we did.

There was another time Chris and I were skiing with my friend Lou. I told Chris before we left the park-n-ride, "Lou has to be back by two o'clock. So we'll take two cars. You can ride with me."

"Two o'clock?!"

"Yeah, don't worry about it, Chris. We're taking two cars." I threw a damp towel over the sparks coming from crossed wires. God forbid that we wouldn't ski until our passes expired for the day, or until Chris would announce, "Jack, my legs are fried. Let's have a couple tree beers." For Chris, a couple tree didn't necessarily mean two or three, it could mean two or seven, or eight, or …

We arrived in Ellicottville without an incident (who counts skidding through a traffic light) and pulled into the HV parking lot. The snow came down in arm loads, heavy flakes, stacking on rooftops like puff pastry.

Chris stepped out of my old red Ford Escape with his freebie pass announcing to the world, "This is going to be greaaat!" Always accepting of delays and tolerant of other's more leisurely pace, he suggested an adjustment in our current tempo of preparation, "What the fuck are you doing? Come on, let's go!" Lou, who had parked his car beside my Escape, looked at me with questioning eyes. Eyes that said, *what the hell kind of craziness did you get me into?*

"Chris, don't rush me," I said.

"*Jaaack*, come on. Life is short!"

So I rushed, got my ski bag, poles, and skis, shut the door and we were good to go. Except for the keys. Fuck!

"I locked the keys in the car."

Chris laughed the big laugh and pulled on his manky rabbit fur hat, the old one soiled with chicken wing grease and beer sloshes. The combination seemed to inadvertently preserve the last vestiges of its threadbare fabric. Chris looked uphill at the spiraling snow. It was a flaps-down day, for the rabbit fur hat.

"We'll deal with the fucking keys later. Fresh powder, Jaaack," he announced with a deep reverent voice. "Lots of fresh powder."

"Chris, I think we better figure out how we're going to get the keys. I'll call Mar to see if she can meet us here with my other set." I said this, but as the words left my mouth I realized having my wife drive through a snowstorm while we were having a grand time skiing was a non-starter. I can't remember if any of us had, or even thought of AAA. It wouldn't have mattered; Chris was focused on first tracks.

"Fuck the keys, Jack," Chris repeated. *I get it, Chris.* "When we're done, Lou can drive us back to the park-n-ride and I'll drive you home. You can get your other keys, and I'll drive you back down." Chris didn't care that it was a 45-minute drive one-way, and that was on a dry road. We'd have to drive back home, back down, and then back home again. I did the calculations. It was a shit load of fucking driving time. I wondered if I'd have done the same for Chris. I hope I would've, but I'm not sure.

Lou whispered through the swirling snow, "What did you get me into?" I knew he didn't mean the snowstorm.

Off we went. Chris waited for us at the chairlift with his ski poles (a foot shorter than they should have been). I'd asked him a couple of times why he didn't get new poles. He laughed. It didn't matter. No matter how many times I told him how to use his poles, planting them in the snow when he started his turn, he'd say, "Yeah, yeah, I get it." But once on the slopes he'd wave them through the air like an orchestra conductor.

Snow gathered in his beard like cotton batting and there was a little pile on top of his soiled hat. Yes, it was going to be great. Chris smiled like it was a breezy day in Saint-Tropez.

There's not much to tell about skiing that day. It *was* great.

On the way home he told me, "Call the Geek. We have to call the Geek."

"Ok."

That's what we did. If you weren't with us, you were against us — and a fem. Fem? Yeah, as in; chicken-shit, wimp, light-weight, candy-ass. Note: my daughter Shaylyn told me, "Dad, I'd get rid of that word, fem. If you leave it in, it's going to offend a lot of younger readers. Trust me."

To which I replied, "Fem has to stay. It's our word. I can't take it out." And then doubt crept in. Shay's right about a lot of stuff. Why did I need the word fem? I told her weakly, "Shay, it's in like six places in the book. I can't change all that stuff. I have to keep it real."

"I'd get rid of it, Dad."

How could I explain this word? We all used it, Chris, the Geek, Mac, me; but why? What did it really mean when we called somebody a fem? Fem was more than a good-natured jab. I told Shay, "When we call each other a 'fem,' maybe it's kind of like a compliment."

"A compliment?"

"Yeah. You know because they (the fems) won't do the stupid, dangerous, embarrassing thing we're all doing. They can think for themselves and not succumb to peer pressure. That's a fem."

Shay listened patiently and then told me, "I'm not buying it, Dad. I'd still get rid of it."

I left it in. Hopefully, when you hear us say, "Fem," you'll understand.

Chris grabbed my phone. "Geek, you should have been here, it was epic. Plenty of fresh powder." The Geek said something, Chris laughed, and he handed me back my phone. I said a few words before hanging up. Maybe next time the Geek would join us—unless he was a fem. Life is short.

Lou drove us back to the park-n-ride. That was the last I remembered of him tagging along with us, but that was okay; not everyone had an appetite for Chris. From the park-n-ride we went to my house, got the keys, explained to Mar that I'd see her in a few hours, and told her to say a little prayer that I'd survive the ride down with Chris. His tires were worse than marginal.

But there was good news. The snow was coming faster, swirling like the inside of a snow globe. I resisted as best I could, holding my advice on safe driving habits until the pimple of my fear erupted, "Chris, slow down! You're gonna get us killed!"

He laughed and tromped the gas pedal to the floor. Predictable. *Good God!* "Chris, do you hear that?"

"What?"

"Your car. What's that *thump, thump* sound?"

"The wheels must be caked with snow. It does that sometimes."

Chris sped forward and, of course, we got there alive, or I wouldn't be telling you this story. Chris's tires spun the whole way up Holiday Valley Road like we were driving in sticks of butter.

"Turn in here," I told him.

"I know."

He didn't slow down (that's for fems), power sliding into the parking lot, and sidling up to my old Escape. I prayed I had the right keys.

"Great day, Jack. See you later," he told me as I got out of his car.

Chris wasn't into lavish declarations of gratitude, so I didn't give him one. I simply said, "Thanks, Chris. Drive safely."

He slammed his door on my last two words.

I pressed my key fob and heard the lock click open on the Escape. *Prayers answered.* I turned to wave goodbye while opening the door. Snow clinging to the Escape whooshed inside, covering my front seat. Chris's shoulders bounced up and down as he laughed hysterically. If I'd been there by myself I would have yelled, "Fuck," and made a big deal out of such a small nuisance. *For God's sake we'd been skiing in the stuff all day.* But seeing Chris laughing, gave me the course correction I needed. I'd save the exclamations of profanity for another time. It was a great day, one I wouldn't forget.

Later that night I received a call from Chris. "Hey Jack. You get home okay?"

"Yeah, safe and sound. Wild ride, huh?"

"Yeah. I just got home."

"You just got home?!"

"Yeah, my tires got all clogged with snow."

The *thump, thump,* thing must have gotten worse.

"I had to drive 25 MPH the whole way. It took me two hours." Chris didn't care about the time it took him to get home, but it probably drove him mad to drive so slowly for so long.

A couple of weeks later I got a Sunday night call from Chris.

"Hey, Chris. What's up?"

"What's the fucking speed limit on the 219?!"

Okay, there has definitely been an incident. My mind raced. Would this involve a clandestine trip to a Southern Tier police station and the posting of a bail commensurate with situations involving misunderstandings between the New York State Police and my good friend Chris?

"You mean on the expressway section?"

"Yes, on the fucking expressway section!" Chris was hot.

"Well …" I measured my words. "I'm pretty sure it's 65 until you get to that stretch at the end, then it's 55."

"That's bullshit!"

Yes Chris, that's bullshit, but they do have some big orange warning signs before you get there advising of the speed limit change. I didn't share this simple fact with Chris. I knew better.

"What happened?" I pictured Chris flooring it up the ramp, blowing through the stop sign, and skidding onto the crossroad with blue and red lights in furious pursuit.

"This little weasel state trooper pulls me over."

"On the expressway?" I hoped he wouldn't tell me he was 30 miles down the road in Salamanca, where his Mazda was finally overtaken by the flashing lights.

Chris didn't answer my question. He pulled the pin on his fury, letting it all out. *That's okay, buddy. That's what I'm here for. No worries, I'm just staring out the window, watching little snowflakes float through the streetlights while listening to smooth jazz.*

"I told the little asshole that this was a fucking speed trap!"

Oh, good Chris, that was good. It's always good to explain your side of the story.

"You said that to a trooper?"

"I've got to drive down to Pennsylvania so I'm at work early Monday morning and this asshole has nothing better to do than pull me over. I got out of my car to see what was taking him so fucking long and he flies out of his car yelling at me to get back in."

"Chris, I'm pretty sure you're supposed to stay in your car."

"That asshole's lucky he had a gun or I would have ..." Chris trailed off. He was losing steam. *Good talk, Chris.*

"So are you driving now?"

"Yeah, I'm fucking driving."

Chris didn't believe in hands free driving. He'd ask me if I had a scorpion in my ear when he saw me talking on my portable Bluetooth. I pictured him with his flip phone up to his ear, left hand on the wheel, and a Whopper in his lap. Probably a Big Orange from Burger King in the cup holder.

"Well I better let you concentrate on your driving. Skiing next weekend?"

"Yeah."

Chris hung up. I prayed that he made it to Pennsylvania without further incident. He was doing what he had to for work. He'd lost quite a few local jobs. I felt bad for him. Chris was a tireless worker, despite times of misguided energy, but never a quitter. If only he hadn't been so damn belligerent. Perhaps he had given a piece of his mind to so many that he had forgotten to save enough pieces for himself. Chris wasn't selfish with his pieces; he gave them to anyone, whether they wanted them or not.

We probably skied the following weekend, drank a couple tree beers, and I would have listened to him tell me about the whole 219 incident, again. This time we probably would have laughed at the end, and as always, it would have been the big laugh.

Wally, me, Chris, Caz, the Geek, and Thad near the
Battenkill River truss bridge – 2002

Battenkill Day 1—Waiting for Wally

"YOU READY, CHRIS?"

He's looking in the treetops again.

"Chris, you okay?

"Yeah."

We walk; Chris is in front of us. A filmy sweat covers me, my shirt sticks to my back, and an irritating stream runs down my spine into the crack of my ass. Chris wears a long-sleeved maroon shirt and blue jeans. There's no talking him into wearing something cooler. We're past that. Who am I kidding? We've never been able to talk Chris into doing anything he didn't want to do. It's always been his way or get the fuck off the highway. We've been okay with that—usually. Most of the time, the Geek and I would look at each other, maybe chuckle, and realize, it was just Chris being Chris.

We walk along a stream. There are no canoes on this little trickle of water.

It doesn't look anything like the Battenkill River, still, I think of those trips. It had been an annual trip. Recently, Bill Shanahan claimed to me that he'd been the one who started the thing back in the late '80s. There'd been the regulars, Bill, Chris, Thad Rice, Mark Moran, Paul "Wally" Sugnet, Tad Kuhn, Mark "Scooter" Hatch, and there had been others that made "guest" appearances from year to year. This would be my first time. It sounded like fun; a lazy canoe ride down a mean-dering river, no Class VI rapids, drink a couple tree beers, sit around a campfire, laugh, and sleep in a tent. I was looking forward to it.

WE WERE taking Caz's van, not because he offered (he would have), but because there was no choice in the matter.

"Caz, you're driving."

"Okay, Chris. Why am *I* driving?"

"Because we need room for the beer. And for the four of us and our stuff, and we can get two canoes on your roof rack. And for the beer," explained Chris.

Caz's wife Mary, a sweetheart of a lady, watched as Chris off-loaded case after case of Labatt Blue from his company issued pickup into Caz's van. I think Mary may have been counting.

"What are you going to do with all that beer?" she screeched.

"We're going to drink it!" Chris answered, bereft of comprehension. How could someone ask such a question?

"Mike?" Mary looked at him with wide eyes and a raised chin.

Apparently, she wanted a word with Caz. They slipped into the open garage while we continued to load the rest of our gear in Caz's van. His back was to us, partly shielding Mary; his head shook up and down, and side to side. Caz wasn't doing much talking from what I could see. Mary was doing the talking, probably gracing him with some last minute canoeing pointers and safety tips. *Sure she was.*

Caz returned to the van looking like he'd received an uncompromising parole decree. He climbed behind the wheel, backed out of his driveway, and headed for the welcoming waters of the "mighty" Battenkill.

The trip was interrupted by a bird. A partially dead bird. It hit Caz's windshield, catching on the wiper blade, and we watched as he attempted to set it free by turning on said wipers. Bird guts smeared the windshield. An omen?

From the back seat, I suggested, "Caz, don't you think you should pull over?" The driver's side of the windshield had become severely impaired by the guts of the shish kebabed bird swishing over the glass.

"Jeeesus, Caz," Chris howled.

We pulled over, got out, and stared at the bird pinned to the glass by a Trico winter blade. One of the bird's wings flapped, or maybe the wind caught it. Caz delicately lifted the wiper. Bird guts hung off the blade like the laces of an old pair of sneakers draped over a telephone line. The bird was no longer partially dead. It was fully dead.

Chris couldn't contain himself, "Caz, just pull the fucking thing off!" He reached past Caz, grabbed the bird, ripped it from the wiper, and flung it into the weeds.

"Let's go. There's cold beer waiting," Chris voiced his time-tested axiom.

That's not to say that Chris was one to wait until we arrived at our destination. It took me years to convince him that open beers in a moving vehicle wasn't in our best interests. He eventually took my advice. Kind of, usually, sometimes. Okay, there was the one time when we were driving through Ellicottville and we saw that cop car.

We continued our journey to the Battenkill, north of Albany, near the border of New York and Vermont. During the six-hour ride there was talk (I listened) about past trips, questions of whether or not Wally was coming this year, and Chris cracked open beers like a chain smoker. I didn't say anything. As with all things Chris, it would only make things worse.

Six hours later, Caz's van bounced over a rutted dirt road into the campground. Empty beer cans surrounded our feet.

We set up camp and when we were done, Chris complained, "The Geek says, we have to go fooood shopping," sounding a bit like Bill Murray in *Stripes*.

"What kind of shopping?"

"Fooood, shopping, sir."

To Chris, this must have seemed like a waste of precious time. Why would we need food, when there was canoeing to do and more beer to drink? He reminded us, "The Geek needs his three main food groups, meat, meat, and meat." We'd heard it so many times before, but it still made us laugh.

Despite Chris's groans we headed to the grocery store. Into our shopping cart we chucked hot dogs, cheese, chips, pepperoni sticks, bacon, and other salty foods that ensured we'd consume all the beer we'd brought.

The Geek picked up a Flintstone-sized slab of steak. Chris snatched it from his hands. "Geeeek! Look at the price! We should've got yellow-tag meat from Tops." Chris had frequently regaled us with his meat stories, proud of his cost-effective yellow-tag purchases at the neighborhood grocer. The yellow tags advise when meat is close to its expiration date. Chris didn't pay particularly close attention to the dates and it was surprising we hadn't all come down with trichinosis, salmonella, Sal Bando, or something terminal from the Italian sausages we'd cook up on his little grill after a mountain bike ride. There were no yellow tags at this store, so the Geek got the steak.

Back at camp we prepared for our first trip down the river. Caz wondered, "Is Wally coming?"

"Fuck Wally," Chris laughed.

With the concern for Wally's whereabouts discarded like a pair of old socks, we piled into the van with two canoes strapped on top. And the beer. All of it! No way was Chris leaving any of it unguarded at the campsite. I wondered about the plan. We had one van. It was a legitimate question. We were driving upstream, off-loading the canoes, parking the van, and then floating ten miles downriver. How were we getting back to the van? I knew better than to ask, but I did.

"How're we getting back?"

"Jeeesus Jack, quit your whining."

Whining? That was whining?

"Wally's coming later," Geek explained. "He'll drive us back."

"Fuck Wally."

Apparently, this would be our new fun phrase for the weekend. What was it that Wally had done, or *hadn't* done that warranted such talk? Was there a back-story? Was it just because he wasn't here yet? Chris kept at it, mixing five of the six essential ingredients for all good jokes. He took aim at a worthy target, mixed in a cup of hostility, sprinkled with some exaggeration, tempered with a pinch of reality and baked with emotion. Surprise was the only missing ingredient. It didn't matter to us; it was still funny.

The Geek and I shoved off in one canoe; Caz and Chris were paired in the other. Four guys, two canoes, two twelve packs of beer. That sounded about right. We shouted back and forth, busting each other's balls, clanking our Labatt Blues, and when we found it necessary to discuss world events, we'd hitch up to each other and float in tandem. There were deep conversations about whether the Bills would make the playoffs next year (or ever), whether we would have to make another beer run (according to Chris, definitely), and again, speculation about whether Wally would make it this year. The question of his arrival was taking on the same suspense as the potential appearance of Mort Guffman in the 1996 mockumentary comedy film, *Waiting for Guffman.* We continued to float and crack open cold beers, which combined with the sound of the river made my bladder feel like a piss-filled balloon. The shoreline was clogged with brambles, but there was a rocky point up ahead that looked welcoming.

"Geek, I gotta piss like a racehorse."

"Chris. Chris!" Geek shouted. "Jack's got to take a leak."

"Jeeesus, Jack," Chris hollered in frustration.

It was coming, so I braced myself. How foolish of me to stop so I could pee in dignity, against a tree. In my mind's eye I saw Chris standing in the front of the canoe, looking like a Roman fountain, pissing into the Battenkill. In fact I had witnessed such a thing while on his sailboat in the middle of Lake Erie. He stood at the bow, responding to the call of nature as my wife looked away in disbelief.

Turning from the tree I had been watering, I saw Chris striding into the rocky shallows, arms up at his shoulders as you do when the water is so much colder than the air, and then without announcement, he dove like an arrow. Swimming hole!

I took off my glasses and waded in. The water felt refreshing, sobering in fact. We didn't stay in long, most likely because it's very difficult to swim in a river and drink beer at the same time.

"Geek, where are my glasses?"

"How the hell should I know? Where did you have them last?"

"I don't remember."

"Jeeesus, Jack!" yelled, Chris.

I thought of a weekend without vision, practically blind around these guys. My God, they'd probably suspend me from an oak tree with an atomic wedgie.

"This is serious," I blurted.

I wanted to reel the words back in my mouth where they belonged. Just what Chris needed, another snarky catchphrase. I'd hear it for the rest of the weekend—and the rest of my life.

He mocked me in a booming voice, "This is serious," sounding like the guy on the radio, proclaiming, *Sunday, Sunday, we're going to turn this place into a giant mud pit.* "This is serious." He said it over and over as I worried about him squashing my glasses while he plodded next to the canoes. "This is serious!" he laughed and his head bobbed up and down.

The Geek and Caz caught on, singing *a cappella*, "This is serious." Sure it was all a big fucking joke for everyone, except me. I found my glasses. They were right where I left them, perched on the bow of our canoe. With my sight restored, and knowing I would never hear the end of it, we shoved off from our temporary port.

Four beer cans popped open as we continued our "blistering" pace down the Battenkill. Chris shouted back to us, "How much beer do you have left?"

"Plenty."

"Jaaack , are you suuure?"

"I'm sure."

It was time to pull over again, because Chris said so. There wasn't a convenient rocky point or sandbar this time, but instead a swirling eddy around a partially submerged tree replete with branches snapped in such a fashion that it appeared a giant had accidentally dropped his spiked mace club in the river.

"How the hell are we going to get on that?" I asked.

The Geek and I grabbed the snaggly branches while we swirled in the eddy. We strained to hold on until Chris snapped. "Paddle forward, Geek!" We were doing it all wrong—of course we were. I was in the front, the Geek in the back. He let go of the branch and attempted to paddle. The eddy frothed, and we twisted sideways, as I held the jagged branch tight.

Boom!

Chris and Caz t-boned us.

"Jeeesus, Jack. Let go!"

I let go and our canoe came about, pounding into the partially submerged log. Caz extended a meaty dockworker's hand and pulled us toward them. Two canoes joined at the hip, banging against the "log of death." "That was easy," said the Geek.

"Caz, you first," Chris motioned toward the log.

"I don't know, Chris."

"Caaaz, just do it."

We must have looked like babies taking their first steps, wobbling from side to side, balancing with outstretched arms, before placing one foot on the log of death while the other was still in the canoe. Miraculously, there were no incidents.

"So *when* is it that Wally is supposed to be coming?"

Really, Caz? Leave it be.

"Later this afternoon," the Geek answered.

"Fuck Wally!"

Yes, Chris. Fuck Wally. All together now on the count of three, Fuck Wally. Is this what we'd distilled ourselves into? Four grown men, (I didn't say mature, just grown) sitting on a log jutting from the riverbank, a collection of fatuous drunks chugging beers, with only the sounds of bird song, rushing water, and the four of us taking turns with our fun new mantra. *What in God's name had Wally done?*

"Fuck Wally."

Thankfully, it replaced, "This is serious"—for now.

"Geek, get me another beer."

The beer was safely in the bottom of our canoes, tethered by ropes at the other end of the log. Like kites in the wind our canoes danced in the patterned flow of the river. The Geek was the first to walk the log. "Here, hold this." He handed me his half-full beer, or half-empty depending on how you view life. We watched. There was great anticipation of a major injury. Wouldn't that be fun? The Geek was up to the task, wrapping his toes around the log like the flexible feet of the Grinch. He snagged a beer. A high wire act indeed. We applauded the Geek; what style and grace he exhibited that day. Who'd be next?

"Careful, that log is slick," the Geek warned us, "It's the Geddy of Death."

Geddy? Did the Geek just say geddy? He was shitfaced, slurring his words. It didn't happen often.

"Geddy?" I questioned. "I'm pretty sure it's not called a geddy."

"Yeah, it's a geddy."

"It's not a geddy, Geek. It's called ..." I couldn't think. I was shitfaced, too. "Well, I know it's not a geddy. You're thinking of Geddy Lee. You know from Rush."

"I still think it's geddy."

It took four college-educated men the rest of the afternoon to come up with the correct word. Jetty, as in: a small pier at which boats can dock or be moored.

We each took our turn walking the log, the log the Geek had referred to as the

Geddy of Death. We watched with the same morbid fascination as spectators at a demolition derby. It would make for a more interesting story if I was to tell you someone slammed their skull against one of the pointy branches and they had to be airlifted to the nearest hospital, but it didn't happen.

We sat on the magical log, told our stories, and we were hilarious. *We were, really.* I have no recollection of what we said that day; all that I remembered was that everything any of us said was funny. Each of us took turns "eloquently" sharing a story. And at the end of each one, we'd all shout, "Fuck Wally!"

On that day the log, formerly known as the Geddy of Death, was renamed the Fuck Wally Log.

As with all good things, they needed to continue. We shoved off from the Fuck Wally Log, cracked open four more beers, and floated. Paddling was optional, more steering, or rather making sure we didn't slam into anything or puncture the bottom of Geek's vintage canoe in the rocky shallows.

As we pulled our vessels onto the grassy land of our campsite a sporty looking sedan rocketed toward us; dust billowed behind on the rutted dirt trail.

Wally?

It was our Guffman.

"Fuck Wally," we slurred in unison.

"Hey, Wally." Chris slapped our friend, Paul Sugnet, on the back. I didn't know why Chris called him Wally; that was a thing Chris started in high school. I never asked.

"Merle!" Wally responded (Merle Haggard, I think). Wally and a few others call Chris, Merle. Another mystery to me. The big laugh came out and we put away our "Fuck Wally" catchphrase.

It'd been a good day. We sat around the campfire watching Caz nod off and Chris held a flame-roasted hot dog in front of his mouth. We all thought that was so funny. It didn't take much to amuse us; we were such juveniles. The fun ended when Caz woke up. He swatted the hot dog into the darkness and announced he was going to bed.

Chris laughed the big laugh, ragging Caz for leaving.

"Caz, Caz, Caaaz, Caz?" There was a musical sing-song tone to his plea.

"Screw you guys," Caz put a twist on the standard, "Goodnight guys, see you in the morning."

Never, I mean ever, should you be the first one to leave this group, serving yourself up as a human sacrifice. In your absence they will mock the living shit out of you. No one will cover for you, they'll pile on like pack dogs. It just isn't worth it, hang in there, always wait for someone else to leave first.

I'm sure you have a few questions. What is the point to all of this? Is there a lesson or two to be learned from these deviants? (Probably not.) We were just doing what we always did.

And ... "Fuck Wally."

Caz, Chris, the Geek, me, Wally, and Thad admiring Thad's shattered window at the Battenkill River campground - 2002

Battenkill Day 2 and 3—Booozzzuh

CHRIS COMPLETES HIS surveillance of the treetops.

"You ready, Chris? Are you okay?"

He looks at me with wide eyes, shaken from a trance. He doesn't answer my questions; his mouth is empty, the words he once used are out of reach, floating beyond the treetops, so far away. There is no laugh at the moment; it'll return, that's for sure, but it doesn't mean what it used to. His feet stay planted as something else catches his attention down the trail. I don't see what it is that could be so interesting, but he studies it hard.

ON DAY two of our Battenkill River experience, Chris cooked breakfast over our campfire, first the bacon to grease up the pan, and then the eggs. He had a metal flipper in one hand and a breakfast beer in the other. Like most of our wood fires, smoke billowed from a punky, moisture-filled "pus log." We'd drag the weighty mass to the fire, intending to feed it to the flames all weekend. For kindling we'd use dry pine branches that popped sparks toward our balls like bottle rockets. When we were done eating, I pointed at the pan with my elbow and told Chris, "You might as well throw *that* thing away."

"Jaaack, Jaaack, Jaaack," Chris scolded me as he trotted to the river's edge with the pan of dried yellow scabs. He waded into the shallow water, scooped some pebbly grit from the Battenkill and scrubbed.

"Good as new, Jack."

"Sure, Chris, whatever you say."

After breakfast, the Geek tested the rooftop straps laced over our canoes and kayaks, hoping to limit the chance they'd take flight when we blasted our way down the swerving roads to our river access point. Chris took inventory, "We need more beer."

We don't need more beer! I didn't want to see those shiny blue Labatt cans for quite a while. Ice picks stabbed me in the eyes and a ball-peen hammer tapped repetitively at the base of my skull. I wanted to curl up in the bottom of the Geek's canoe and float away my hangover. I kept those thoughts to myself; I knew better. It pissed me off that Chris looked fresh as a wildflower, gazing into the cloudless sky, and informing us, "This is going to be great."

Maybe if I could've removed my eyeballs from their sockets it might have provided some relief—but of course that wasn't possible. I had no tools with which to pry an eyeball, and even if I had, there wasn't a safe place to store them for when I'd need them later. This was "serious." Why had I thought I needed to keep up with Chris last night? I was an idiot.

After a short ride we pulled off the road and parked near a well-maintained truss bridge. The river was maybe 80 feet wide at this point, the water was shallow, and there wasn't so much as the tiniest ripple on the surface. It was a perfect access point. *I can handle this.*

The sun felt like a hot iron on my back. Sunscreen would have been nice, but with so many other important things to pack (toothbrush, shirt, shorts, sneakers, hat, beer …) how could I remember sunscreen? I feared that by the end of the day my skin would be as red as a boiled Battenkill langostino. My shirt provided some protection from the *blistering* sun, but didn't stand a chance against Chris's *blistering* taunts of sarcasm. I wore the shirt anyway. "Have another beer, Jaaack. You'll love it." Apparently, Chris must have heard the banging in my skull.

A fly fisherman watched the scene from his position along the shore, tilting his head in our direction, like a pet beagle, perhaps trying to figure out if there was any purpose to our silly antics.

We floated tethered together, the Geek and me in one canoe and Chris and Wally in the other, and Caz in his kayak. "That looks like fun," the Geek said, pointing at the fly fisherman. "Great day for that."

"Geek—don't make eye contact," advised Chris.

Yes, Chris we know. God forbid we don't want to waste time talking to strangers.

The Geek ignored Chris, "Catch anything?!"

"Nothin' to brag about," the fly fisherman hollered.

"Great day, huh?!" the Geek continued his small talk.

"Geeeek, Geeeek," Chris muttered, jabbing the Geek with his paddle as he looked at me. I wasn't getting involved.

"There's a storm brewin' boys. Big one. Other side of that ridge. Over in that *die-rection*," the fisherman pointed with the bill of his hat.

I looked up. I suspect we all looked up. The brilliant sun shined through gathering clouds that hung on a baby blue sky like sheets out to dry. The fisherman smiled at us, a smile salted with a dash of, *Good luck boys, I hope you know what the fuck you're doing.*

"Really? You think?" the Geek asked.

"I don't think, young man, I knows. Seen this sorta thing a hun'ren times," the fisherman said.

He was busting our balls.

"Come on Geek, let's go," Chris commanded, rolling his eyes and giving me another look.

We paddled on, not prepared for much of anything, other than drinking and floating. Wisecracks ricocheted down the Battenkill, echoing off tree trunks while we looked for significant landmarks. Where was the Fuck Wally Log? We'd been in mirror-flat water for the last half hour. The kind-hearted river understood our limitations and was taking it easy on us. How nice. We had no worries in our sturdy canoe, so it was with riotous laughter that we absorbed the rippling waves that started to bounce off the hull of the Geek's canoe. *Doomp, doomp, doomp.* It was becoming more work to keep our craft on course. Remember that scene in Jurassic Park where the water glass vibrates, tiny concentric waves of water announcing the approaching stomp of *Tyrannosaurus rex*? Yeah, it was kind of like that. *Doomp, doomp, doomp.*

"Hey, Geek, look over there," I raised my paddle and pointed. Our bow swerved left as if the canoe wanted to head back whence it came, trying to tell us, "I'd turn back if I were you."

"Yikes," exclaimed the Geek. The Geek says yikes during such times—and he loves weather. The wind kicked up, stronger, dropping the temperature. Our canoe continued to resist our efforts to keep it pointed downstream. It was like a dog heading to the vet, pulling hard against its leash, wanting to go any direction but there. We should have listened to our floating mutt.

"Get under the bridge!" I yelled to the Geek.

The storm spit on us, tasting us with the tip of its rainy tongue before mashing us in its toothy maw. Wally paddled furiously in the bow as Chris, in the stern, attempted to rudder them to safety.

"Hydraulic cushion, Geek! Watch for the hydraulic cushion!" Chris shouted. I'd heard him use that term before. I didn't know what it meant and had never asked. Around Chris, some things were better left to figure out on your own. Finally, over seventeen years later, I found out what it meant. It came up in conversation with his brother Brent, an avid fly fisherman. He was explaining fishing pools to me, "It's because of the hydraulic cushion."

"Yeah, your brother used to yell that on our canoe trips. What's that all about?"

"It's when water rebounds off a rock in the river and pushes back upstream a bit. The combination of the current and the water rebounding off the boulder forms calm water behind the rock. That's hydraulic cushion."

"Oh, that's what it is? Your brother loved that term."

"Yeah, guess where he learned that from?"

He didn't have to tell me.

By now you know how this turned out. Chris stood up to the gods that day, as always, and he won, with his arms spread wide, absorbing all that they could throw at him. He tempted them to take another shot at all of us, "Is that all you got!"

Chris won, but the storm took its toll on me. My body shivered, sheathed in gooseflesh as we got back in our canoes and Caz in his kayak, paddling down river through the calm after the storm (cliché, but true).

"Geek, I'm freezing."

"Fem."

I should have known better.

Chris and Wally headed for another bridge ahead. This one looked cool, as in neat, not as in, freezing my ass off, hypothermia, what the fuck did Chris get me into this time?

Chris climbed out and started up the bank. Foolishly, I questioned what he was doing. "Are we getting out?"

"No Jack, we're not getting out, we're paddling," he answered sarcastically. It was a dumb question.

"Chris! I'm freezing my ass off."

He ignored my request, but it was a reasonable alternative to being called a fem. I followed as we all scaled the river bank and huddled inside the covered bridge. Our bivouac provided shelter from a second round of rainfall, musically *plink, plink, plinking* a final "ta-da" on the bridge's roof. I felt like the weakest link of the polar bear club, a fish packed in ice.

Without explanation, Chris jogged to the other end of the covered bridge and circled back to where we stood and watched. *What in God's name was he doing?* Was this the second leg of some kind of bizarre triathlon he'd dreamed up? He came up with stuff like that.

Chris ran by, explaining, "Gotta get our core temperatures up." We followed, trotting in single file, five of us under the covered bridge, warming our cores. After the drumming rain stopped we slid into our canoes and kayaks, and once again, paddled through tranquil waters, until we came to yet another covered bridge.

Teenagers perched on the banks, shouting. It was a taunting shout, egging on someone we couldn't see. We floated under the bridge to get a better vantage point. Splash! Without warning, like a bag of potatoes with a head, something, or someone, cannonballed into the water. A face gurgled to the surface with one arm extended. The "young punks" on the river bank hollered for someone else to take the "plunge."

The sun burst through the clouds. Chris took this as a sign from the heavens and on cue climbed onto the bridge's roof. He inched his way so that he was perched on its edge over the center of the river. It was time to show everyone he wasn't to be outdone. Chris looked down at us, smiling that goofy smile. Caz looked up and hollered, "Chris?" It was a one-word question, short for, *What the fuck are you doing?*

First, I prayed to God he didn't kill himself. This probably hadn't been necessary since I'd learned, recently, he'd been doing this for years. He had even goaded Wally into doing back-flips. Second, I prayed this would be the end of it; no way was I taking a turn at this show of insanity. I hate heights and there were boulders under the river's surface that could bust you up. Call me a fem all you want, but I wasn't jumping off any bridges. Chris loved it, smirking at us.

The punks whooped it up, "Do it, dude."

He stood with his feet together, twenty feet over the water, as we watched from the shore. Chris bent at the knees and pushed off from the roof. To me it seemed as if he hung in the air for an eternity, before knifing, feet-first into the blackish water of the Battenkill. The spectators roared their approval. "Joey, you gotta do it now. You gotta, dude. That guy did it." *Maybe Joey's "gotta do it," but I sure as hell don't gotta.* No fucking way. Chris was crazy and we loved it! *Did you see that guy? That was our buddy who jumped off the bridge. Pretty cool, huh!*

Chris waded to shore, "Who's next?"

Please, please, don't look at me, Chris. Thankfully, I wasn't next. And on that day, no one was. It was all Chris. We climbed back in our canoes filled with bravado and waved goodbye to those that lined the shore.

Chris instructed us, "Beers up, beers in," and we did.

I looked at the rolling empty beer cans in the bottom of Wally's and Chris's canoe and once again, we floated hinged together. Chris hollered, "Let go," as the river branched in two directions. Like Yogi Berra, when Chris saw a fork in the river, he took it. He and Wally went right; the rest of us went left. We came to the end of the small island dividing the river and somehow the rest of us had arrived there before Wally and Chris. At first there was no sign of them. Then—there were signs. They floated by us, some were white, some were red, but they were predominantly blue. Labatt Blue. Beer cans littered the river. Obviously, there had been an incident.

Chris's and Wally's canoe floated bottom side up just below the river's surface. They bobbed next to it, arms draped over the hull, hair pasted to their foreheads, and in no hurry to right their capsized canoe. The Geek, Caz, and I waited for them in the shallows, standing in the river, each with one hand on the gunwale of our canoe and the other snagging empty beer cans before they floated past. It was with pomp-infused merriment that Chris and Wally righted their canoe, scurrying in the shallows, grabbing the empties and firing them into their empty canoe, *doink, doink, doink.* What a rollicking good time we were having on the good old Battenkill. Tornadoes be damned, make sure to retrieve and recycle your empties, replace all divots, and fuck Wally.

It was another hour before we made it back to our campsite. The storm had passed; replaced by late afternoon sun that warmed our cores, warmed our spirits, and made us feel happy, so happy we decided to crack open a celebratory beer. Tubular meat sizzled on a makeshift grill over our smoking campfire. Amazingly, our tents were as we'd left them, except for a bit of water in the bottom. *I told you we should have closed the flap, Caz.*

LATER THAT night Thad Rice and his college roommate, Steve Block, showed up. We told them how we had stood up to a tornado and looked forward to another trip down the Battenkill the next day. Steve, perhaps anxious to make sure he fit in with our group, boasted of past kayaking expeditions. *Careful Steve, Chris is eyeing you up like yellow-tag meat. For your sake, I sure as hell hope you can live up to your words.*

The next morning we arrived at the truss bridge. It was starting out as another sunny day, but we were now well aware of how fast things could change. Steve suited up. I didn't realize there was a need for such a thing. The rest of us wore swimming trunks, or ragged shorts with tank tops, or t-shirts. Steve was taking things *seriously*, wearing a form-fitting vest he called a paddling jacket, along with black skin-tight neoprene pants. On his feet he wore boots with grippy tread. *Those babies would have come in handy on the Fuck Wally Log.*

Chris vomited hysterical laughter on unsuspecting Steve. "Jeeesus, Stan, you're wearing that?"

Stan? Was that his name? I thought it was Steve.

Chris looked at Steve. Steve looked at Thad. *Good luck, Steve, I hope your kayak has airbags, or better yet, maybe you should head back to the van and get your Swimmies.*

"Steve, it's Steve," he clarified for Chris.

"Steve?"

"Yeah—Steve."

Chris found this to be funny. He slapped Steve on the back sounding like the snap of a wet towel on a bare ass. Steve stumbled forward and gave Thad a *Who is this guy?* look. Or, was it a, *I want to get the hell out of here* look? I'd seen those looks before and wanted to tell Steve, don't worry, you'll survive. You might have to pay a visit to a rural hospital, whose head surgeon goes by the name of Flinders McFly, but you'll survive. That is, unless you go mad from tormenting ridicule. Otherwise, the survival rate around Chris was surprisingly high. I wanted to explain all of this, but there wasn't time. Chris hollered, "Let's get going, there's cold beer waiting."

Steve eased into his sleek racing kayak. Its lines were in bold contrast to our sturdy forest-green and stop-sign-red canoes. He was raring to go, to show us what he was made of. I'd seen this act before. It seemed Chris had a way of either scaring the shit out of people, or making them think they had something to prove, to put on a good show. *Good luck, Steve.* We floated no more than five minutes, when we observed our first incident. Steve, paddling lickety-split, took the lead, looking good, gliding with confidence, until he wasn't there anymore. *You were right Chris, this is going to be great.* Steve had been swallowed by a twisting eddy, flushing him below the surface like a turd down a swirling toilet.

He bobbed next to his swamped kayak. Steve wasn't happy. The rest of us *were* happy. Chris was *very* happy. He lived for that kind of stuff.

"How are your booties, Steve?" Chris asked with the big laugh.

Later Steve would tell us, "I was taken aback by the current." *Taken aback? Who talked like that?* It would be our new catchphrase. For years after, when we'd be surprised by something, something not all that "serious," we'd shout, "I was taken aback," and laugh, remembering the day Steve was "taken aback" by the Battenkill.

When we arrived at camp later that afternoon a bocce game commenced in the field grass where we had parked our cars. It was evident that the combatants had a blatant disregard for the rules outlined by the United States Bocce Federation. The weighty bocce balls were hurled aloft in all directions. Wally flung the pallino over the top of Thad's SUV, signaling the start of a new frame. It nestled in the wet grass about twenty feet from me.

"Caz, just throw it. Nothing's going to happen," instructed Wally.

The nicked red bocce lay at his feet, waiting for action. Without a thought of future consequences, he picked up the weighty ball in his meaty paw, gave it a cursory inspection, and flung it far in the air. It hurtled high into the darkening night sky; a thing of beauty. If you're a bocce aficionado you're screaming, "Hey, he can't do that. That's an illegal volo. The United States Bocce Federation (USBF) strictly outlaws the high arcing throw of a bocce ball beyond the centerline of the court, due to safety considerations and to prevent damage to the courts." Caz ignored this forbearance, acting as if he didn't give a damn about volo restrictions. For God's sake, it seemed like he was spitting on the rule book.

The bocce ball followed a path shaped like a rainbow, a beautiful ellipse until ... *booozzzuh!* The ball slammed through the back window of Thad's SUV. Glass shattered into a billion diamonds. And inside the SUV—was Steve. I'm sure he was taken aback.

"Shit!"

Caz was regretful. Thad was pissed. Chris was hysterical. If only Caz had heeded the USBF's regulations. Never volo—especially near your buddy's SUV.

"*Booozzzuh.* Did you hear that?" Chris mimicked the sound of the bocce ball hitting the SUV's window. "*Booozzzuh.*" Chris loved his new onomatopoeia. It sure beat the hell out of boom, or wham.

We all liked the new word. Except Thad—and Caz.

"Why the hell is Caz so upset? I'm sure Thad has glass coverage," I mumbled to the Geek. I thought it'd been a stroke of good luck that it sailed immaculately through his rear window instead of bludgeoning his roof. The ball lay in the rear of Thad's SUV, looking up at us innocently, like a puppy that had pooped the carpet.

Thad gave Caz a dressing down. *What the hell. Thad—let it go already. The storm's blown through, it's a beautiful night, let's not put a damper on the rest of our time together.*

Chris stepped in, with the big laugh, defending poor Caz. "Jeeesus, Thad.

What the fuck? It was an accident. Forget it. Beers up, beers in." Chris looked at me, "Jack? Where's your beer?" I grabbed one from the cooler, popped the top, and clanked to the truce.

Caz skulked to our tent. *Shake it off, buddy.* I tried to talk to him. He moaned about how pissed his wife, Mary, was going to be once he told her what he'd done, and the ensuing surgical procedure involving his balls she'd be scheduling for him. *Really, Caz?*

I tried to reason with him. "Caz, don't worry about it. Mary won't care. I'm sure we'll all laugh about it tomorrow." Caz didn't laugh about it tomorrow, and still doesn't, but we did, and still do. And we had a new word! An onomatopoeic word, *booozzzuh*, for Christ sakes! How cool was that? We should've contacted Webster's.

The rest of the night we recapped the good times we had. We'd been "taken aback," capsized canoes, jumped from covered bridges, and fought a tornado. It had been epic. It was always epic. Chris made things epic. I rested with one leg hanging out of my comfy sleeping bag. One more time I tried consoling Caz. He didn't want to listen. Most likely, he was thinking about his pending surgery to remove his balls, and whether or not there'd be anesthesia.

I looked through a slit in the side of the tent, telling him, "Hey, at least it's not raining." I fell asleep looking at a sky bursting with stars, until … I was woken by pitter pattering on our nylon tent. My first thought was that Chris was wandering in the dark, searching for a tree (or a tent) to piss on. But it wasn't Chris, it wasn't piss, it was raining, and it was coming down harder. Not good. By morning, Thad's SUV would have an onboard swimming pool. He was going to be so pissed. I went back to sleep. I had no more words for Caz. .

The next morning we all laughed and repeated our new word (all except Caz and Thad)—*booozzzuh*. When we were ready to drive home our separate ways, we took a moment to stand by the rear of Thad's SUV and admire Caz's "handiwork." We were all smiles. Chris pulled Caz's arm toward the smashed window, making him point to what he had done, as if rubbing Fido's nose in the mess he had made. *Booozzzuh.*

Front - Sam Yu, Chris, Jobe Wheeler - Back - Mac McCready, Caz, the Geek, Arty Aungst, and Alex at Sprague Brook Park - 2007

Punctured Lung

CHRIS LOOKS AT us while he catches his breath. He doesn't have the stamina he used to, so the Geek and I do a fair amount of standing and waiting.

"You ready, Chris?"

"Yeah."

He turns from us, hop stepping down the incline we just summited, walking through an area of downed trees. Nature has exacted its revenge on this chunk of woods, once filled with beefy trunked trees, guardians of this mature forest, standing like Methuselah. A tornado swept through here last year and in a matter of minutes destroyed what nature had built over decades. Why this tree and not that one? It looked to have been in good health, but now, its partially uprooted trunk lodges in the crook of another behemoth. Green leaves grow from the uprooted tree. It's not ready to die; branches reach skyward for the light, hoping to survive in its new form. Several larger branches have splintered from its trunk, crushing adolescent trees below, but not reaching the short saplings. These fingers of new growth stretch toward the sun filtering through new holes in the shredded canopy.

"Geek, look at that one," I point to a toppled maple. Its trunk is riddled with woodpecker holes and white fungus the size of dinner plates sprout from the decay. Nature is taking care of business, but it'll be quite some time before this area of the forest has healed.

The Geek points at another tree, thirty feet from the trail, "How about that one?" A large branch on the hundred-foot tall tree is severed twenty feet from the base. It bends toward the trunk, forming a splintered hinge. The Geek says, "It looks like a hammock."

"It'd be cool if we could get up there." But not even the Geek is tall enough to crawl into this hammock. I think about what it would take to get up there and what a neat picture that would make with the Geek lounging in the hammock-hinge of this fallen tree. In the past, Chris would have insisted we figure a way to get up there. And I would have insisted on taking a picture.

Chris stands a hundred feet down the trail from where we are. He's done taking a break and starts down the path.

"Hey, Chris, wait up!" I yell toward our friend, the one in the long-sleeved maroon sweater and blue jeans on this 85-degree day. He stops, turns his head, and looks back at the Geek and me. He has no words, but I imagine him thinking, what the fuck is it now, Jaaack?

"Hey, Chris, you should come back here and check this out. It looks like a hammock," the Geek hollers.

Chris stares with wide vacant eyes, his mouth tight. We don't expect much, but this time he doesn't even say, "No." I miss the days when Chris would have barreled through the brush, told Geek and me to give him a boost, and climbed into the splintered mass. And then, I would have taken his picture. I could hear him, "Jaaack is taking his fucking pictures, again." He'd climb down, and then we'd look at my "fucking pictures." Today there'll be no climbing into a splintered hammock; there'll be no "fucking pictures."

Life *is* short.

The Geek and I catch up to Chris. We stair-step down a tricky section of the trail, carpeted with snarly roots that take a hard left through a narrow section at the bottom. It's lined on both sides with sturdy trees. I pause, trying to determine which one it was, the one that jumped into the middle of the trail, six or seven years ago.

"Remember that one, Chris?" I ask. "This one." I tap the bark of a thick pine. It withstood the winds of last year's tornado. And before that, it withstood Chris.

WE DIDN'T ride at Chestnut Ridge Park often, but it was convenient for our annual Father's Day ride. The date was June 15, 2008. We had a good group this particular night, six of us met at the Newton Road parking lot, looking to break a sweat, rag the shit out of each other, and drink a couple tree beers when we were done. Chris was already on his bike killing time, peddling around the blacktop and riding up and down the parking lot berm that borders the woods, while the rest of us pulled our fat tires from their racks. Our bikes laid scattered on their sides (you don't have a kickstand on a mountain bike—unless you're a fem) as we pulled on our riding gloves and helmets. Chris didn't wear a helmet. "It's a false sense of security, Jack." *Sure thing Chris, whatever you say.*

He couldn't take our leisurely pace any longer."Are we fucking riding, or what?! Come on let's go! Life is short."

The Geek and I looked at each other and smiled as Caz adjusted his seat. He was always adjusting his seat. Usually it was during the ride. There was nothing wrong with Caz's seat, but it provided a sneaky excuse for him to catch his breath. It was better to fake a mechanical malfunction than tell Chris you needed to take a break.

"A breaaak! Jeeesus, Caz. You should be well rested. You're riding so slow," Chris would tell him and laugh.

We were off, Chris in the lead and the rest of us followed. As usual, Chris stopped every so often, in order that he wouldn't get too far ahead of us—and to allow us to grab a breather. Despite the back of my neck throbbing and my heart pumping wildly I made a conscious effort to hide my gasping from Chris. He took pleasure in seeing that kind of shit.

"Come on Geek—we're waiting," he yelled as soon as he saw the Geek coming up the trail.

Chris never seemed to get tired or break a sweat.

"Where the fuck is Caz?!" he bellowed after we'd gathered like a stretched slinky.

We smiled, grateful none of us was the last man. I don't know who started it, but bringing up the rear became known as, "The Curse of the Last Man."

"He's coming," the Geek answered. I think he had a *problem* with his seat.

Way to go, Caz, you crafty bastard. I hope you're recharging back there because you won't get a break when you catch up. We saw Caz approaching over a rise; he was walking alongside his bike. Not good. For Chris, it was a mortal sin to be seen walking your bike on the trail. "Caz, that's not a walker, it's a bicycle," he yelled.

Caz wasn't smiling. He was probably thinking; why in hell did I let Chris talk me into coming out to ride tonight? I don't need this shit.

"Everyone ready?" Chris looked at us, laughing. "Caz—you should be well rested." "The Curse of the Last Man." Now you know two curses, "The Curse of the First to Leave" and "The Curse of the Last Man."

"Caz, Caz." Chris smiled. It was coming, a volcano of laughter. It was fun to laugh at your friends, right? Chris had the big laugh; we were the chorus. It was a dry track that night. I rode with confidence, faster than usual, but knowing full well there was no way I'd pass Chris; he wouldn't allow it. He'd just as soon run me over the edge of an embankment before he'd let that happen. He rode faster, I rode faster. Chris pulled the best out of me—and sometimes the worst. He had a special knack for getting through tight spaces and didn't let silly obstacles, like boulders, brush, or ditches dictate his path. It was that way on the bike trails, or anything else for that matter.

I wanted to keep up with him, so that when we stopped, he'd tell me, "Nice riding, Jack." It felt good to hear those words. Chris didn't toss compliments around like loose change into a tip jar. And he'd remind me to look ahead, don't look down, "Don't sweat the small stuff, Jack." I concentrated on the trail, glimpsing at the drop ahead. The gap between us was closing; my shocks absorbed tangled pine roots, thump, thump, thump. Chris would also remind me, as Jobe Wheeler first warned us, "Don't look where you don't want to go, Jack." His words were, so many times, like grains of sand irritating the inside of an oyster, but if you listened carefully, they might become pearls of wisdom. Unfortunately, on this night, Chris forgot his own advice.

Wham!

A crash is such a waste unless there are witnesses. Nobody wanted to *hear* about how badly you smashed into something. We wanted to actually *see* it. *Sure, sure, Caz. Were you actually on your bike or did you just trip while you were walking next to it?*

I got to see this one. Chris slammed full-speed into the trunk of a large pine at the bottom of the hill. I stopped next to him and jumped from my bike. He wheezed on the ground. This was "serious." I'd never seen Chris "do" wheezing. I hunched over him, just Chris and me. Strange noises came out of him.

"Chris, are you all right?" Of course he wasn't all right, but I was in full panic mode. What the hell was *I* going to do about anything? I knelt next to him. "Chris, can you breathe?" Another dumb question.

Chris didn't answer. The crash knocked the smart-ass right out of him. We'd have to look for that later. The rest of our group arrived on the scene; none of us had any idea about what we should be doing for our friend. So we stared at him, continuing to ask if he was okay. It was the best we had. Chris got to his knees, and then to his feet; that was good. He must've just got the wind knocked out of him.

"I'm good." He picked up his smart-ass laying at his feet. "Thanks for all the fucking help." Chris grabbed his chest. Maybe he should've put some dirt on it. Rubbed it in real good. Dirt could heal things.

"What happened?" the Geek asked.

I told everyone how Chris had slammed into the tree, dropped to the ground, his bike had rolled forward a few more feet, and then, the bike, sensing there was no need to carry on without a rider, tipped gently on its side. We joked about how the tree must have darted into his path, coming out of nowhere to take him to the ground. There were a few chuckles, but the big laugh had been knocked into next month.

We rode on, but things were different; Chris was riding in the middle of the pack. The first creek crossing was a typical stop. We gathered there and I asked the Geek, "Where's Chris?"

"I don't know; I passed him a while ago."

That was odd. When he finally caught up to us, we asked, "Chris, are you okay?" It didn't take the head of pulmonary sciences at Buffalo General Hospital to see that something was wrong with Chris's breathing. We asked again, "Chris, are you okay? Maybe we should get you some help."

"No, you guys keep riding. I'll take the road when we get to Seufert." Chris winced.

We were now at the halfway point, riding out of the woods, onto the road near the entrance to the Eternal Flame trail.

"Are you sure, Chris?"

"Yeah, finish the ride. I'll wait for you guys in the parking lot."

We should have followed Chris. A lot could have happened in the next 45 minutes while we lollygagged our way along the trail and Chris coasted down Route 277 back to the Newton Road parking lot. We were idiots. But Chris said to ride on, so we did. Our concern for Chris was so "great" that we only had time for dozens of pictures.

There's a cool spot coming down a steep grade next to a do-or-die 45-degree angled cliff. At the bottom, jaws of a craggy creek threaten serious injury if you were to go over the edge and a slick wooden bridge crosses in front of a small waterfall. It's quite picturesque. I waited at the top, leaning my bike against the crumbling sedimentary rocks and set up to photograph everyone as they took their turn navigating the descent, turning on the bridge, and peddling up the steep climb on the other side.

Alex and the Geek femmed out as they got near the bridge, pulling up short, and getting off their bikes where the path was as narrow as a case of Labatt Blue. I got a couple of nice pictures of them standing on the bridge waving up to me with the waterfall trickling behind them. It'd be a nice picture to hang on their refrigerator. Caz was next. More than once he'd been accused of GQing it for the camera, smiling, posing, looking good for the paparazzi. I was ready, and then something happened. I snapped the picture with my small Olympus digital. What did I photograph? Caz disappeared and I heard the sounds of metal on rock, percussion sounds from a band named Mercy Flight. Caz climbed out from under the bridge, belting out a steady stream of f-bombs. I stashed my camera and rode down for a closer look.

"Fuck, Jack!" Caz let me have it. Apparently he'd almost killed himself, styling on the bridge, slipping down the incline and landing with the bike on top of his bloodied legs. Had I gotten the picture?

I listened to his opening arguments, politely letting him finish, before I readied myself for a well thought out rebuttal. Caz explained that the whole thing was my fault, arguing that he wouldn't have fallen if not for me taking his picture.

"It's my fault, Caz? Why is it my fault?"

"I would have never tried to ride that bridge."

Caz had been the one asking me every time we paused, "Jack, did you get me in that one?" *Sure Caz, it was my fault. Whatever.*

"So did you get me?"

"What?" I questioned.

"Did you get me riding down?"

Really, Caz? I pulled out my camera. I couldn't wait to see the picture of Caz free-falling from the bridge. That one I planned to put on *my* refrigerator. It was a disappointment. Damn. Chris would've loved that one, but it was dark, blurry, and Caz was out of sight. The Geek could be seen pointing into the gorge with the others standing nearby looking disinterested.

Caz complained for the rest of the ride. I let him. It would pass.

When we got to the Newton Road parking lot Chris was waiting. A good sign. *Beers up, beers in. Right Chris?*

Caz continued to rag on me, telling Chris how it was my fault that he almost killed himself. I was getting close to having enough when Chris offered his opinion. "Mike, shut the fuck up. It was your fault. It's over." And it was. *Thanks for the support, Chris.* We had one beer each and Chris announced it was time to go. That was unusual. Chris was never the one to end the day, the night, the late night, the early morning.

The next day, I called to check on him, to see if I could get the big laugh out of him. It didn't usually take much. But there was no big laugh. He told me that Jen had to take him to the emergency room that night. He couldn't breathe.

"Really? So what was the matter?"

"Punctured lung."

"Punctured lung! Geez, Chris. Now what? Do you have to have surgery?"

"No. They want me to rest for a couple of weeks."

"Oh." I wondered about Chris resting for a couple of weeks. I didn't see it happening. I said a prayer for his wife, Jennifer. He'd be like an angry wasp caught between two panes of glass. *Good luck, Jen.*

I called the Geek, "Did you hear about Chris?"

"No."

"He's got a punctured lung."

"Whaaat?"

"Yeah."

I decided it was time to buy Chris a helmet. If he didn't wear it on his head maybe he could strap it across his lungs the next time we rode. The following week the Geek and I went to his house and presented him with the helmet.

"False sense of security, Jack," Chris reminded me in his booming announcer's voice followed by the big laugh. He was feeling better.

"So when can you ride again?"

He widened his eyes, motioning with his head toward the kitchen, "Jen wants me to stay off the bike for a while."

"That's probably a good idea, Chris," agreed the Geek.

Recently, I learned from Jennifer that she had come home that night and found Chris lying on the couch in his muddy mountain bike clothes. He was having trouble breathing, but he decided to go to bed and see how it felt in the morning. She was scheduled for varicose vein treatment the day after Chris's crash. Jennifer told me, "You know, the veins-veins-veins-guy? Chris had gotten himself to work, but he called me later. I told him, 'Chris, I'm in the doctor's office.' He told me, 'I can't breathe. I'm getting stabbing pains in my chest.'"

I asked her, "So then what happened?"

"I can't remember for sure, but I know Dr. Karamanoukian, the veins-veins-veins-guy is the one that called in a referral to get Chris scheduled to see a doctor about his lung situation." And then I suppose he went back to the business of making Jennifer's legs beautiful once again.

Chris had told us he had a punctured lung; I suppose it could have been that or maybe a collapsed lung. Either way, the situation was life threatening. Jennifer explained, "they inserted a syringe to remove the air from the injured lung so it could fill with air again. And later they inserted a chest tube to make sure the lung stayed inflated." She told me how that didn't stop him from going to work the next day with a bag (I assumed part of the chest tube apparatus) stuffed down the front of his pants, or attending his son Troy's sports banquet the following evening. *Good God, Chris, you never told us about any of that stuff!*

The Geek and I told Chris to get well quick, but not to rush things. We had the whole summer in front of us. We had a few more laughs about Chris's crash and looked forward to the next time we'd be together. I hoped it would be soon and that Chris would be wearing his new helmet, defying a false sense of security.

Bill Schupp, me, the Geek, Mac, and Chris at Liverfest in Ellicottville - 2009

Chris on Golf

We're past the section of the woods thrashed by the tornado, walking the rooty terrain next to a farmer's field. Not much to look at here. We've stopped talking, lost in our own thoughts. I wonder what the Geek is thinking? I wonder if Chris *is* thinking? What's going on in there? Does he have memories? I hope so. Maybe they're buried in the undamaged section of his brain, in a place that he can access in a way that we don't understand.

I'm through with my deep thoughts.

"Hey, Geek. When is it you're retiring?"

"April, 1, 2021."

"I thought it was 2020."

"Nope. April Fool's Day 2021."

That is *so* like the Geek.

"What're the chances we're going to get you to join EACC (East Aurora Country Club) when you retire?"

"Maybe. That *would* be fun playing with you guys."

"Yeah, it'd be cool having a Class of '76 foursome, you, Mac, The Doctor, and me."

"Hey, did you hear Schuppy had another hole-in-one?"

"Really?"

"Yeah."

I have no further comments on the hole-in-one matter. I guess it's cool when you get one, but what else is there to say? You swung the club, striking the ball, causing it to fly through the air, landing on short grass, and it rolled in a hole.

"Hey, Chris. You remember when you got your hole-in-one?"

He looks at me like I asked him if he remembered the day he was born.

"You were with Geek, right?"

Chris musters up a, "Yeah," validating my premise that there really *isn't* much to say about a hole-in-one.

IT WOULD seem that golf and Chris had nothing to do with each other—well, almost nothing. In one way or another everything has *something* to do with Chris. He either has a passion for it and has an opinion, or thinks it's bullshit and has an opinion. There's very little in between. It keeps things simple. I don't have a problem with that, but it's quite possible I may be in the minority. Chris had a knack for ruffling feathers, fur, skin, whatever it was that you were wearing; he was an equal opportunity ruffler.

There's no big story here. Chris would tell it like this, "I got a hole-in-one. The End."

I've heard the story before, a tale without trimmings, but I needed to confirm the facts. Facts are important. What with all the time and energy I've spent, digging for the details about Chris's life, I thought it best to get this right. Great effort has gone into cultivating these words, the stories about my friend, to ensure they are 100% historically accurate. And in so doing, I have dredged all emotion and prejudicial viewpoints from this discourse. *Sure I have.*

Fact one—Chris had a hole-in-one at Minerva Hills on number three. The Geek confirmed this.

Fact two—Chris thinks golf is mostly bullshit. I confirmed this as can my friend Bill Schupp, who during the infancy of his relationship with Chris, made the mistake of admitting he was golfing yesterday, and the day before that. *How dare you, Bill? Do you have no shame? You, wearing your Sunday whites looking like the Good Humor man striding up the 18th fairway. How do you live with yourself?*

"Gaaaulf?! Gaaaulf?!" Chris questioned Schuppy as if he'd told him he'd joined a bingo club. Bill endeavored to regale us with tales from his last golf outing at Bandon Dunes, but Chris cut him off with the big laugh and questioned, "When was there ever a good story that had anything to do with golf?" He went on further, telling all of us, "I'll wait until I get really old to golf." I doubt that Chris will get that old. Old enough to experience the civilized behavior, the etiquette, the politeness in the country club dining room, the proper dress (I'm sorry sir, no cargo pants allowed on the golf course, no jeans allowed in the club house, no ripped-to-shreds shorts you've been riding the trails with, no underwear that you haven't changed while hiking the 46ers, no manky rabbit fur hat), and the overall good feeling of privilege being a country club member. *Sir, I'm sorry, but I'm going to have to ask you to vacate the premises.* For all of this, and so much more, Chris won't get a country club membership card. And I'm quite sure he's sincerely okay with that. If he was able to find the words, he'd probably tell us, "I don't have time for all that bullshit."

Fact three — Schuppy has three holes-in-one. He's got the signed scorecards to prove it, and one that's in a frame. Big fucking deal. Back to the research lab and the spreadsheets. Jaaack, Jaaack, you can't figure out everything with a spreadsheet. Hold on Chris, you're going to like this one. I did the calculations, worked it all out. You actually have a much greater percentage of shots that have resulted in a hole-in-one. Based on Schuppy's 40 years on the links at an average of 90 rounds per year and your approximately eight rounds of golf during your entire life, Schuppy's percentage of holes-in-one is a pathetic .02%, whereas yours is a robust, 1.39%.

Let's move on, shall we? Yes we shall. The scene was Minerva Hills Country Club. Chris hit a decent tee shot on number two, landing twenty yards to the side of the green. Yeah, yeah, Schuppy, I know. It's a good shot for duffers. Unbunch your knickers and just listen. Chris pulled out a wedge, or some kind of lofted club that looked like it had the proper design to get the ball airborne. He snatched said ball off the turf and propped it on a tee. That made things so much easier, increasing the chances of a nice wedge shot; who cared if that's against the rules? It made things more fun. The ball floated in the air, etching a parabola against the lush landscape of Minerva Hills CC, before trickling on to the green and into the hole.

"Great shot, Chris! Nice birdie," yelled the Geek.

"Isn't that what you're supposed to do? Get it in the hole?" Chris was not "taken aback" by his delicate chip shot (it had been, after all, struck while on a tee).

The Geek finished out with a dandy seven on the par three and suggested to

Chris, "If I were you, I'd quit now. You'll never have a better shot than that." But Geek, you aren't Chris; nobody is Chris, so you can just stuff that logic of yours into your cargo pants and get ready to tee it up on number three.

Chris probably thought, *there's cold beer in my bag, but only two. There's a whole bunch back in the car. The Geek's giving me permission to quit.* Decisions needed to be made. He might have studied his golf bag, not for the right club, but to check on the beer. Indeed, the two beers were safe and secure. "Let's play another," he suggested.

Chris had first-shot honors by virtue of his courageous chip-in on number two and therefore got on his knees, jammed the tee into the Minerva hard pan, and placed a dingy white ball, the color of an old man's teeth, on its perch. For luck, I suppose, he rotated the ball so the words Titleist were replaced by Delia Cadillac. He took a practice swing. Then without pretense, he swung his lucky 8 iron with the dry-rot-grips. *Thwack!* He'd done it again.

"Nice shot, Chris."

It wasn't a high arcing beauty, but it headed in the direction of the hole, not just the short grass on the green, but the hole! Chris watched with mild interest.

"That's going to be close. I think it might be in the hole!" The Geek yelled as if Chris had just won the lottery.

The Geek was up next, and with unparalleled muscle memory hit his tee shot into the woods—twice, and swore—twice. The Geek was running low on balls. He had a half dozen left, but two had smiley-face gashes on their covers. The two "golfers" walked up the fairway without the Geek taking another shot.

Amazingly the crack maintenance crew at Minerva had yet to whip the dew from the greens. It looked like a mouse had dropped from the sky near the front of the green, scurried toward the hole, and in the process, had created the shape of a hooked Roman nose. *Good shot indeed, Chris.*

He'd made a hole-in-one!

"Now you *really* should quit," advised the Geek.

But he didn't. Can you blame him? At that point he was probably hovering around 2% holes-in-one per shot attempted.

Chris's Top Ten Golf Tips

1. Never keep score.
2. If you have a bad lie, put the ball on a tee, or make up a better lie, one that someone might actually believe.
3. Laugh.
4. If you find someone else's ball, don't ask questions; just put it in your bag.
5. Rag on anyone making a bad shot—even if they're not playing with you.
6. Laugh some more.
7. Keep plenty of cold beer close at hand.
8. Don't take gaaaulf seriously.
9. Laugh again.
10. Life is short, don't waste too much of it playing gaaaulf.

Even if you don't play golf, take note of these tips; they'll improve your game of life.

Chris's high school yearbook picture (they didn't spell his last name correctly) - 1976

Where Does Your Dad Live?

WE CONTINUE DOWN the path, Chris leading, one measured step after another, until he stops and turns to look at us. Maybe he's worried that we aren't behind him.

The Geek looks at me, "I guess we're stopping."

"How are you doing, Chris?" I ask.

"Good."

Good is good.

"Hey Geek, stand over there with Chris. It'll make a cool picture." I point to the boney carcass of a fallen pine tree. Its needleless branches look like the ribcage of a brontosaurus skeleton. "Geek, move more to the left. Chris's face is in the dark." Chris isn't interested in my directions, or my pictures, so it seems. That's nothing new.

The Geek tells him, "Chris, move over this way a bit." He looks at the Geek like he's told him there's a pinecone in his ear. The Geek grabs Chris by his maroon sweatshirt and pulls him closer.

"Perfect. One more." I look at my phone. "Great! That's a good one." In the picture the Geek and Chris are smiling, each with an arm draped over the other's shoulder. I hold it out for them to see.

"Looking good, Chris." The Geek taps his finger on the screen and the image disappears. Without a word, Chris turns from us, continuing on the trail. So the Geek and I follow.

I stuff the phone in my pants pocket, making a mental note to text my dad the picture; I make it a point to give him regular updates on my visits with Chris. They're different from when I'd tell Dad about the outrageous details of our crazy adventures. He's known Chris almost as long as I have. I've heard him on several occasions recount the time Chris showed up at my high school graduation party with a covey of my shit-stirring classmates. He arrived in his Chevy Corvair van (*Unsafe at Any Speed*), with its 10-inch-wide, supposedly decorative white stripe wrapped around an oxidized blue body. It was a real beaut, no doubt one of Chris's $100 wonders, some of which weren't even worth that much. Paul (Wally) Sugnet had told me about a few of those acquisitions: there was the junker Chris bought and convinced him to tow home with his brother's brand new Ford Mustang, and then there was the less-than-sea-worthy trawler with an in-board motor that sank during its maiden voyage on Canandaigua Lake. *What fun!*

On this particular night the Corvair had provided reliable transportation to my graduation party, and in typical fashion, Chris was on time. He leaned against the Corvair, parked in front of our house, beer in hand, waiting on his hosts. I'm certain Mom was aghast at the scene forming in our front yard, as our family of six pulled into the driveway on Park Place. Dad probably wasn't a Chris connoisseur back then, but like some who acquire a taste for fine wine, foreign films, or abstract art, Dad at first acquired a tolerance, and later a fond appreciation for Chris. He'd listen raptly to my accounts of our canoe trips, mountain bike rides, snowshoeing and skiing adventures, and of course, the incidents. Every story was punctuated with an exclamatory incident. So, seven or eight years ago, it was only with moderate surprise, that Dad asked me, "Chris is going to visit *me?*"

It started when I received a call after work on a Friday afternoon, "Hey, Chris. To what do I owe the honor of this call?"

"Where's your dad live?"

"Boise, why?"

"I know that! *Where* in Boise?"

"Umm, what's going on, Chris?"

"I'm out West. I want to visit your dad."

Okay. First thought—what a marvelous gesture Chris was suggesting. Second thought—I had to warn Dad. Fast! I wasn't concerned that this visit was unprecedented. Dad would be thrilled to see Chris. It's just that even if you hadn't had rain all summer, as happens in Boise, and you saw storm clouds forming on the horizon, you'd think hooray, but still, you'd want to make sure your windows were closed and you brought in the newspaper you were reading on the back patio with your afternoon martini so that things wouldn't get ruined. Yes, I needed to warn Dad.

While these thoughts rumbled in my head I continued my conversation with Chris. I needed to get some basic facts. "That would be great, Chris. My dad would love that. Where are you now?"

"I told you, out West."

"Yeah, I got that. Where out West?"

"Idaho."

I could see I wasn't going to get an accurate global position on Chris's current location, so I tried a different question, "When were you planning on going to see him?"

"Now."

Hmmm. "Why is it you're out West?"

"I'm calling on a customer. We sold them this piece of shit and I'm the one they expect to make it work."

"Oh."

"Yeah, if we don't get this thing up and running by the end of the month, they're threatening to return everything. These fucking engineers don't know their ass from a hole in ground."

"Uh, huh."

While Chris waxed poetic about his profound affection for the engineering society, as he was prone to do, further thoughts fermented in my alarmed subconscious. I wondered if there'd been an incident in the Mountain Time Zone. I should've asked, but I didn't. It wouldn't change anything. Chris was visiting my dad, whether I gave him his address or not.

"I'll text you his address."

"Jack, I don't do fucking texting!" *Oh, yeah, thanks for the reminder.*

"Are you ready? You got something to write with?"

"Yeah."

I gave him the address. "What time do you think you'll be there?" I wondered if this would be a Code Red, Orange, or Yellow. Dad would need a little time to get ready for the nimbus blowing in his direction.

"I don't know, Jack. When I get there, okay! I gotta go."

"But, Chris, I …" He didn't hear my words; probably snapping his flip phone shut as I shouted my last words.

I called my dad immediately, "Hey, Dad. How are you doing today?"

"Good. How are you doing?"

"Great. I just got a phone call from Chris."

"How *is* Chris?"

"Good, Chris is good. He's coming to visit you," I blurted.

"Chris is going to visit *me?* When?"

"Today. I just got off the phone with him and I gave him your address. He's out your way on business." I said the words softly, suddenly feeling like a teenager again, and I had to figure out how I was going to tell Dad I'd screwed up. *Hey Dad, umm, I was accidentally doing donuts in the plaza parking lot and then I accidentally slammed the backend of the car against a light post.*

"Okay," Dad took the news in stride. "Do you know what time he's coming?"

"I don't know; I just know it's sometime today. You know Chris."

"Yes, I *know* Chris." Dad chuckled.

"I better let you go. Good luck," I said, feeling like I was giving Dad a send off on a space mission. I hoped he'd be okay and that he wouldn't have too much trouble reentering our atmosphere.

That was the last I heard from either Chris or my Dad until early the following week.

When I asked Chris about his visit, he told me, "Your dad's house is as neat as a pin."

"So what did you guys do?"

The big laugh. "Drank a *couple tree* beers and watched some baseball games. Your Dad loves baseball."

"Yes, he does." *My dad drank a couple tree beers?* I visualized him napping on the couch while Chris raided the refrigerator.

"I stayed overnight."

"You stayed overnight?"

"Yeah. And then I took your dad to lunch the next day, before I took off."

"It sounds like you had a good visit."

"Your dad is great, Jack."

"Thanks, Chris."

My conversation with Dad uncovered a few details Chris hadn't discussed with me. "Hey, Dad. I heard Chris stayed overnight. How did that go?"

"Good." Dad laughed, gathering himself.

I could tell there was a story that needed telling; I couldn't imagine what Chris and Dad could have talked about for that many hours. Wait, yes I could. God help me. I hoped there was some modicum of a filter on what Chris might have said. Hopefully, my dad did most of the talking. Who was I kidding? There wasn't a chance.

"So what did you guys do all night?"

"Well, he showed up at the front door with a twelve pack of Keystone." I pictured Chris posing with the beer, cradling it in his arms like one of those photos from the '60s of a tight end catching a football. Dad continued, "He handed me the beer and said, 'Here Bill, I brought you a present.'"

"Yeah, that's Chris. How many did you guys drink?"

"I had one. And part of another."

"What about Chris? How many did he have?"

Dad paused, laughing, "Quite a few. I think he took three with him when he left the next morning."

"He didn't leave them for you?"

"I wasn't going to drink them. I didn't care."

I wasn't passing judgment on either of them. You see, I'm a numbers guy, I just had to know, it helped me form the picture of their night together. I could see Chris reclining in my dad's leather lounge chair, having a couple tree beers and a couple tree more, sharing stories as my dad patiently listened while sneaking glances of a ballgame on TV.

"He said you guys went to lunch. How did that go?"

"Well—*I* had lunch. He had a couple of those tall beers. I asked him, 'Chris, do you think you should be drinking all that beer if you're going to be driving?' and he told me, 'Bill, you gotta stay hydrated.' I told him, 'You know, Chris. You can do that with water.'"

Dad laughed, I laughed, and I was glad to have a friend who would take the time to visit my dad. I hope when Dad visits me this summer we can repay the favor. I'll drive Dad over for a visit at Chris's house, but this time we'll skip the twelve pack of Keystone.

Chris, the Geek, and Alex at the top of the Wall at Holiday Valley - 2008

Memorial Services for an Atheist

W<small>E VEER OFF</small> the trail—time for a potty stop. Chris strides forward like a zombie, straight-lining his way to a large bathroom constructed of mortared stone. It was built during the Great Depression, a make-work-project of the WPA (Work Projects Administration), part of FDR's New Deal agency. The WPA provided work opportunities for millions of unemployed men to carry out public works projects. The sturdy walls have withstood savage Western New York winters for eight decades, but the roof is in need of some major work. I respect those that toiled on this great building, but we don't really give a shit about any of that today; stopping here is just part of Chris's routine. The Geek tells me about the Bills' quarterback, Josh Allen, and some of their new players. I don't know the team like I used to, but I like hearing the Geek talk about his passion for the Bills. We take turns hollering through the walls, "Chris! Everything okay in there?"

"Yeah."

It's always good to check on your buddy, but Lord knows what we'd do if he yelled back, "No." We don't know what goes on behind the stone walls; hell, I've never even been inside. Maybe he's in there praying.

B<small>ACK IN</small> February of 2005 I received a call from Chris, the first of several to tell me that a parent of someone we knew had died.

"Hey Jack, did you hear Wilma's dad died?" Chris asked on the other end of the call. He was talking about our friend Keith. Chris called him Wilma (his last name is Williams), but the rest of us call him, The Doctor. Keith is *The* Doctor, but he isn't *a* doctor. It's a nickname he acquired while pitching for our softball team, the Big Fighting Weasels. That's the kind of name you earn when your consistent twelve-foot loft notches a few strikeouts in slow pitch softball. He became The Doctor, as in Dr. K, as in Dwight "Doc" Gooden, the New York Mets flame-throwing pitcher during the '80s.

"Yeah, Chris, I heard. I talked to Keith yesterday."

"You're going to the memorial, aren't you?"

"Yeah, I'm going. Are you?"

"*Yeees,*" Chris answered, as if I'd insulted him by asking.

I was surprised he was going since he didn't know Keith that well. But memorial services were one of Chris's things. He was a stickler for them, even though he was lukewarm at best, about his belief in God. It wasn't that important to Chris whether or not Keith was a close friend. It only mattered that we had grown up together in East Aurora and he'd suffered a loss.

Thad Rice had seen that side of Chris. He'd told me recently about a time back in high school. "We were at a party. It was our senior year. I remember it was after soccer season. It was a big party and of course there was a lot of drinking and the typical craziness. Chris was in a corner. He was crying. I asked him what was the matter and he looked me in the eye and asked, 'Where were you guys?' I didn't know what he was talking about. He repeated, 'Where were you guys? Nobody was there.' I still didn't understand until he told me, 'At my father's funeral.'" Thad choked up a bit as he recounted the story from over 40 years ago, telling me, "I never forgot that. It stuck with me." He went on to tell me how he had told that story in his capacity as an educator, to never make that mistake, to not miss the opportunity to be there when someone needs you. That's the way Chris lived his life. He was always there; you could count on him.

Inside Howe Funeral Home, Chris and I stood in front of metal folding chairs in the back row. I saw The Doctor standing in front and waved to him. He raised his hand to me and then looked down. The Doctor didn't look well, dabbing his face with a white hanky.

It was with a sincere lack of discretion that Chris blurted to me, "Wilma is huuuge!"

The Doctor had put on a few pounds. Apparently, Chris hadn't seen him in quite a while. I felt bad. Keith is a good guy and I knew Chris didn't mean it as it sounded, but the words were harsh for such a solemn occasion. I looked at Chris, my eyes wide, and waved my hands out in front of me, like an umpire giving a limp safe sign.

Chris laughed and sat down as the service started. The minister had some opening words, which prompted Chris to jam an elbow in my ribs and laugh. I can't remember what it was that he thought was so funny. So many things amused Chris and he was especially quick to laugh at other people. It could have been the minister's voice, what he was wearing, maybe he had a silly haircut, or all of the above. A memorial service wasn't about to deter Chris from laughing. My lips stayed tight. I didn't say a word, but that didn't stop the elbowing. I looked to my right; there was an unoccupied chair at the end of our row. I thought about moving, but that would have meant jostling my way past Dave Shifferle, his wife Lisa, the Geek's brother-in-law, Tom, and a few others I didn't know. The elbowing stopped so I stayed in my seat.

Chris was the common denominator of my propensity for poor seating choices at memorial services. He was like your favorite sneakers, the ones that you were wearing when you stepped in purple gum melting on a hot sidewalk. After walking a bit, the gum wore off the surface, and you forgot about it. Except when you walked on someone's snow white carpet and were reminded that the gum was still there, squished into the crannies of the sneaker's sole. You'd look around, hoping no one noticed, and if they did, you'd say, "Sorry." Yes, Chris was like those sneakers. You wished they didn't have gum stuck to the bottom, but still, they were your favorites. A perfect fit for walking through life, but definitely not for everyone, especially if they were foolish enough to have a white carpet.

I SUFFERED a more recent lapse of seating judgment at Mrs. McCready's memorial. What a classy lady she was. We were all there for her son, our friend Mac, jammed into the pews of Baker Memorial. Earlier I had seen Wally in the parking lot.

"Hey, Paul, how you been?" Back then I didn't call him Wally; as I've said that was a Chris thing.

"Good. It's been a while, huh. What's up with you? How you been?"

"Good, everything is good, Paul."

We both laughed even though neither of us had said anything funny. He slapped me on the back and I introduced him to my wife. Wally had probably met her before, but it seemed like the right thing to do. He was in lively spirits as we walked into the church.

Once inside he spotted Chris. This gave rise to uproarious laughter. Yes indeed, it was all fun and games inside the shadowy darkness of reverent Baker Memorial Church. This would've been the time to rid myself of my purple gum sneakers, but I didn't. We slid into the polished wooden pews and I found myself sitting directly in front of Chris and Wally. Please God, I begged, if you're here today. Do something. Slap a piece of righteous silver duct tape over Chris and Wally's mouths, or maybe find it in Your power to give them temporary laryngitis.

Apparently, God was busy with other stuff. Chris and Wally talked through the whole service until sonorous sounds from the organ's bulging pipes filled Baker Memorial. Mrs. McCready loved organ music. Depending on your appreciation for instruments with 610 pipes, it was either a stirring grand finale to the service and a profound send off for Mrs. McCready, or it was just a bunch of hilarious pressurized air. Chris and Wally cast a vote for the latter, erupting like Krakatoa. I hoped Mac hadn't noticed. Despite the embarrassment, I still wore the sneakers with the purple gum. I wear them today, but the gum is mostly worn off.

INSIDE THE confines of Howe Funeral Home Chris sat quietly as the minister let us know that The Doctor's sister wanted to say a few words about her dad. I didn't know The Doctor's dad, but I knew that he was a big wig at Moog, Inc., in the aerospace division. His sister delivered a poised synopsis of her dad's life, about how smart he was, and how he was so well-respected and liked by many. Mr. Williams sounded like a pretty cool guy and I felt bad that I'd never gotten the chance to meet him. Chris listened intently.

The Doctor's sister concluded, "Dad wasn't much of a church guy. I'm not even sure if he believed in God." The elbow returned and Chris nodded toward The Doctor's sister. *Yes, Chris. I'm listening.* I couldn't imagine what she was going to say next. It didn't sound like it was going to be anything religious.

THINKING ABOUT Chris and memorial services, calls to mind how I'd routinely get a call from him during the week, telling me of his plans for that weekend. Sometimes I had conflicts; he understood — kind of. Except when it came to Sunday church services. Chris has a gauzy relationship with God.

"We're riding Sunday at 9:00, Jack."

"Chris, I can't go. I have church."

"Chuuurch?!"

One day, I suggested, "You know—we could go to church and *then* ride."

"Okay. What time?"

What had I just heard? Had Chris just said okay to my invitation to join me at church? I asked him again, to make sure I had heard him correctly, and then gave him directions telling him to meet me in the church parking lot at a quarter after nine the next day.

I saw him when I pulled in, standing by the side of his car with a shit-eating grin.

"Hey, Chris." He laughed. We shook hands. "What's so funny?"

He responded with another laugh, apparently understanding the irony. *He* was waiting for *me* in *my* church parking lot.

It was kind of funny, but I felt progress was being made. Chris had come a long way since that day ten years ago, at Grace Camp in the Adirondacks Mountains, when a busted valve on the propane tank caused us to lose heat in our one-room cabin. I pleaded with him not to use a Bible as a fire starter (he didn't) and here we were today, in a church parking lot.

"What time did you get here?"

"Nine."

"Nine? I told you quarter after."

"Yeah, so I'm early."

As we walked through the open front doors and waded through the parishioners gathered in what the church calls their "fellowship mall," Chris turned to me and said, "Jack, you know I'm an atheist?"

"Yeah, yeah, Chris, I know. We're working on that."

We went inside. Chris looked everywhere and I'm sure it wasn't what he expected. The music started, one of my favorites, "It is Well with My Soul." The lady behind us sang loudly — and badly. I said a quick prayer. Please God, make sure Chris doesn't say anything that mortifies, or do anything that horrifies—just this once. My prayer was answered. The next song started, its words boldly displayed on three large video screens. I sang and peeked out of the corner of my eye to see if Chris was singing. I couldn't tell.

After the song he nudged me in the ribs, "You know, Jack, there are four cold IPAs waiting for us in my car."

I looked at him, wide-eyed, shaking my head yes and no at the same time. As in; *Yes, I know you have cold beer in your car, and no, now isn't the time to be talking about cold beer.* I nodded with my forehead toward the front where the pastor was about to speak.

Chris covered a chuckle that gurgled in his throat.

When the service ended and we were safely outside, I asked, "So how'd you like it?"

"It was good. I liked it. The music was good. But what was the deal with that lady's singing? Jeeesus, it was horrible." And then he sang a couple of words, imitating the woman quite well. *Chris remembered the words! Maybe he had been singing.*

"Good. I'm glad you liked it. You know, you can come again if you want."

Chris laughed. Apparently, I had said something funny, and he reminded me, "Jack, there's cold beer waiting."

We rode at the Ridge that afternoon. Chris had two IPAs. I had one.

It was six months before he went to church again. He came with his son-in-law, Dan Glover. Chris loved the music, but I don't know if he ever found God. We prayed for him, and we still do. I know it would take a miracle and maybe God is all out of miracles for Chris. It might have taken Him most of His energy just to get Chris to come to church. But I hope You are with Chris now; he needs You more than ever.

THE DOCTOR'S sister was wrapping up, "I asked my dad. 'If you don't believe in God, aren't you worried about where you're going after you're gone?'" She paused before telling us, "Dad told me that he hadn't been all that concerned about where he'd come *from*, and for that reason, he wasn't concerned about where he was *going*."

Chris loved those words and thought the same way; he never seemed too concerned about tomorrow, or where he was going in the future, it had always been about today.

The Geek, unknown, Troy Kelley, Bill Steinwachs, Rick Ohler, Jack Norton, Chris, Lance Norton, Mac, James McCready, Jimmy Landhal, and Spencer McCready at the Geek's pond - 2009

Hockey Night in Colden

*You've got to know the rules before you can break 'em. Other-
wise, it's no fun.*

—Sonny Crockett, *Miami Vice*

Sonny Crockett could have learned a thing or two from Chris when it
came to going against the grain. But I wonder what would have happened if it
had been possible for Chris to meet Sonny and compare notes with him. He might
have encouraged Chris to pull up stakes and live on his sailboat that he moored
next to the empty grain silos in the City Ship Canal off Fuhrman Boulevard. He'd
mentioned it to me more than a few times, "You know, Jack. I'd be happy just
living off my boat." I think Chris loved the idea of its simplicity, and maybe he
had a little Sonny Crockett in him. The undercover agent benefited from the lack
of a fixed address, keeping him "off the radar," making him harder to find, and
even when his *St. Vitus Dance* was docked at its usual berth, Sonny's watch-gator
Elvis ensured that anyone who *did* find him was given a hostile welcome. Yes, I
do believe the two accomplished rule breakers would have had a lot to talk about.
Today, however, Chris is in a different place, far from floating leisurely on his
sailboat, *Toons II*, far from making plans to break a rule or three.

He stands peacefully in the shade of old-growth trees outside of the stone bathroom. There are a variety of trees in the park, including beech, maple, oak, and
cherry. Sadly, there are no mature chestnut trees in Chestnut Ridge Park. Wiped
out by a blight, they have been absent from the park for several decades. Hopefully that will change for future generations. In celebration of Arbor Day 2018, approximately 50 American chestnut seedlings were planted. That's cool, but today
we're not thinking of the chestnut trees. The Geek and I wrap up our discussion
about the Bills, debating their prospects for the coming season. He's optimistic. I
say 4 and 12, but what do I know? Chris isn't engaged in our football discussion;
he's looking up the trail, and without a word he takes off.

"I guess Chris is ready to go," I say.

"Yes, it appears you are correct," the Geek laughs and we take off after Chris.

We come upon a section of the trail that runs parallel to the park road. Chris stops, appears to weigh his options, and then walks toward the road.

"Hey, Chris. Go this way!" I holler. The Geek and I hurry our steps, jogging to catch up to him. "Chris, why don't we stay on the trail? This is a really cool section. It runs along the creek the whole way." I point toward the creek bed, lined with shale, its flow reduced to a trickle. I tell him, "We'll still end up at the same place."

He looks at me, at the creek, and back at the road. He's not having any of it. Nothing new there, he didn't often take my suggestions; why would he start now? Maybe he thinks I'm messing with him, paying him back for all the times he told me: "Jeesus, Jack, quit your whining and just get back on your bike, we only have a little ways to go; Jeesus, Jack just ride over the rocks; Jeesus, Jack, just keep walking there's no ice on the other side of the mountain—just don't look down; you're going to love it; it's going to be great."

"Come on Chris, let's go over here. It'll be good." The Geek has my back on this one. Chris gives him a stare that seems to be saying, So you're in on this, too? "Come on, Chris." The Geek gives a little wave like he's motioning to his dog, Puddles.

The Geek and I start walking up the trail, looking over our shoulders to see if Chris is following. He's not. He's standing like a soldier at attention. We walk further, stop and wait. He looks at us, ignoring all that we just said, and then turns without a word, heading up the road.

"I guess we're hiking the road today," I say. The Geek and I turn in pursuit, following quickly. The drapes have closed on the days of going off-road, staying off the beaten paths, and Chris smirking at us, holding a Labatt Blue in one hand and our plans for the day in the other. We hike up the road, dripping in sweat. Chris has to be melting under his maroon sweater over a black t-shirt that's visible at the collar. My McCall, Idaho, t-shirt is sopping wet and the crotch of my underwear acts like a catch basin for the runoff. If only there was a whisper of a cool breeze. Snow, even. How about Hockey Night in Colden?

"Jack, we're doing Hockey Night this Saturday."

"What time?" I asked, thinking fast, trying to come up with an excuse why I couldn't make it.

"It's Hockey *Night,* Jack. We'll be around all night." And probably a good chunk of the following morning, or at least until the paramedics had left.

"I'll have to check, Chris. I think I might have something going on that night."

"Jaaack, Jaaack." Most years I stayed away from Hockey Night in Colden, the bone-breaking, beer swilling, shots-of-exotic-liqueurs-drinking night of boot hockey that resulted in bent fingers, welted ankles, damage to intestinal linings and missing entries in the catalogue of our collective memory. Eventually, however, Chris would talk me into coming, as he did so many times for so many things.

The original venue for Hockey Night was Chris's expansive front yard in Colden. Winds whipped across the playing surface like dust devils on the high plains, carrying the lightweight inflatable ball, our "puck", over the packed snow. After those games we'd stand around a bonfire the size of a teepee. Chris accumulated shit all year to be burnt to a crisp in his funeral pyre of crap. I wonder what sort of carcinogens we had inhaled from the smoke that billowed from a yellow laminated bathroom vanity, a broken stepladder, vintage Rossignol cross country skis, sections of a white picket fence, and a variety of colorful objects that had the possibility of burning at extreme temperatures. The resulting teepee looked like a giant Christmas tree with all manner of flotsam and jetsam festooned onto it. We were celebrating victory. It wasn't about winning or losing the game; the victory was about standing without assistance, eating and drinking without the aid of a feeding tube, being able to clink our cans, and in unison saying, "Beers up, beers in."

Eventually the venue moved from Chris's endless front yard in Colden to a cozy patch of sloping ground at his new house on North Davis Road in East Aurora. It could be argued that, at times, the game more closely resembled a rugby match than a hockey game. Of course this satisfied Chris's desire for full-contact anything. He'd remind us so often, "You know. When we played rugby, we would just bash the shit out of each other. And when it was over, we'd stand together, and drink." *Yes, Chris. We know about your rugby.* I can only imagine what a psycho he'd been on the pitch. Maybe all the head bashing factored into Chris's current condition, unable to make an obvious decision to wear short sleeves on a hot and humid summer day.

Hockey Night was not to be confused with our pond hockey events. The venue for *our* Winter Classic was the Geek's pond in the field behind his house. The pond actually belonged to Knox Farm State Park, but we'd always thought of it as the Geek's pond. The pond hockey games occurred with the same forewarning of Cousin Eddie showing up in his ramshackle RV in front of your house at Christmastime.

"Pond hockey tomorrow," the Geek would tell us, or perhaps it was Chris who would call some of us.

"How's the ice?" I'd ask.

"Smooth. We got it shoveled off yesterday. It's going to be cold for the next couple of nights."

"Perfect. See you tomorrow night. Want me to ask Schuppy?"

"Sure."

We'd tie knots in busted skate laces, tape the cracked blades on decades-old wooden hockey sticks, and expose Buffalo Sabres souvenir hockey pucks to possible loss in the snowbanks piled around the pond's edges. Puddles chased sliding pucks, burying his snout in the snow like he was sniffing for the table scraps that the Geek so often fed to him. Most of the time he found the puck.

Snaky orange extension cords, hung on six-foot step ladders, plugged into caged trouble lights that provided as many shadows as light. The Geek had hauled a few benches out to the pond, allowing for a place to lace up and have a couple tree semi-frozen beer slushies when we needed a break. When the ice needed clearing, we'd grab the shovels, skate in tandem, and "Zamboni" the snowy ice shavings off to the side.

The cast of characters, etching parabolas in the pond ice, at our last event included the Geek's brother, Jack, in from Alaska, the McCready boys (Spencer and James were great skaters despite their dad sliding around in his galoshes, a legendary booter), Chris's son Troy, Bill Steinwachs (another class of '76 high school buddy), a few interlopers, me, the Geek, Chris — and Rick Ohler.

Rick is well known around town, with more than a tinch of celebrity status, the result of his many pithy columns written for the local *East Aurora Advertiser.* On this night he looked like Max Patkin and Hans Brinker's love child, gleefully wedging cold feet into his Bauer skates, artfully jamming his blue jeans behind the skate's tongue and protective heal, and topping off his throw-back look with a Buffalo Sabres woolen tuke. Rick was ready. The Clown Prince of Hockey's garb belied his skating ability, as he gracefully circled the ice, scrawling stylish commas in the pond ice, chasing pucks, banging into us when we got in his way, and stopping quickly on the toes of his old skate blades. He was like the rest of us, wanting to pot a puck or three (a hat trick), drink a beer or three (not a hat trick), and avoid taking things too seriously. The frigid single-digit temperature was no match for the warm feeling that filled us. The primary goal of it all was to share an experience with our family and friends.

"Rick, you have to write about this! It's epic!"

"Maybe," Rick answered, not so sure it was epic *enough.*

Rick did write about it, or at least briefly alluded to that particular day. He gave it one paragraph in his article "Frozen in Time" that was republished in a collection of amusing anecdotes in his book titled, *Have You Lived Here All Your Life? "...Not Yet."*

> Like minutemen we assembled for a nighttime pond hockey game just outside the village at a pond on Knox Road. We set up halogen work lights, dragged out some benches and beer coolers and a grill for hot dogs, and had ourselves a roaring good skate.

Initially I was miffed. One paragraph, come on, Rick, epic deserved more than one paragraph. Maybe Rick had developed a more mature palate for the taste of epic. Then I got it. He was protecting the sanctity of the event, like the conservationist he is, realizing some things were best appreciated in their natural state, unfettered by others, and perhaps those wanting to quash the whole thing, specifically the New York State Parks Department. It was that, or he had felt his brief words had said what needed to be said.

Hockey Night was quite different from pond hockey. It didn't involve skating and required no equipment, other than a stick. For this particular year's edition of Hockey Night I wore more equipment than I did skating on the Geek's pond. I was going for a laugh, wearing my old white hockey helmet, hockey gloves that had been feeding the mice in my attic, and shin pads still scented with eau-de-musty-locker-room.

I walked into Chris's kitchen and in the time it took Buffalo Sabres announcer, Rick Jeanneret, to say, "La-la-la-la-la-la-LaFontaine," Chris spotted me. He loved my look (I think he did), pointing at me, laughing hysterically. It was a contagious laugh, everyone caught the virus, and I hoped, like our mothers taught us, that they were laughing with me and not at me.

My silly appearance disguised the primary reason for wearing decades-old hockey equipment. Protection. I was guarding against an early exit from the game due to an undisclosed lower body injury, or upper body injury, or middle of the body injury. Things happened at Hockey Night. I can't remember who it was, but the previous year someone celebrated after the game with a swollen paw the color of an eggplant. It might have been the result of an axe like chop across his hand from a CCM hockey stick.

Chris ordered us to head outside. I grabbed my stick, an old Sher-Wood (sure-to-break) wooden stick. You had to go with wood on Hockey Night. The flimsy plastic blades that you melted into a curve in your oven and screwed onto a salvaged wooden shaft just didn't cut it. When you had to blast the rubbery ball we used for a puck through a pile of snow you needed the oomph of wood.

Chris had expended significant effort to arrange hay bales, looking like giant rectangles of Shredded Wheat, so that they rimmed the snow-covered field. Two openings at each end served as goals. The hay bales also provided the possibility of a soft landing if one of your buddies tried to hip-check you into next week. So that we could better see who we were bludgeoning, he dangled portable halogen work lights from the tree tops, giving everyone an unhealthy gray appearance.

We slapped the ball around as the captains picked their teams. Schuppy, whom I'd convinced to come along, was on my team. I told him, "Don't worry. You're safe. They don't know you well enough."

"What do you mean?"

"You know, if they knew you better, they'd be slashing you across the wrists and stuff like that. You'll be fine, just don't call too much attention to yourself."

"Great." Schuppy shook his head.

Shit! Chris was on the other team. *Don't make eye contact. Don't make eye contact. Don't make eye contact.* I planned to hang back in the weeds, stay out of the action; there was no need to be a hero.

Bang! I saw the white light, you know, as in, I saw stars, and my spine made that same cracking sound you make with your knuckles, only a lot louder. It felt like I'd run into a tree. I must not have been "skating" with my head up. Chris had clobbered me, face planting me to the snowy turf. And then he hovered over me. Waiting. I knew as soon as I tried to get up he was going to give me a two-handed cross-check across the back. So I stayed down. Wally blasted the "puck" from our goal and it squirted across crusty tundra, stopping near the blade of my stick. For a moment, Chris became more interested in slapping the ball away from me, instead of bludgeoning me into the muddy snow. I scurried away like a chipmunk from under a cat's paw, reminding myself to be more careful the next time.

My helmet was plugged full of cold slush, causing my brain to jump the tracks of sanity, and dream up scenarios of payback. *When you least expect it, Chris.* What was I thinking? The ball found my stick. Slap shot! Score! Take that! I paraded around like a peacock, stick high, as Chris smirked, telling me, "Nice goal, Jaaack."

That wasn't so smart.

Play went on. Chris moved onto meatier prey, like his brother-in-law, Andy. Andy is built like a block. Chris rammed him full-speed, tilting him up on one leg like a stunt car balancing on two wheels. Andy regained his balance and gave Chris a solid shoulder, sending him into the hay bales, proving that Weebles wobble, but they didn't fall down. No one seemed very concerned about scoring.

It was the Broad Street Bullies versus the Hanson brothers from the Charlestown Chiefs.

I saw my chance. I might not get another. Chris was racing up the side, chasing the "puck," sweeping it forward toward our goal. I blind-sided him with all the ramming-speed I had, driving Chris off his feet. We tumbled over the hay bales, entwined like adolescent bear cubs wrestling for the fun of it. Something hard smacked me in the mouth; it was Chris's boot. My tongue tasted blood oozing from a mashed lip.

"Good one, Jack," Chris told me as he got to his feet. He extended a snowy mitten, offering to pull me up, and like a stooge I reached for it. He pulled his hand back and I tumbled backward.

He howled, pointing, "Nice lips, Jack!" I touched the bloody pulp with a tentative finger and knew I needed to go to the "locker room" for repairs. My lower lip felt like a gummy worm.

"That's a beaut, Jack." Chris's head bobbed up and down, and he continued to laugh while he watched me bleed out. Play stopped. Rubberneckers took a casual look at me before play resumed. There was no spinal damage, so of course it was hilarious.

I came back outside in time to see that Chris had dislocated Wally's finger. I didn't get to see how it happened, but it was enough to satisfy Chris's thirst for body maiming. It was a relief to me when he declared the game was over and we headed to the relative safety of the Kelley's kitchen.

Inside, postgame celebrations commenced. We raised the Ratzeputz, just one of the nasty liqueurs Chris acquired during his travels overseas. If you look at the bottle of 58 proof schnapps, you will note it contains root ginger. And if you do a bit of research, you will find that fresh ginger is said to be beneficial to the stomach. In this case—I think not! Hockey Night participants sampled many of these bitter beverages, even one made from the extract of avocados, then challenged themselves to "keep it down." And of course there was always Chinese wine. Chris shamed me into taking a swig of that nasty shit. I wimped out and knocked one back quickly, trying to get it past my tongue before it knew what was going on. It made my face hurt.

Schuppy looked at me with sealed lips and shook his head. I knew what he was thinking. *I can't believe these are your friends. Chris is a maniac. And no way in hell am I drinking any of that crap.* In the corner of the Kelley's kitchen it appeared that one of the younger guys had a tummy ache. *It has happened to the best of us, young fella. You'd best head outside, rookie, and puke it up. Better luck next year.*

Yes, for better and for worse, these were my friends. Most of them for over 50 years, poking me, jabbing me, encouraging me, there in need, the best friends you could ever hope to have and Chris was the nucleus.

Chris, the Geek, and Alex playing bicycle polo in my side yard - 2008

The Skunk Whisperer

W E CATCH UP TO Chris on the road. He's waiting at the top of Heart Attack Hill.

"Time for a break, Chris?" It's the Geek's turn to ask dumb questions.

"Yeees," he laughs. *That's why I'm standing here. Jeeesus. How many times are you fuckers going to ask me that?*

He's doing pretty well with his stamina today. A few years ago he would have insisted we run back down and do it all over again—three times. He loved the punishment. I suppose Chris's logic was, that by comparison, it made everything so much better when it was over; like pounding your thumb with a hammer because it feels good when you stop. I wonder if all of these things that Chris called "punishment" were tests, to make sure he could endure, or maybe he just loved to laugh at the rest of us gasping for breath and bruising our bodies. He'd stuck by this logic in everything he did; he loved it, and sometimes when the throbbing wasn't too painful, we did too. My hope for Chris is that there is something better for him at the end of this latest punishment.

We don't have much further to go until we're back at our parking spot. Chris loops us off the road. And—we're back on the trail. He must be following the donut crumbs he left earlier in the week when he hiked the trail with his brother, Brent. Chris loves his sweets.

I remember years ago—it was a small thing, but I thought at the time it was a strange clash of incompatibility. At the midpoint of a local winter hike, Chris had offered me a Hershey's Kiss wrapped in silver foil while we took our beer break. That brief moment said a lot about Chris, and if you weren't paying attention to the little details, you'd have missed it. In one hand you had a brash beer-slugging man's man, and in the other you had a guy delicately handing you a piece of chocolate gripped between the tips of his thumb and forefinger.

As the disease has worsened, we've begun to understand what we had previously written off as Chris being Chris. Things that only we, his closest friends, tolerated: his blaring laugh at the most inappropriate times and places, a laugh that caused those unaccustomed to Chris to wonder if they'd missed the punchline of an obscure joke, a laugh as out of place as a smile on a crucifix. *What was that doing there? Had that always been there, and if so, how did we not notice that before?*

We now understand that decisions have to be made for Chris. There'd be no more afternoon six-packs of Labatt. There'd be no more driving. Jennifer sold his car, and not long after, she sold his boat. It was what Jen had to do—the disease took the rest. No longer do we hear Chris hollering, "This is bullshit." What I wouldn't give to figure out how to throw this whole fucking thing in reverse, to make it all go away, so we'd have our imperfect crusty friend back, just the way he was.

I WASN'T there for the family sit-down, if there was one, about the curtailment of his precious beer consumption. Even if you don't believe in miracles, you still had to marvel how after all these years, Chris stopped drinking and started pounding sweets—candy, cookies, brownies.

There was the evening I took him to a church benefit event. He loved the fellowship, the dinner, the music, but especially the dozen Cokes and the dessert table piled with sweets. He made his way back to our table balancing like a high-wire walker, slipping through the crowded room, while holding a mountain of cookies on one plate and a carefully balanced stack of silver-pouched York Peppermint Patties on another. I wanted to cheer as the plates landed safely on the white linen tablecloth. Foolishly, we thought he had heroically brought some for all of us. We were wrong. He curled his arms around the plates like a dog guarding a tray of pig's knuckles.

"Chris, you look like Buddy the Elf." I'm not sure if he picked up on my reference to Will Ferrell's character. He just laughed. And then plowed through the sweets like a wood chipper, until all that remained were wadded pieces of silver foil and cookie shavings.

And so it's without substantive evidence or discovery, that I made the assumption that the sweets were replacing the converted carbohydrates from a couple tree beers in his body's quest for glucose. Chris no longer drinks beer—a bet none of us would have taken. It might seem odd, with all I know about Chris, that I never got around to asking, how, or why, this came to be. And now, it just doesn't seem important. What I do know, is that he'd go to insane lengths while on a sugar pilgrimage. It was 2013 at our second-to-last Liverfest, when perhaps he was at the beginning of his "conversion" from beer to sweets. He was on a sugar rampage, yelling, "Did anyone bring cookies?" I watched Chris pillage the kitchen cabinets in my Ellicottville condo, afraid he was going to pull a door off its hinges. "Don't you have any fucking cookies or something?"

"Chris, I told you—there's nothing. Go into town and get dessert if you want something that bad." I knew that wasn't happening.

He continued to forage and found a box of Honey Nut Cheerios left over from the last year of the Clinton administration. His hand rustled through the plastic and pulled out a cupped hand of little O's. The overflow bounced to the floor and scurried for cover under the couch, out of sight from the cereal predator. Cheerio dust filled the air as he picked up speed with his feeding hand. Another epic Liverfest was in full swing.

But I'm getting ahead of myself. There's so much to tell about Liverfest. A glossary of terms might help.

> Liverfest – an annual gentlemen's retreat honoring our favorite organ meat, rich in so many vitamins—chicken livers.
>
> Dead mice – a mainstay of the Liverfest menu featuring jalapeño peppers (tails included), filled with cream cheese, garlic and spices, wrapped in bacon, and baked at 350°—until dead.
>
> Liver lasagna – the centerpiece of the Liverfest menu. Made by arranging several layers of liver, onions, and bacon in a baking dish.
>
> Bicycle polo – like real polo, only with bikes and croquet mallets, what else were you thinking?
>
> 38 – the optimum volume setting on a sound system to best rattle the window panes while Neil Young's screechy but resonant voice blares "Cinnamon Girl."

It was a time of deep introspection. *Sure it was.*

I was on the phone with Chris and told him, "We're meeting at the condo at 4:30." Schuppy and I had tee times at 10:30 that morning. I figured that would give us enough time to get back and prepare for the onslaught.

"4:30? Why 4:30?" Chris squawked.

I should've just lied. That would've been so much easier, but my mouth betrayed me, "Because Bill and I are golfing tomorrow afternoon."

"Gaaaulf?! Jaack, why in the hell would you want to play gaaaulf?"

"Because I *like* to," I attempted to dodge Chris's verbal avalanche.

"Jeeesus, Jack. Gaaaulf? What kind of good stories ever came from playing gaaaulf?"

I said, "Maybe Schuppy will drive the cart into one of the little ponds today."

The big laugh came out. "Bill? Drive the cart into a pond? Mr. Safety? Right."

So we settled on 4:30, kind of. I knew the situation would be fluid. *Beers up, beers in.* Bill and I played our round of gaaaulf. It took a bit longer than we planned, but still it should've given us time to get back before the arrival of the entourage, except it didn't. Like I said, the situation would be fluid. It was always fluid.

Chris, his nephew Alex and the Geek, were waiting for us on the second floor deck. First thought. Seeing beer cans balancing on the railing, I figured I'd forgotten to lock the door and they'd been trashing the place all afternoon. Second thought. I saw it now; they'd pulled the Geek's van under the deck and somehow had hoisted themselves up and onto the second floor. Third thought. Why the fuck did they feel it necessary to get up on the deck? There was nice green grass, a paved parking lot, a concrete walkway—all fine places to set up their chairs and coolers. Why? It was my high school graduation party revisited. Chris's van parked in front of my house, classmates hanging-out on the front porch drinking beers, and the ring leader, Chris, smiling his smirky smile.

"Well, we're waiting." He sounded like Judge Smails in *Caddyshack. Yes, I suppose you are.*

They clinked cans, "Beers up, beers in."

Chris looked down from the second floor deck at the minions of his kingdom and proclaimed, "Get the fucking door open, Jack. Let's go, there's cold beer waiting."

I had invited my new son-in-law to join us for the weekend, exposing him to the potential hazards of hanging-out with my life-long friends. What had I been thinking? Worlds were about to collide. The others arrived. It was a good crew for our 3rd Annual Liverfest: Chris; the Geek; Alex; Schuppy; Arty and Judd, father and son and Chris's in-laws; Caz; my son-in-law, Jesse; and me. We stowed our overnight bags inside and put the food we'd brought on the counter or in the fridge, wedging it around pillars of beer bottles and beer cans. Someone had brought a growler. Probably Caz.

We loaded a cooler with beer and headed out to the back end of the golf driving range on the other side of the parking lot where, until the sun tucked behind the mountains, we commenced gaming. We weren't at risk of flying golf balls. At least not high risk. No one ever seemed to hit it that far; and we were at least three epic bocce ball heaves away from our vehicles, which minimized, I didn't say eliminated, the chances of a *booozzzuh* reenactment.

The driving range was relatively level ground with short grass that provided us a fine playing field for croquet, Kan Jam, bocce, and whatever new game evolved once someone (Chris) got bored with the rules. Although that was pretty much a certainty, I carefully went over the rules of croquet while everyone paid close attention to ignoring me.

I pulled a mallet from the wooden box containing the pieces to my grandma's antique croquet set. "Remember this, Chris?" I waved the splintered handle of a destroyed croquet mallet in front of his face. The other half, the business end, lay in the box like a body in a coffin.

Chris looked at me with his goofy bug-eyed look. It was the one that silently said, *Yeah, I remember, but I'm pretending I don't.*

I played along, "Remember, Chris? Bicycle polo?"

He burst into beer-lubricated laughter.

"Remember? You broke my grandma's croquet mallet."

The broken mallet incident had been a couple of years prior to that year's Liverfest. What had started out with a casual game of couples croquet in the side yard at my house in Hamburg, devolved into shenanigans. It took us over an hour for one game and that exhausted Chris's patience. He'd had his fill of me telling him when he could hit and which wicket was next in the zig-zagging course of play.

"Jack, how many bikes do you have in your garage?"

"Why?"

"Let's play bicycle polo."

"What?"

He made his way to my garage, disappearing into the gloom, rummaging, making sounds like there was a family of raccoons rumbling in my garbage cans. Alex was in there with him. They emerged with my two mountain bikes, letting them fall to the grass before heading back in. Next they wheeled out Mar's bike with the *Ahhh* comfort seat and Shay's mountain bike with 20-inch tires. *Who is going to ride that?* Alex jumped on Shay's bike, looking like a Shriner in the Memorial Day parade. *Oh, that's perfect.*

Four bike riders circled the yard, attempting to club a croquet ball with Grandma's wooden mallets. There were mostly swings and misses. The Geek pinged his mallet off the spokes of the bike Chris was riding. *Don't worry about it, guys. It's only my new mountain bike. Eric's Cycle Shop should be able to repair any damages and have me ready to ride by next weekend.* I wanted it to stop, but there was zero chance of that happening, unless there was an injury warranting a 9-1-1 call. So I laughed the same way you might at that relative of yours you tolerate being in your house around the holidays; the one that loses control of his red wine and spills it on your new sofa. So I laughed, and I watched.

Chris retaliated, stabbing the Geek, like a matador. Instead of the traditional "suit of lights," the colorful sequined costume worn by bullfighters, Chris wore pajama pants and a white t-shirt. He continued to jab at the Geek, attempting to impede his progress toward the croquet ball, resting harmlessly under a wicket. The Geek got to the ball and gave it a whack, sending it toward the flower beds.

There were rules in this game. Simple in theory. Try to hit the ball and while doing so: avoid hitting yourself in the ankle, avoid stabbing another rider with the sheared-end of a broken mallet, avoid riding through the flowerbeds, and take it easy on my fucking bikes. The rules were in place because of Chris. I prayed we wouldn't need to call the first responders.

Chris gave up his pursuit of the croquet ball and focused his attention on running into the other riders, using his mallet in such a way I should have whistled him for a two-minute slashing penalty. He smashed Grandma's 100-year-old heirloom mallet across the head-tube and front shocks on Geek's bike. The mallet handle shattered.

"Jack, this one is broken." Chris held the splintered stick in one hand, "Sorry." He handed me the handle. I looked at the useless mallet lying in the grass like the bladed-end of a broken hockey stick. I picked it up, making a useless attempt to jam the handle back into the mallet.

When they all left, my daughters asked me, "Dad, why did you let them take Mom's bike out of the garage?" and "Is Chris a crazy man?"

My answers to both were, "You just don't understand." I had said those words so many times to so many people when they had asked me questions about my friend Chris.

So now do you remember, Chris?! Of course he did. And he was so sympathetic, responding with the same irreverent tone he typically saved for discussions about religion. "Jack, it's a fucking croquet mallet. Sometimes they break. It was worth it." Yes, I suppose in Chris's logic of such things, it was. Well worth it. And now there was another story to tell, not at all like a boring *gaaaulf* story.

WE PLAYED croquet on the Ellicottville driving range, rocketing balls in total disregard of the designated pattern of the wickets. Chris questioned, "What fun is that, Jack?" It had turned into a game of, *Let's see how far I can hit this fucker.* I thought it best to gather up the wickets and mallets before there was another fallen soldier in Grandma's croquet set. We moved on to Kan Jam, but only four could play, so the others broke out the bocce balls. I checked over my shoulder to make sure we were still catapult-distance away from anyone's car.

Kan Jam ended quickly, Chris wasn't into it; how much damage could you do with a Frisbee and a couple sheets of plastic rolled into cylinders? It was so much more fun with the potential chance of mayhem that came with bocce balls in flight. Eight of us hurled two-pound balls at the helpless pallino. Some balls dented the peaty earth with a thud and others skittered by our feet after hitting hardpan. It made for rollicking laughter, especially when a ball caught someone flush on the ankle.

We played our games until the amber lights of the ski resort and red brake lights at the traffic signal near the Burger King glowed in the darkening sky. Dusk settled over us like a host subtly telling his guests that the party was over. I asked the Geek, "What's he *doing*?" I pointed at Chris, on his haunches, 50 yards away from us in the middle of the driving range. Schuppy stood next to him.

"Is that a skunk?" Arty asked.

Of course it was. Chris approached the skunk with the same level of caution one might employ with a golden retriever puppy. I called out to him, "Do you really think you should be getting that close?" I took a few cautious steps in his direction. "If you get sprayed you're sleeping in your car," I said, as if that was going to change anything. For a moment, I think Chris might have heeded my warning; he stood up, and took a few steps away from the baby skunk. But then I realized why; he picked up his beer can that he'd left in the grass. And there was another odd sight, Schuppy (Mr. Safety), squatting a short distance from the skunk as Chris stood directly behind him sipping his beer. The gathering skunk family stood their ground, presumably looking for a handout, or a sip of Chris's Labatt. From where I stood it looked like one of the skunks was a miniature baseball pitcher, staring at Schuppy on his haunches, looking for the sign from his catcher, while Chris prepared to squat in the position of a baseball umpire behind Schuppy. I snapped a picture.

Schuppy stood up and Chris moved closer, talking to the skunk. But the skunk had nothing good to say about any of us, and so as he was taught, he kept his thoughts to himself. Still there was danger. If he pointed his hind quarters at Chris, I was heading back to the condo and locking the doors. Chris tossed something toward the skunk; a peace offering. It appeared to be a pretzel rod. The skunk took the offering in his tiny paws, stood up holding it, and sauntered off, happy that he had made a new friend.

We picked up our beer, left the games outside with the skunk family, and prepared to move the party indoors. The sun set behind the hills, spilling purple on the horizon as Chris turned from the Mephitidae family, content that his work as the Skunk Whisperer was finished for the night.

Chris sampling the eats at Liverfest - 2012

Liverfest

"W HY'S HE GOING in there?" the Geek asks as Chris veers off the road, plowing through the brush. He's on auto-pilot.

"That's the way we always go," I tell the Geek. Despite no evidence of a trail, it's Chris's trail. A brambly shortcut that intersects the marked path a few hundred feet ahead. It's as if Chris has a GPS microchip embedded in the deepest folds of his brain, hidden from the disease, allowing him to maintain his trail sense. Maybe the disease is so preoccupied with stealing his memory, his ability to negotiate the smallest descent, his bowel control, and his speech, that it hasn't gotten around to his sense of direction.

It seems like he still enjoys our company. He doesn't say anything unless we ask him a question, but he greets us with a big smile, and waits for us with the innocence of a four-year-old being picked up for a trip to the zoo. There won't be any thank-yous for us today, but that's okay. In the past, if the Geek or I had organized an outing, he might've complained; there was always something not up to his specifications for life on the edge. Still, he never missed the chance to say, "Hey, thanks for setting this up, Jack. It was great!" Sometimes he'd get downright sappy with Geek and me, breaking out his misty-eyed-friend speech, telling us, "You guys are the best. I don't know what I'd do if I didn't have you guys for friends."

He'd try to go on further until the Geek would shut him down, "Yeah, yeah, Chris. We know we're great." And then we'd all laugh, knowing in our private thoughts that we *did* have something special. We *still* have something special— only different.

INSIDE THE condo in Ellicottville I headed upstairs for a shower, a tactical error on my part. The recommended protocol for damage control demanded that Chris not be left unsupervised in the kitchen. He'd brought his "big knife." It was prudent to watch your fingers while he chopped onions in the same fashion you'd use a paper cutter, levering the wide blade up and down. My knives weren't good enough, didn't "cut it" with Chris. "Jack, these knives are bullshit."

Bacon popped in two frying pans, splattering grease against the tan walls behind the stove; the oily drips creating expression art. The ownership group for our place won't appreciate the abstract creativity; insisting, instead, on a fresh coat of paint. And I hoped that by the end of the month the smell like the inside of a Denny's would be gone.

"Chris!" I yelled.

"Yeees?"

He answered with the equanimity of a crisis center operator. Unless the authorities were involved, Chris typically displayed a mental calmness during the most dire of situations and in that regard, would've been well-suited to man an emergency hotline. Except that he might have answered calls with advice like, "Jeeesus, just get over it, life is short," and top it off with the big laugh.

That calm-in-the-eye-of-the-storm demeanor did come in handy now and again. There was the time a few years ago when I almost made the front page of the tabloids: *Man Gives Birth to Alien Baby.* We were mountain biking on the Holiday Valley Race Loop, near the top of the mountain, ready for our descent at the end of our ride. A cool morning had turned muggy, and I had exhausted my water reserves, riding on fumes, while trying to stay on Chris's ass. Sometimes I could see him, sometimes not. I pushed down on my front shocks and then pulled up on my handlebars, attempting to jump over a log lying across the trail. I'd ridden over that log before, it wasn't a big deal. But this time I felt something bulge from my abdomen. I crashed the bike, landing on my side. It felt like a baby's skull, or maybe a foot was trying to force its way out of my gut.

Chris wasn't far ahead, but I couldn't see him. I called out for help, hoping he'd hear me, "Chris! Something's wrong with my stomach! Chris!!!" Within seconds he was on his knees at my side. I thought that maybe what I was feeling in my abdomen was only in my mind; maybe he wouldn't be able to feel what I felt. "Something's coming out of my stomach!" I hollered, putting my hand on the knobby dome protruding near my waist. I was fairly certain that I was about to die at the top of the mountain, near the Eagle Chairlift. My mind raced through a list of body parts that could rupture: gallbladder, appendix, liver (ironic), spleen, intestine. It would be a cool place to die, at the top of the trail on my mountain bike, but I wasn't ready yet.

"Jeeesus, Jack. There's an alien poking out of your gut."

It was a situation that required a resolute hand, able to push the unwanted protuberance back whence it came. And of course no serious situation was complete without emotionally incontinent cackling. Chris pushed the bulging bubble back into my abdomen as if he was kneading rising bread dough. It was at that point that I became reasonably confident that I wouldn't die—not there at the top of the mountain, not on that day.

Afterwards, we sat together in the dirt, looking at each other, laughing at how silly it all had been. Now that I wasn't going to die.

When the other riders approached us lying in the trail, Chris laughed and explained, "Jack had an alien poking out of his stomach. I had to force that fucking thing back inside. Jeeesus!"

I was glad it was Chris that had been there, staying calm, knowing what to do, saving me from something I didn't understand, something that could have been more "serious" than misplacing my glasses. I remember mentioning the incident months later during a routine physical. Dr. Deberny told me I had probably suffered a hernia and that the weakness in my abdominal wall muscles could be easily corrected with surgery. I'd already had one hernia surgery; this time I decided to "ride things out." Dr. Chris had stuffed my guts back where they belonged.

It's been over ten years since that day. So far so good.

In the Liverfest kitchen, pans sizzled on electric burners across from the counter where it appeared there'd been a botched autopsy. Bloody liver lay waiting on plates, in bowls, whatever was handy, and raw bacon, like strips of skin from a cadaver, coated the marble countertop. Next to the assembly line of uncooked meat were fully baked dead mice (refer to the glossary of terms). The mice cooled in their own grease on metal sheets while Arty and Alex filed by, admiring them silently, as if they were lying in state.

The dead mice were a Chris Kelley original, one of his proudest creations. It was as if he'd constructed himself as a food: a dash of fun, something you wanted more of, until you ate one that stabbed your mouth with a dagger of heat, settling on your tongue with a scrambled combination of pleasure and pain. Despite the pain, despite the heat, we always went back for more. We also ate more dead mice.

"Chris, *what* are you doing?!" I screamed too hysterically for a guy's weekend.

"We're cooking liver," Chris answered.

Schuppy held his hands in front of his face like a surgeon ready to be scrubbed. I looked at him. *Couldn't you have done something to contain this mess? I expected more from you.* Schuppy spread his arms wide and gave me a standard-issue shoulder shrug while Jesse stood next to Chris, smiling, like a psycho partner in the bloody massacre.

"Huh?" I lost track of what I had said.

"You asked me what we're doing," Chris repeated my question, "We're cooking liver." He looked at Jesse, his eyes moved side-to-side, and then he let it out. The big laugh. Now everyone was laughing, except me.

Chris looked at something on the counter through the cheater glasses perched on his nose while Jesse shook a few drops of Worcestershire sauce into a clear mixing bowl from my lifetime-supply-sized bottle of Lea and Perrins®. *Were these guys actually following a recipe?* They were not. While they stood at the counter, geysers of grease exploded from pans of bacon. *Schuppy, where are you? Caz?*

Chris calmly turned back to the stove, forking greasy bacon onto paper towels. Maybe the event should have been named Bacon Fest. The meat candy was in everything: the liver and onions, the dead mice, and the Geek's scallops. All were ensconced in bacon. I removed a heavy lid on a red-glazed kettle Chris had brought. A combination of raw potatoes in the center were surrounded by boiling cheese magma, some of which had hardened along the edges, creating an igneous rock-like coating. So we had vegetables covered.

I endeavored to restore order to the kitchen, but was met with the standard, "Jack, stop your whining, don't worry about it." Chris laughed as he sent more bacon strips cannonballing into the pans filled high with a wading pool of grease. *Splish, splash, bacon takin' a bath.*

I needed a cold beer. I don't think I said anything, keeping the thought in my head, or maybe I *had* said something, but either way, Chris shoved a pre-popped Labatt in my hand.

"Beers up, beers in," he said to all of us. After the third one I no longer saw the grease, didn't smell the Denny's grand-slam-of-bacon, and sat down to a feast of liver lasagna, dead mice, scallops wrapped in bacon, burnt potatoes, and a couple tree cold beers. Life was good.

Chris wolfed down the nitrite-wrapped organ meat with the unhinged jaw of a snake, inhaling it with such speed that it caused a weird clacking sound to come from his mouth. None of us had ever asked him what *that* was all about. I don't know why. It certainly wasn't because anything was too embarrassing, or sacred within our group.

It was time for one more beer. I saw that someone had brought Corona; that explained the lime slices on the counter. I wedged a sliver of green into the bottle, eyeing Chris and took a refreshing swig. He stared back. *Here we go.* "Fruit in beer?! Why would you put fruit in your beer?" Chris bellowed.

"Because it tastes good, and because — it pisses you off," I explained.

Chris loved it. We clinked, or I guess we clanked, his Labatt Blue can against my Corona glass bottle. *Beers up, beers in, my good friend.*

Mystery hands, Alex, Jesse Hunt, and Chris arm wrestling
at the Ellicottville condo – 2011

Feats of Strength

CHRIS STOPS AT an intersection on the trail. He looks back at the Geek and me, wearing a painted smile, pondering his options. He knows where to go, but sometimes he takes a minute to be sure. It's either that or he's contemplating fucking around with us, bolting in a new direction, one that causes us to take off after him yelling his name. He does that sometimes. We're close to the end, it's been a good hike, but my legs lost their battle with the shredding briars along Chris's shortcut. Blood leaks from superficial flesh wounds on my calves; maybe that's why Chris wears blue jeans.

I could never have seen this day coming, a day where the Geek and I are responsible for Chris. Today it's up to us to make sure he's safe, to get him back home, to see that he has a bathroom break or whatever he does in there.

We are far removed from when it was the other way around. Although Chris was the one typically responsible for our predicaments, he was also the one I counted on to get us out of them. I remember thinking once, if I was stranded on a deserted island, Chris would top my list of those I'd want with me. Not because we could coexist for very long—there were limits to such things—but because his presence would have given us the best chance to get off the island. My challenge would have been harnessing a creature with the bullheaded perseverance of a fly *bomp, bomp, bomping* against a window screen, the resourcefulness of a wood-gnawing beaver, and the brute strength of a Brahma bull. It would've been a challenge filled with opportunities for incidents and I'd have had to endure his nettling opinions before, during, and after every survival undertaking — but we would've made it off that island.

I'm thankful I was never confronted with this scenario, but it would've been interesting to see how we embraced another opportunity for "epic," so we could have told the others how we'd survived. That is, if we didn't kill each other before we finished constructing a life raft fashioned from logs and island debris.

The life raft was how I'd imagined we would've gotten off the island—until recently. I've reconsidered our chances for success. Wally told me a story about the two of them foraging through the junk pile behind Delevan Electronics out on Quaker Road in our senior year. The goal—build a creek-worthy pontoon boat. They bound barrels together with rope and dragged the thing down to Cazenovia Creek. Whether it was damaged in transport, or never had a chance, is open for speculation. What I do know is that the whole kit-and-caboodle disintegrated as soon as it hit the lazy current of Caz Creek.

Times are different now. Today, *I'm* the first one to say, "A cold beer would taste *so* good right now!"

"It sure would," echoes the Geek.

Chris laughs, but I'm not certain it had anything to do with what I said.

Maybe I'll have one when I get home, and toast a good day with my friends. It would be better if we were together, sitting on a log, sipping a couple tree beers, and telling our stories. We used to do so in conversation filled with jabberwocky, the language we'd cobbled together over a lifetime, a language only we could fully appreciate. Yes, a beer would taste good—even if it was a light beer.

"WHO THE fuck brought light beer?!" Chris fished the intruder out of my refrigerator like he'd found a sardine in his six-pack. Liverfest 2011 was in full swing with a menu consisting of salty and greasy; what was someone thinking? Light beer? Nobody fessed up. The truth. It was me. I'd been trying to pawn-off the stray Miller Lite all summer.

Tangled arms wrestled for dominance on the kitchen counter. How did these things start? Frank Costanza would have been impressed at our version of "Feats of Strength." There was no need for a formal "Airing of Grievances;" we did that as a matter of course. Eight hands locked together in a new sport—team arm wrestling. I recall Chris and Jesse on one side of the kitchen counter and although I'm not certain, Alex and Judd on the other. Jesse and Alex bared their teeth in a half-grimace half-smile, closing their eyes, filling the room with unfettered laughter. Chris was cheating. One foot was clearly off the floor. Where was his honor? I waited for a winner, four arms thudding hard on the marble countertop, but the participants agreed to a draw. And then Chris pulled a fast one. As Alex and Judd relaxed their grip, he curled his arm hard, yanking Jesse's hand with his and slamming Alex's and Judd's arms onto the greasy countertop.

Okay, so they were done with that. Maybe we could do something a bit more civilized. There had to be a game on TV we could watch. No need. The bell rang, signaling that the "Feats of Strength" had moved to the hardwood—Greco Roman style. The four of them had dropped to the floor, teams had disbanded and it now appeared to be every man for himself. Chris had Jesse in a headlock, they squirmed on the floor, and Jesse's heavy work boot banged against the wine rack. Another item I needed to add to the growing list that was titled "Items Requiring Maintenance." Chris won the best two out of three falls. The wine rack came in a close second. "Are we going to hit the town?" the Geek asked, as he relinquished his ringside seat to Arty.

"Get your bikes, we'll ride into town. Come on." Chris headed for the door. Time was wasting. He was not a patient shaman. "Come on. Let's go!" He watched the Geek grab a piece of cold liver lasagna without the nuisance of a fork, going at the slippery liver with his long pincers. The Geek loves to eat.

I had to take a leak before we went to town, but the downstairs bathroom door was closed. I knocked. "Anyone in there?" There was no answer. I opened the door. *Whoa!* The stench made my eyes water. Someone did a number four—shit squared, a flatulent miasma of marsh gas billowed from the bathroom. "Good God. Who dropped the bomb in here?!"

Chris was down the hall, his back turned to me, shoulders shaking up and down in uncontrolled laughter. "Chris! What the hell? You couldn't even use the courtesy fan?" It smelled like rotting intestines mixed with eau de skunk.

I flicked on the ceiling fan and shut the door. We left the condo, some of us piling in the Geek's van while Chris chaperoned Alex, Jesse, and Judd on their bikes. Vans are faster than bikes, even if it was Chris riding, and so we arrived at the Ellicottville Brewing Company (EBC) first. We sidled up to the bar. Time passed; there was no sign of Chris and his posse. I worried that there'd been an incident.

"Here they come," Caz pointed toward the door. It was apparent that Chris was about to saturate us with an explanation of their tardiness.

"What took you guys so long?" the Geek asked with a chuckle.

That initiated the launch sequence. 10-9-8-7-6... "Those fucking cops have nothing better to do than stop us on our bikes."

"What happened," I asked needlessly. The story would be told whether we wanted to hear it or not.

"This asshole stops me and asks if I realized I was breaking the law. I said, 'Breaking the law?' And he said, 'You're supposed to have a light and reflectors on your front and rear fenders.' And I told him, 'This is a fucking mountain bike. There *are* no fenders.'"

Oh, perfect. Good rebuttal, Chris. That was telling him. Good Lord! I imagined a SWAT team assembling into position outside EBC.

"And then the guy gets an attitude." Chris continued.

Imagine that. Alex, Jesse, and Judd were silent. Jesse looked at me like a teenager who had stayed out past his curfew. *Don't worry, Jesse, I know it wasn't you.*

Chris's less than flattering views of the men and women in uniform—law enforcement, our armed forces, homeland security, even the security detail at the Buffalo Bills games—are not shared by me. Please understand, and don't take it personally, it's just that you fine folks represented an obstacle to Chris's good time. Think of it like a bull seeing red, the bull charges. I believe Chris couldn't control himself; the disease was already busy at work, and you, the fine men and women in uniform, were an early target. There'd be others.

Chris was on a roll, telling us, "Finally, this asshole says, 'I'm letting you go, but you need to get reflectors and a headlight on your bike if you're going to ride at night.' A fucking headlight?! Reflectors?! These lazy sons of bitches need something to do down here."

It seemed like Chris was well on his way to filling that gap in the work schedule of the "lazy sons of bitches" of the Ellicottville Police Force. *Good luck to both parties.* The story was finished, for now, we all had a beer, and the guys did a nice thing for me. They chipped in and bought me a black t-shirt with "The Liver is EVL" written across the front. EVL abbreviating Ellicottville, but doubling in its meaning nicely. *You guys are the best.* I had the t-shirt for a few months before it suddenly disappeared. I suspect a certain member of my household decided it should be properly disposed of; too bad, I liked that shirt.

The beers back at the condo were already bought and paid for and there wasn't much going on at EBC, so after obtaining a quorum we took a vote and decided to head back. Chris was in abstention. Typical.

"See them out there? They're watching. They're waiting for me." Chris pointed at the police car idling near the corner of Monroe and Washington Street. *Huh?*

"They're waiting until we leave."

I saw them at the corner, but they were always there at this time of night, keeping the peace. I suppose for them, it was like shooting drunken fish in a barrel. Those foolish enough to zigzag down Washington Street as they left the bars ran the risk of a personal escort to the Ellicottville PD. Good thing we were heading back on Martha Street. We were so smart.

Chris guided the young bucks to their bikes as the rest of us climbed into the Geek's van. We headed down Martha Street, and there was a flash in front of us, like the Headless Horseman, Chris zoomed in front of our headlights. There was no sight of Alex, or Jesse, or Judd.

"What the hell is he doing? You almost hit him!" I yelled.

I hoped Chris was planning an off-road route back to the condo. I doubted those "lazy sons of bitches" on the Ellicottville Police Force would want to trash their police cruiser in pursuit of Chris over a single-track mountain bike trail, but they might throw it in high gear across the golf driving range.

We arrived at the condo without incident. Chris and the bikers came inside shortly after us. Surprise, the "lazy sons of bitches" had stopped Chris, again.

"What happened?"

"They said they were letting me go with a warning. A fucking warning! Jeee-sus!" *Another warning? Had it been the same guys?*

Alex and Judd followed Chris into the living room. Alex slid a Neil Young CD into the player. Chris had finally figured out how to adjust the volume and cranked it to a level one notch below where your ears would start to bleed.

"Where's Jesse?" Nobody heard me over the twangy guitar and high pitched whine of "Down By the River". I asked again, "Chris, where's Jesse?!"

"How the hell should I know?"

This wasn't good. A mental image formed of my son-in-law behind bars in a cell next to the town drunk. How was I going to explain all of this?

"Chris. What happened? Wasn't Jesse with you?"

"I don't know." He strung out each syllable.

I walked outside; my image of the jail cell vanished as I saw Jesse ride up to the garage. He smiled at me. "What happened?" I asked.

He told me about how the cops pulled over Chris on his bike. Jesse continued, telling me about his own on-the-spot-decision to ride off the road and hide behind some tall bushes in front of someone's house. He waited until the coast was clear before riding back. Everything was okay. It was good to know I had a smart son-in-law.

"Okay, good. And Jesse, one more thing."

"What?"

"We don't tell anyone. Okay?"

"Yeah."

Inside, "Cinnamon Girl" blared. I told Chris to turn it down. Why did I bother?

"38! Alex, keep it on 38."

Some listened to Neil Young and some tried to sleep. 38. It would become a catchphrase for everything loud, everything obnoxious, everything we loved about our time together. 38. It continued all night.

In the morning all was silent. I turned on the TV, tuning it to SportsCenter. I saw the volume still set to 38, but the commentators' mouths moved without sound.

"Chris, what the hell happened to the sound?"

"I couldn't figure out how to turn it off. So I pulled all the wires out of the speakers."

Yes, he did. Chris was always able to solve a problem. It was good having a friend that could solve problems. Sometimes.

*Chris, the Geek, and Mark Norton near Grace Camp in the
Adirondack Mountains - 2009*

The Labatt Winter Blues

I KNEEL, MAKING sure the angle is perfect, and touch the screen on my phone. *Click.* How cool is this, a mushroom the color of a pumpkin. "Hey, Geek, check this out," I holler, but he doesn't hear me. He's a football field in front of me, walking next to Chris. Steadying my phone, I take another picture before they disappear behind the trees at the bend in the road. I cup my hands around the phone, shielding the sun's glare. They're barely visible, dwarfed by the 100-foot trees framing the road, two specs on the horizon, two of my best friends near the end of our hike. The metaphor isn't lost, heavy inside my being like a bag of polished gemstones. It seems we just got started and here we are rounding the corner, heading downhill toward the parking lot.

I shove the phone into my pants pocket and jog to catch up. They'd wait for me at the car, but I want to walk the last steps with them. Emotions well up inside. *Good Lord, Jack, pull it together.* No way do I want to sidle alongside them with tears running down my cheeks. Like a fem. I catch up and show the Geek the mushroom picture. Chris stops to look, too. This is a new development. *Chris is interested in my pictures?*

IT'S BEEN over ten years since our Adirondack winter hike with the Giant. The Giant is the Geek's oldest brother, Mark. He's also the tallest—six foot seven inches. The four of us trekked uphill toward Grace Camp with Chris in front dragging our provisions on an orange plastic toboggan. The trail was wadded with muddy leaves where the snow should have been. Chris aligned the toboggan such that he could pull it across three logs bridging a meandering stream of winter runoff. I was on the other side of the primitive bridge, setting up like the enthusiastic photo journalist that I am. Chris, always respectful of my desire to chronicle our expeditions, shouted to me on from the other side, "Instead of helping, he's taking fucking pictures."

You were wrong, Chris. I wasn't taking "fucking pictures." I was recording a "fucking video," capturing your words forever in our personal time capsule. And look at you now, you dickens, taking an interest in my mushroom picture. Who would have guessed? Not me.

It was 2009. We'd done this, I don't know, maybe three or four years in a row. The Geek and Chris had been at it longer, if you included the lean-to days. I had passed on those. The joy of hiking all day, getting hogged up, returning to a freezing open-air structure (fires aren't allowed in this area of the Adirondacks), stripping off sopping wet clothes, standing buck-naked in the cold while pulling on dry clothes wasn't my thing. It sounded *a lot like fun—only different—*from my point of view, mainly the latter. Only after their guarantee of a heated room at the day's end were they able to convince me to join their winter hikes in the Adirondack High Peaks. One room, six bunks, six slim vertical lockers, six smelly guys, propane heat, dank socks, underwear, and yesterday's hiking clothes drying over our heads on a cat's-cradle clothesline. This was Grace Camp.

The Geek had summited over 30 of the 46 Adirondack (ADK) high peaks (elevations over 4,000 feet); he was well on his way to being an official ADK 46er. My hiking goals were less lofty: see some cool scenery, spend time with the crazies I had chosen as friends, experience minimal butt chafe, and avoid frostbite. I'd been fairly successful on most counts. This year it was just Chris, the Geek, me, and Mark. At the outset of our expedition, Chris started referring to Mark as My Giant. All of us remembered the funny Billy Crystal movie by the same name. Mark is a good guy. He'll do anything for you and defines the term, "gentle giant." He accepted his trail moniker with aplomb.

Mark didn't hear (or ignored) Chris's orders, telling all of us what to schlep out of the back of his pickup and onto the plastic toboggan. In mock disgust, Chris moaned, "I need a new Giant," quoting a line from the movie. At least we were pretty sure Billy Crystal had spoken those words, and if he hadn't, he should have. Mark would hear us speak those words many times throughout the trip. It didn't get old. In fact, it aged quite well and became our Cabernet Sauvignon, sipped with good cheer at every appropriate occasion.

The weather had been unseasonably warm the previous week and there was no precipitation in the forecast. As a result, this year's trip was shaping up to be Miami in the mountains when compared to my first winter hike. I'd received zero instructions on that initial trip regarding equipment that would've proved handy (dull toothed snowshoes are not a substitute for crampons), proper clothing (cotton doesn't wick), and footwear (ten-year-old Timberland's just don't cut it.) I had never been snowshoeing, so while picking up the snowshoes I was borrowing, I asked Chris for some guidance. He responded with all the insight he felt I needed, "It's fucking walking on snow, Jack. Jeeesus."

Things I learned over "winter vacation in the ADK:"

1. Waterproof boots are not a luxury item. Had my brain been leaking fluid thinking my old Timberlands would be a good choice? They absorbed water like a sea sponge. The skin that had peeled from the tops of my toes, the result of cotton socks rubbing on the leather inside my water-soaked boots, scabbed over a few times before healing in late July.

2. Don't fool around with Mother Nature. She'll make you pay. I showboated with my shirt off and a beer-bloated belly in 50-degree sunshine. She had the last laugh in Act II. An abrupt scene change that included a refreshing 30-degree temperature drop and a blinding snowstorm that took me by surprise. I walked in the black-as-tar night wearing sunglasses (nobody said we'd be hiking after dark) and it felt as if we were snowshoeing in wet concrete; my legs were out of steps. I asked the Geek how much farther. He toyed with me, "A couple of hours." I laughed like a death row inmate. "No really. How much farther?" He didn't laugh. Fuck. Months later, my infatuation with numbers caused me to weigh the chance I had of dying that night while wandering in the dark. If it hadn't been for the Geek's headlamp and Arty Aungst's encouraging words, I estimated it was 50% when factoring 10% for wet clothes, 5% for thirst and hunger, 5% for cold feet, 10% for lack of sight, and 20% for raw stupidity.

3. If you're afraid of falling to your death, stay off the rocks. Seven hours into our hike we'd come upon a sheer rock face. I didn't recall seeing this in the "brochure" and asked the Geek about alternatives. "We have to go up and over, or we'll have to turn around and go back the way we came." Again, fuck! I took a few steps up. The worn teeth on the snowshoes I'd borrowed from Chris were of little use on the sheer rocks. I didn't want to risk scaling the rock, only to get up so high before skittering down and smashing my head open like a pumpkin dropped from a second story window onto a concrete driveway.

THIS YEAR'S weather wasn't shaping up to be anything like that first year. At the trailhead, known as The Garden, we battened down the essentials on our toboggan, fastened our gaiters (this would prove to be ridiculous), and hoisted 50-pound packs onto our shoulders. The sign at the trailhead reminded us that snowshoes or crampons were mandatory. Chris laughed at the sign. The sign responded with a blank stare.

We surveyed the woods in front of us, realizing that Mother Nature is a prankster. All around us was a patchwork quilt of ice, mud, snapped branches, and leaf litter. It wasn't her best work. Holding the last case of Labatt to load on our toboggan, I pointed with a bent elbow, and asked anyone willing to listen, "How're we going to drag our stuff over that?"

"What do you mean, *we?*" Chris snapped at me. "Since when have *you* dragged the toboggan?" Chris made a valid point. I'd offered in the past, but usually it was when we were almost at Grace Camp. The toboggan was Chris's cross to drag; he embraced the muscle straining punishment like Schwarzenegger hoisting sagging barbells. I discontinued my line of questioning and strapped on my snowshoes.

I'd bought crampons after last year's hike. It seemed like a smart purchase when considering the little confidence I had in the teeth of my snowshoes to hold fast against the howling winds that pushed me across ice shelves at the top of

Little Haystack. I visualized, in vivid Technicolor, my glorious sliding death-descent, banging my skull on ice and rock in a rousing percussion solo. It didn't actually happen—but it could have. Good thing I'd brought the crampons this year, bad thing that I had decided to leave them in the truck — the truck that we wouldn't see until Sunday. *Do I want to lug these things around? Yeah, you never know. Screw it, I won't need them.* I should have put a spare brain in the space I'd saved by not taking the crampons. What an idiot I was.

We were halfway through our three-and-a-half-mile trek to Grace Camp. My snowshoes had held up admirably over the muddy trail. I kept them on so as not to slip on the ice patches that Mother Nature had sewn onto the rutty holes in her landscape. Chris, opting out of snowshoes and crampons, pulled the sled wearing hiking shoes. For most of the trail it had been the right call. The further we went into the woods, the less ice we encountered and off the trail were the vestiges of crusty snow, like pieces of a stale doughnut.

But the conditions changed once again. Chris was the first to attempt making his way up a patch of glassy ice with an angle that you'd call gentle in the summer, but, iced over, presented a real challenge. He wedged one foot against a rock in the trail, but when he took his next step he glided back to us with the grace of a baby giraffe walking on a floor covered in marbles. He tried again without luck.

"Chris, I think you're going to need your snowshoes on this section," the Geek suggested.

"I'm not putting on my *fucking* snowshoes." I wondered why Chris and his snowshoes weren't on speaking terms. Had there been a misunderstanding between the two parties?

Until now, the Giant had been content to watch our histrionics like a spectator at a carnival. He spoke for the first time since commenting on our level of intelligence when the plastic toboggan flipped, tits down, in a soupy septic sludge. "You want to try my Yaktrax?" asked the Giant.

Chris, always ready to disdain the advice of others, ignored the Giant. He tried again, inching his way sideways up the ice, before sliding backwards and slamming into the Geek. *Why couldn't we divert around this granite edifice coated in ice as smooth as a cat's eye marble?* I knew better than to ask, but that didn't stop me, "Why don't we just go around the ice and up through those trees?" I pointed, with a gloved hand, at an incline void of snow. Narrow streams of winter runoff slithered beneath the leaves like wisps of venomous water moccasins. My suggestion to take an alternate route fell on deaf ears, but Chris responded to the Giant's earlier suggestion. "Give me those fucking Yaktrax."

The Giant stood with his back to Chris, telling him, "They're in the top pouch of my pack." Chris reached up, on the balls of his feet, and pulled the Yaktrax from the Giant's pack. He took off his own 50-pound pack, unhinged himself from the cross country ski poles fastened to the toboggan, and with the graciousness of a teenager given twenty bucks by his mom for a pizza, fastened the *fucking* Yaktrax to the bottom of his boots.

Well would you look at that! Those things really work. I wish someone would have suggested that earlier. Thanks for your patience, Mark. You are a good Giant.

"I smell beer." I said. I wasn't imagining it, wasn't summoning a pleasant thought as we closed in on Grace Camp. I actually smelled beer. As usual, nobody listened. What did I know? And so we continued our trudge. Chris had done his typical yeoman's job pulling the toboggan, wearing his new best friends, the Yaktrax. It wouldn't have been in good taste to ask Chris if he wanted me to take over toboggan duty, now that we were at the bridge, a few hundred feet from Grace Camp. No, not in good taste at all, "Hey, Chris. You want me to pull the toboggan for a while?"

The joke was lost in the ice drips off the wood planked bridge. Chris blared for all to hear, "Jeeesus, Jack! Thanks for the fucking help when we're almost there." The Geek laughed, Mark laughed, I wanted to laugh, but we were still too close to the bridge and the water looked cold. I lowered my head and tromped the last few steps toward Grace Camp.

"I'm so starved I could eat a Utica pizza," I joked while un-strapping my snowshoes.

"That pizza was shit!" Chris replied.

We all laughed and remembered a road trip a few years ago. Alex's brother Sam had told us, "We gotta stop in Utica. They've got the best pizza."

The *best* pizza? Really? Okay, we all agreed, we'd give it a shot. Why not, we were all hungry and we were going right by Utica. What the hell.

We knew something wasn't right, from the moment we stepped inside. There was no one in the place. It should've been all the warning we needed. Still, we ordered at the front counter and sat down at long folding tables. *What was this?* The guy who had taken our order balanced one rectangular cooking tray on another before setting them on our table. He walked away, but was within earshot when Chris wondered, "Where is the fucking pepperoni?"

The answer came quickly from our "waiter." While walking back to the front register he said from over his shoulder, "It's under the cheese." *Under the cheese?* Chris pried up what looked to be a white Kraft single. Sure enough, there were pepperonis hiding under there. The sauce tasted like watered down ketchup. *Wow Sam?! Just how drunk were you when you had this world famous Utica pizza?*

Chris summed it up that night the same as he did standing next to the front porch of Grace Camp, "That pizza was shit!" There was no pizza at Grace Camp and so we settled for beef jerky and trail mix. Dinner would come later, it was time to crack open a few well-deserved beers. Chris pulled the shiny blue cans off the toboggan. Before we cracked one open, I could smell the lager's bouquet of hops blended with malted barley. Peculiar? I had a good sense of smell, but ...

"Shit." Chris exclaimed.

He licked his fingers and gave his hands a cursory pant's wipe. "They're full of fucking holes!" He explained, in case we didn't hear him, didn't catch his drift, "The cans are fucking leaking."

Chris yanked another Labatt Blue from its soggy case. The cardboard slid off the cans like a snake shedding its skin. He held the beer aloft, twisting it back and forth. It looked like a kid's toy sprinkler you'd set up in the yard on a hot summer afternoon. Beer squirted out of tiny pinholes in the side of the can. He picked up another, and another, and another. They were like beer snowflakes. No two alike, each with its own unique beer sprinkler squirting pattern.

Geek and I looked at each other. Cautiously, we inched closer to have a look. I speculated on the potential for a hurled beer can. I took a few steps toward the toboggan to see for myself. Chris was losing his mind, firing off f-bombs in rapid succession. The situation was too fresh to make jokes; it needed to ferment for a while, so I stepped back and busied myself with my pack. I kept a watchful eye for anything hurled in my direction. I didn't think about it then, but if an admission ticket had been required for events with Chris, it would have come with a disclaimer on the back similar to that of a baseball ticket that warns, to at all times, be aware of the action on the field and vigilantly watch for potential flying objects hit or thrown directly at us in a fit of anger. Furthermore, these objects were capable of causing injury.

Chris, never one to be wasteful, chugged the self-draining beers before any more was lost to the forest floor. The aluminum beer cans, as thin as Wal-Mart Christmas tree ornaments, had been no match for the gritty aggregate boulders on the trail leading to Grace Camp. They must have been banging against the rocks as our flimsy plastic toboggan twisted its way through nature's obstacle course. It had been that, or the squirrels had been taking pot shots at our provisions with miniature blow darts. *I told you guys I smelled beer!*

I inspected the stacked cases sitting in our orange plastic toboggan. They looked back at me, ashamed of themselves, unable to hold up over the treacherous journey to Grace Camp. I didn't reprimand them, they wouldn't understand.

Chris was on his knees, cradling one of the wounded soldiers from the vastly depleted battalion. His lips pressed to the can as if attempting to apply mouth-to-mouth resuscitation. But it was too late. This one had been too badly wounded. He stacked it on the porch of Grace Camp, the first pillar of a soon to be pyramidal mausoleum of the fallen. A bead of fizzed beer, or was it a tear, dripped from Chris's chin as he dragged the toboggan of the dead, closer toward the mass grave site. The cooling temperatures had frozen the amber blood of their wounds in the ribbed bottom of the toboggan. *Don't cry Chris.* I put a hand on his shoulder. We were in the middle of the woods, our beer supply had taken a hit, but by my count we'd survive.

Beers up, beers in.

Alex, the Geek, Sam Sowyrda, and Chris at Grace Camp - 2008

ChapStick

OVER THE LAST few years, Chris's behavior, his social boundaries (what few had been there in the first place), and his running-with-the-bulls-approach to obstacles, real and perceived, have been unraveling like a sweater caught on the burred edge of your front door's strike plate. His personality had never been a trim and tailored fit. There were times when alterations were prudent; that is, if you wanted to "wear him out in public" without embarrassment. We were used to all of that. We had been, for years, putting up with his thorny diatribes because we couldn't resist the beauty of the wild flowers that were our adventures with Chris. What we can't handle now is his increased indifference to his day's activities. Now others remind him to eat, to use the bathroom, to wear a jacket on a cold day, and to drive him places where others will watch over him. Those places include Aurora Adult Day Services. I don't know what goes on there. Maybe someday I'll visit him there; we'll see. There is nothing that could prepare me to see him in those surroundings, a once proud Bengal tiger roaming free, now with his stripes fading, pacing, and looking at me with empty eyes behind the bars of his cage. The disease is very good at building cages.

I wonder how much more the disease will take from him. It's not something I've discussed much with his family. And back when he was capable of communicating what was going on inside of his brain, Chris and I never discussed it. Early on, I wasn't aware of his diagnosis, but I had suspected something wasn't right. I remember the last time we were together down in Ellicottville when he chose not to join us for a snowshoeing expedition to Little Rock City, instead opting to stay back and watch college basketball, telling me, "Jack, I'm in the worst shape of my life. You guys go, I'll be fine." Looking back, it was like Lou Gehrig deciding, without fanfare, not to play that day, thinking he was just tired, not realizing it was something much more, an incurable disease.

Chris's disease is good at reminding us that silence is not always just silence; it can be the inability to communicate. It reminds us that standing still is not always just a lack of motion, it can be the inability to cross a two-foot-wide stream. I witness this new reality and a part of me dies as the Chris we knew leaves us, piece by piece. It's our time to do what we can for him, spend time with him, and do things that remind us of the times we used to have. What we don't do is console him by telling him how sorry we are. He probably wouldn't understand, and if he did, he wouldn't want it that way. The time for consoling has passed. That had been reserved for things that were "serious."

As SERIOUS, for instance, as losing a significant quantity of beer during our first day that year in the ADK with the Geek and his brother, whom we called the Giant. We tried to calm Chris, telling him, "It'll be okay. We'll get through this together, somehow." *There's more to life than beer.* I kept my thoughts to myself. It was too early for that type of talk; he was still in mourning over the lost beer, drained through the sieve-like cans of Labatt.

Back inside Grace Camp it smelled like the boys' locker room of EA Middle School. For the next three days, we would eat and sleep inside what smelled like a pair of Converse Chuck Taylors from the 1970s. I staked claim to one of the bottom bunks, exercising my right to quick and easy access to the outhouse perched on a bluff directly behind Grace Camp. For me an outhouse visit was an exhilarating night-time excursion that involved shuffling in cave-like darkness through the obstacle laden one-room cabin, down icy steps, and sliding in camp slippers over packed snow. At the end of my trip, I'd fill my lungs to max capacity like a deep sea diver. I hoped I had enough oxygen, that I hadn't dived too deep, and God forbid if I couldn't find the toilet paper. That miscalculation could prove costly.

"Hey guys. Take a look at this." The Geek was on his haunches near the sink. He held up a box of Ohio Blue Tip matches with a hole in one end. He tipped the box and a dead mouse slid out, dropping to the wood floor. *Thwip.* "No Cannabis Vodka under the sink this year," the Geek said, making reference to last year's discovery. The vodka bottle had been empty, but in keeping with its brand's name, a previous camper had either decided to pay it forward, or like a squirrel, had forgotten where he had buried his roach. Stuffed in the top of the bottle had been a ready-to-toke clip of marijuana (matches not included). Chris, Alex, and the Geek had smoked the bejeebers out of that thing, bringing towering Alex to his blithering knees. This year there was no cannabis clipped to a bottle of Cannabis Vodka; maybe the mouse had smoked the last of it.

As in previous years, we didn't linger very long at Grace Camp. There seemed to be a complete disregard for letting our Giant catch his breath. There was more hiking to be done. I would have been okay hunkering down for the rest of the afternoon, enjoying a well-deserved ale and a hot meal of whatever the Geek and Chris had brought for dinner. They had other ideas, suggesting a trail with a name that forecast possibilities for incidents. "You guys want to trek up Big Slide." *Perfect.* I can't say that I thought about the life insurance notice from the AICPA sitting in my stack of bills at home, but maybe I should have. At the moment I had been more concerned with how many steps I had left in my legs that day.

I knew the trail he was talking about. It wasn't long, but it was steep. I wanted to say, *Really, didn't we just get done with a three-hour slog over leaves and muck? Can't we just eat some cheese and have a couple tree beers.* But I kept the thoughts to myself, avoiding the risk of being called a fem.

Chris didn't have to remind me, but he did. He looked up at me, while kneeling to strap on his crampons, "Jack, we have to punish ourselves. You'll love it."

Yes, Chris, I know. The food will taste better. The beer will taste better. There was no point in complaining. I knew better. So I said, "Okay," knowing there were no alternatives. I'd have to suck it up, otherwise he'd have us sprinting laps up and back to Johns Brook Lodge.

The sun bore down on the last remnants of snow and ice in a tall pine near Grace Camp and a hunk of slushy snow flopped to the ground near the Giant. He didn't flinch. The Giant rested against the pine's trunk, ready to go, stripped of the rigging from his 50-pound pack that had given him the appearance of an elegant Spanish galleon. The Giant smiled a *giant* smile and shook his head, "You guys are insane." *Thanks Mark, compliment accepted. It's good to be acknowledged as insane by such a noble Giant.* Yes indeed, we were insane, led by the King of Insanityville, our friend Chris.

The Giant pulled out his ChapStick, applying it to weathered lips. "Don't ever let Chris borrow your ChapStick," I advised him, as if this was something that he'd actually consider.

"Okay," he answered, waiting for the rest of the story. The Giant knew there was always a *rest of the story.*

It wasn't really much of a story. It was better classified as a go-to and a warning. Whenever one of us pulled out their lip balm, they'd be reminded, "Don't let Chris borrow that." As the story went, Chris was experiencing a severe case of rump rash, to the point, as he described, his asshole was rubbed raw. Chris, out of options, had *borrowed* the Geek's lip balm, coating his butt liberally with the healing ingredients of carnauba wax and camphor. Perfect. Problem solved.

The Giant laughed, silently sliding his lip balm into the top of his jacket. He looked down, making sure he'd securely zipped his pocket.

"You guys are wearing your crampons?" I asked, directing my question at the Geek.

But Chris answered for him, "Yes, we're wearing crampons. That's why they're on our fucking boots."

My mistake, sorry, I hadn't properly phrased it as a question. I thought of trying again. *Why are you wearing your crampons? What is it you're expecting that snowshoes can't handle?* The Geek must have seen the look on my face, and explained, "The snow is hard-pack. These will be easier. And there might be some ice."

Some ice?

"Do you think I should just wear my hiking boots?" I asked.

"I thought you brought your crampons?" said the Geek.

"I did, but I left them in Chris's truck."

Geek gave me *the look,* before advising, "I wouldn't just wear your hiking boots."

I saw that the Giant had taken back possession of his Yaktrax, so that wasn't an option. I looked at my snowshoes propped against the porch of Grace Camp. Chris had heard enough, "Just put on your fucking snowshoes, Jack!"

We headed up Big Slide, poles in hands, heads down, Chris in front followed by the Geek and the Giant. I hung back in sweeper position so I could take pictures.

I hollered to the front, "Chris, hold up. Let me get one of you guys climbing up that ice." I knew what he was thinking, *Jack and his fucking pictures.* It was useless. He looked at me over his shoulder, like a deer taking notice, but then losing interest and sauntering on, continuing his climb up the mountain. The Geek and the Giant obliged me, hamming it up with a pair of big smiles for the camera.

The hike was easy on packed snow, but the snowshoes were needless and clumsy. On the positive side, I had conserved energy by not schlepping the 400 grams of crampon-weight from the truck to Grace Camp. I reminded myself, in case I had forgotten—I'm an idiot.

Chris indicated that it was time for a break. He didn't say anything, but I could see him; up ahead, looking back at us with disgust dribbling from his chin. We were going to get an earful. We weren't maintaining the pace. His pace. *There's cold beer waiting,* even though most of the half-full cans were chock-full of dings and dents. The barrage was brief, "You know Jack; we'd be at the top by now if you weren't taking all those fucking pictures. Jeeesus!" *Right.* I framed a picture of him sitting on a lichen-covered boulder, holding his water bottle in a gloveless hand and his rabbit-fur hat (flaps up) perched on his head like a bird's nest. He took a swig and turned away from my camera lens, making a sour face as if he'd swallowed a bug.

We continued up, encountering deeper snow and wider spans of ice as we gained elevation. The Giant wore his blue gators. They weren't necessary in the current conditions, but he was styling the look. The trail got progressively steeper and the melt-off near the top caused hard-pack snow to run off the rocks and freeze at the lower levels. We took short, choppy steps on the glassy surface, one behind the other, as if chained at the ankles like prisoners of the Adirondack High Peaks.

"I'm going back," the Giant informed us.

"What?!" Chris couldn't believe it. "I need a new Giant," he said and we all laughed.

We were close to the top and I couldn't believe the Giant was heading back. I guess he had had enough of our insanity for one day. I watched him navigate his way down like a baby deer on newborn legs. "We'll see you back at the camp, Mark," the Geek shouted down to his brother. The Giant raised one arm and gave us a parade-float wave and in less than a minute he vanished from our sight. One down, three to go. We continued to the top.

"Wow! Nice view, huh?" The Geek spread his arms like a condor. We stood on massive boulders, the leviathan shoulders of this bald summit. The sun had completed its work on this section of the mountain, completely melting the snow, ice freezing in shaded areas below, and icicles hanging off rock outcroppings like dragon's teeth. Not much was said at the top; we were captured by our own thoughts. *What a day! I'm glad I have friends that do cool stuff.*

Chris stood near the edge of a hundred-foot drop, perilously close to the brink of disaster. Our vertiginous position on the mountain top made me light-headed as I crept up behind him to get the optimum angle for a cool picture. He stared into the abyss, perhaps trying to see Grace Camp below, making sure our reserves of cold beer weren't under siege. While Chris looked below, the Geek, inspired by the winter sun, warmed his alabaster skin. He sat, shirtless on a boulder, munching on a bag of homemade trail mix. We didn't stay long at the top; for us, it had always been more about getting there than being there. It was like that with most things we did. Maybe that's why Chris paces so much now, because he needs to be on the move, and he's frustrated that he can't do what he used to, his essence ransacked each day.

We started our descent. Thankfully, the trip up hadn't been as risky as I'd feared; the gritty snow and ice had provided ample traction for my snowshoes and I'd been able to navigate around a few narrow sheets of ice that sluiced down the trail. I hadn't paid close attention to the route. The Geek and Chris had been there before; it was my responsibility to be an able follower and to not take too many *fucking pictures.* But now I questioned, "Why are we going this way?" I knew for certain that we hadn't come up this route and it looked like we we're about to descend a frozen waterslide.

"This way is shorter," explained the Geek.

I could see that much. There was no doubt that this way would indeed get us down faster, but I began to wonder:

1. During our descent would we exceed the speed of an Olympic bobsled?
2. Had anyone given a heads up to the Keene Valley Paramedics Team that their services might be required this afternoon, at, or near, the base of Big Slide?
3. Would there be in-flight beverage service during the trip down?

I hate heights. Actually, that's not true. Height is okay, it's the falling from said height and then smashing my skull into papaya pulp. That's what I hate. Chris and the Geek, equipped with crampons, jammed metal teeth into the icy shell that encased boulders. I stood on a ledge wearing my cloddish snowshoes. *Great call bringing my crampons a couple hundred miles across state, but leaving them a few miles from where I could use them.* Another reminder, I'm an idiot. "Geek, I can't get down there in snowshoes." I pointed with my hiking pole.

"Can you get down to here?" He stood on a ledge of sheer ice, as wide as my snowshoes, hugging the top of a boulder with a fingernail grip.

"No. I'm going back up and coming down the trail we came up."

"Jaaack, just do it," Chris hollered at me from ten-feet below where the Geek stood.

Chris subscribed to the cautious motto; when in doubt, do something. I *was* going to do something. I hollered back, "I'm turning around."

"Jack, step there," the Geek reached up with his hiking pole, tapping the ledge below me, "and I'll throw you up my crampons."

What a friend. The Geek was willing to take off his own crampons in order for me to have a fair and equal opportunity to kill myself. "Okay," I said, backing my way down on my belly, hoping the teeth of my snowshoes would slow my slide. I stuck the landing.

Chris wasn't impressed. "Come on, Jack, let's go. There's cold beer waiting."

Yes, I know, Chris, but I'd like to drink it from the can and not through an intravenous feeding tube. I strapped on Geek's crampons. Dangling my feet over the edge, I tried to touch the surface below. This time I didn't stick the landing, the crampons ripped free from my boots and I crumpled in a heap on the ledge. I guess I hadn't properly fastened them to my boots; *I'd done it all wrong.* The good news was that I wasn't rocketing down Big Slide like an out-of-control luger.

I made it back alive, in one piece, or you wouldn't be reading these words. Instead you might be reading different words; maybe they'd be Chris's words, words documenting the day of my demise, words filled with regret. *Remember that time on Big Slide when Jack busted his head open on the rocks and died — and he ruined our Adirondack trip?*

Chris, me, and the Geek at the top of Mount Marcy - 2009

On Top of the World

We're at the end of our hike in Chestnut Ridge Park. There are no beers to be had so I say goodbye to Chris, but he's already climbed into the passenger seat of the Geek's van, ready to ride. I look at him through the rolled up window and this time holler goodbye, but he looks straight ahead. Gone are the days when we would have hung out for a while and he dragooned us into having one more beer, and then one more after that one. I miss those days when Chris injected his brio into all of us, and what he lacked in panache, he made up for with a boundless zest for life. A zest that, at times, could cause people to stare, like they might at a misbehaving preschooler in a fine-dining restaurant. *Why did you bring him? Can't you get him under control? He's ruining it for us!* And as if by staring, they'd think that would fix things.

"See ya, Geek." We shake hands and I look at Chris waiting in the van. "Good luck," I say, hoping the Geek doesn't have too much trouble explaining to Chris that he needs to get out of his van when he gets him back home. Why is it like this? We had so much left to do.

That evening we were safely inside Grace Camp sharing stories after the first day of our Adirondack winter hike. No one at a loss for words, except the Giant, who sat pensively at the indoor picnic table. Maybe he was plotting to swipe Chris's truck keys in the middle of the night and do the old skedaddle on us. "Jaaack, come on. It's too early to go to sleep," Chris hollered from his spot at the table. I'd had enough fun for the day and enough of Chris's pithy sayings until tomorrow. I wanted to slide off my bunk, grab the shiny blue can of Labatt from his hands, and hurl it out the front door, but I didn't. I feared the consequences. Messing with Chris's beer would only escalate things. I needed to hunker down and endure his annoying verse.

"Jaaack, Jaaack." Now the Geek was involved.

They alternated saying my name, like lumberjacks on a two-man cross-cut saw ripping across my forehead. The sharp teeth sank deep into the part of my brain that craved sleep. I repressed burgeoning homicidal urges, covering my head with the clothes I had piled up for the next day's hike. They smelled like they'd been hanging in a musty basement. Chris and the Geek continued to call my name; it was a game of who'd crack first. They'd laugh if I got up and joined them at the table, but they'd persist calling my name, if I didn't. I kept the clothes over my head, allowing for a small opening so I could keep tabs on what they might be plotting. I knew it was better not to say anything and hope they'd get tired of the whole thing. So why was it that I blurted? "Shut the fuck up! I'm trying to get some sleep."

They laughed, and continued in chorus, "Jaaack, Jaaack."

"Anyone up for a night-cap?" The Giant swung his bottle of Maker's Mark like the pendulum on a grandfather clock.

The Geek rummaged under the sink and found a red Solo cup. He tapped it upside down on the table and blew a cleansing breath into his makeshift shot glass, scattering particles of unknown origin. Bourbon would complete the sterilization process. The Geek extended his arm in the direction of the Giant like he was begging for spare change. The Giant poured him a double.

"Chris?" The Giant offered him a knock from his swinging bottle of bourbon.

"That stuff tastes like shit!" Chris responded. He belched and slammed an empty Labatt on the wooden table. *Dooonk.* Chris opted out of the bourbon shot. We could always count on him to make responsible decisions. I'm sure he didn't want to be hung over for our hike the next day. *Sure, that was it.*

I heard the door open. One of them was going outside to take a leak. It must have been Chris because I could hear the Geek talking to the Giant. The door hinges squealed and I heard footsteps come back inside. Someone turned off the light and finally I'd be able to get some sleep — except I couldn't. It was so quiet that I could still hear the echo of them calling my name, imploring me to join the party, like horrible song lyrics that wouldn't leave me, burrowing into my head. A brain worm.

Jaaack, Jaaack, Jaaack, Jaaack, Jaaack, Jaaack.

In the morning the sun got up before us, poked its head inside Grace Camp and laughed at us. *It's time to get up, boys.* The sun headed on its way, filling the rest of the sky with glorious warmth. We stuffed our daypacks with essentials. Chris had our lunch, which consisted of jerky, cheese, crackers, and a couple packets of smoked salmon. The rest of us carried water, trail mix, and extra layers of clothes (I'd learned my lesson.) Surprisingly, there were no breakfast beers.

We started our trudge to the top. At the onset, it didn't feel like we were going up. The first couple of miles or so were relatively flat and when we did climb, it was immediately followed by a descent. The plan was to summit Mount Marcy, the highest point in New York State. The Geek had been there before and told me, "It's a long hike, but it's easy."

I'd heard those words before, so I asked, "How far is it?"

"About five or six miles—one-way."

"Oh."

I quickly computed ten to twelve miles and added another six. The extra six represented the amount of miles the Geek had probably subtracted from the total to ensure that I'd join them. It's not that I'm a fem, I loved this stuff—except when it crossed the line, the line when it became, *a lot like fun—only different.*

"And it's a bald summit. Should be some good views today," the Geek added.

The sun cast long shadows on the trees as we walked past Johns Brook Lodge and over a few creek crossings, some with bridges, and some without. I snapped a picture of the Giant on a metal bridge, hoping the cables held while he pushed the tensile strength of the rusty steel to its limits. It bounced and swayed with every giant-step, but he set foot safely on the other side. The bridge had been Giant tested, which was always good.

"Hold up guys. I need a minute." I was already out of energy and all I could think of was lying down and taking a nap.

"Jeesus, Jack," Chris consoled me.

"Just give me a few minutes, okay!" Like a Tesla recharging, I stood with my eyes closed, facing the sun, plugging into its warming energy source. "Okay, I'm good."

A steep incline was within our sights as we walked past felled birch trees, their stumps protruding from the snow like spearheads. "Beaver dam." The Geek pointed off to the right. We explored the area for a few minutes before continuing on our way. I thought of the beavers, wishing I could have seen them at work, cutting down trees with their teeth, walking on their hind legs with a mouthful of timber, and artfully weaving it together into a cozy little home. The beavers were pretty cool.

"Did anyone bring TP?" Chris stopped on the trail, grinning at us like he wanted to tell us a secret.

"Here." The Geek handed him a flattened roll of toilet paper. These guys thought of everything. I wondered about the things I might need that I hadn't brought. Crampons were one thing, toilet paper was not. Too much Wisconsin extra sharp cheddar and not enough beer had me stopped up until we returned to Western New York. Chris had no such issue, gamboling joyfully off the trail to take his morning crap. I was envious of his evacuation system.

"Let's go," he said as he returned wearing a shit-eating grin (not-literal, I hoped).

"Everything work out okay?" I asked. We all laughed. No further words were required.

Chris stopped to refill his water bottle in the creek. "You're going to drink that?" I asked. No way was I drinking water that hadn't been boiled. I remembered our buddy, John Hitchings, a few years ago, had used his water purifier with iodine tablets. Still he'd succumbed to the joys of giardia, also known as beaver fever. This "weight-loss program" is an intestinal infection caused by microscopic parasites found in, among other places, backcountry streams. Its benefits include abdominal cramping, bloating, nausea and bouts of watery diarrhea. It usually clears up within a few weeks. Poor Hitchy lost twenty pounds by the time it had finished having its way with his personal plumbing. *Yeah, go ahead. Drink all you want, Chris; throw caution to the wind. Just make sure it's downwind ... and you have plenty of toilet paper.*

Our next stop was lunch. The guys allowed me to take their picture, posing next to iconic Slant Rock, a huge boulder left by receding glaciers. *Thank you glaciers, you did nice work.* We took off our snowshoes and climbed the backside of the rock, carefully walking single-file to its highest point, a narrow tip of rock twenty feet off the ground. I was first in line followed by Chris, the Giant, and the Geek. As if on command we lowered ourselves onto the snow, using gloves and jackets as butt insulation from the wet snow. I looked at Chris. He was smiling. *Why are you smiling, Chris? What are you plotting?* I scooched away from the edge of the rock.

Chris pulled our lunch from his pack and commenced doling out rations of cheese and crackers. His gnarly hands touched everything, the hands that a few hours ago were touching … *Oh, God, please remove this vision from my head.* Chris palmed me a saltine loaded with a thick cut of white cheddar. I took it. What the fuck, a little shit on a cracker never killed anybody. Had it?

On top of Slant Rock, we basked in the sun, roosting on its narrow perch, retelling stories from past hikes. We told them because they were funny. And we told them to remember, the mundane evaporated from existence, the indelible framed with laughs, and bolstered by embroidered tales of suffering. We talked about the time Arty, the Geek, and I hung back on Little Haystack, watching Alex, his brother Sam, and Chris as they attempted to jab their way to the top of ice-covered Haystack. From our vantage point they looked like lice crawling over a surface of whipped meringue. And we remembered the time five of us had struggled (I was the fifth, responsibly chronicling the episode with my Olympus camera) to pull five feet of six-foot five-inch Alex out of the snow he had broken through. The false floor had covered the tops of 15-foot blue spruce trees. Alex's snowshoes tangled in the evergreen's branches beneath the snow's surface. The more he thrashed, the more ensnared he became. I steadied my camera, ready to snap a picture of the next victim to break through the snow and asked, "How about a rope?" I was informed we didn't have rope. *We carried toilet paper, but we didn't have a rope?*

Tranquilly, the Giant indulged our story, asking, "So what happened to Alex?" The story didn't have a surprise ending; a helicopter wasn't summoned to airlift him to safety, nor did we leave him behind to be eaten by bears. I guess in that sense, it wasn't much of a story, a had-to-be-there type of tale.

The Geek answered his brother's question, "Eventually we pulled him free."

"Did anyone else break through the snow?"

"No."

The Giant seemed disappointed.

We finished our lunch, backed down Slant Rock, feet first, and readied ourselves for the ascent of Mount Marcy. "Okay, lads, have a good time. I'm heading back." The Giant had once again reached his limit for the day.

"What?" Chris couldn't believe it.

Maybe the Giant was thinking of his Maker's Mark, waiting patiently back at Grace Camp for someone interested in an afternoon nip. "I need a new Giant," Chris feigned disgust. We all laughed. The line was still funny. It would always be funny. We said goodbye to the Giant and an hour later began our climb up Mount Marcy. Wow! What a sight it was that day, bathed in bright light, blanketed in white snow, and framed in a primary blue sky. Its size deceived. There was a smattering of hikers scattered on the trail near the top, that from our lower vantage point, looked like pins on a wall map. The Geek and I posed for each other, taking pictures along the way to the top. I also snapped a few of Chris, capturing a strong back and internal wiring that always required him to be in the lead. At the steepest section of the mountain, I handed the Geek my camera. He took a cool picture of me, snowshoes at a 45-degree angle with the incline of the trail and Whiteface Mountain in the distance.

Rock cairns, created by previous hikers, artfully dotted the top. One plaque documented that the mountain was first summited in 1837. We were three of many who had been there, but this was our day, a special day at the top of New York State 5,344 feet above sea level. Since the Giant hadn't made it this far, it was the Geek that was the tallest point, at 5,350 feet and four inches.

I selected a worthy-looking candidate, from among the other climbers standing at the top, to take our picture. Chris covered his heart like he was about to pledge allegiance to something. Our unsuspecting photographer was patient as I asked him, "Can you take one over there? And make sure you don't cut our legs off." I'm sure he knew I meant in the picture and not literally. The right leg of Chris's nylon pants billowed in the wind. In the picture it looks like he has a deformity; one leg appearing to be four-times the size of the other. And I'm on a raised portion of rock so I'm almost at eye-level with the Geek. It's a great picture with two of my best friends. We hadn't climbed Mount Everest that day, but it felt that way to me. And as always, we did it together.

Near the edge of a snowy precipice, a telemark skier we had passed on the way up readied for descent. *He's going down there?* The skier glanced over his shoulder and without fanfare, shushed over the edge. In less than a minute he was consumed by the tree-line below. *Wow, how cool! I'm surprised Chris hasn't suggested this. He'd love the punishment of the uphill climb on skis. Maybe next year.*

Nobody said it was time to head down. It was an internal clock thing, a silent cue that it was time to leave this incredible place. We fastened our snowshoes and pulled on our packs. The wind continued to pick up, causing Chris to place his rabbit-fur hat back on his head, this time flaps down.

Three and a half hours later we were back at Grace Camp. As we approached the cabin I envisioned the Giant, in a Maker's Mark induced coma strapped to the ground, like Gulliver surrounded by Lilliputians. The camp was quiet.

"Mark," the Geek called out for his brother.

We stomped up to the stairs and onto the front porch of Grace Camp. There he was, standing near the stove. Our Giant.

"Hey, Mark. So what did you do with the rest of your afternoon?" the Geek asked.

"Well, I read a few chapters of my book, drank a little of this, (the Maker's Mark tick-tocked in his big hand), and I took a nap."

"Nice."

"And I got all of this ready," he said, spreading his hands over the preparations he had made for our dinner. "I would have started cooking, but I had no idea when, or if, you idiots were coming back."

We laughed—even Mark. We loved our Giant.

Chris at Chestnut Ridge Park - 2017

A Change of Plans

I'M HIKING SOLO at the Ridge today. A hundred feet from the trailhead I slide down a small embankment, landing on my ass. I'm okay, but something is missing. The laugh. It's a laugh that, for years, pissed me off, but at the same time reminded me not to take myself too seriously. Chris would have reminded me, I had fallen, but *there was no spinal damage, so it's funny.*

I need to be more careful. My crampons would have helped back there, but they wouldn't be a good option for most of the trail. Snow covers soupy mud, crusted in places, but mostly the ground sucks at my feet, using its slippery tricks to pull me down. *If a man falls in the woods, and no one sees him, can you still hear Chris's laugh?* I am confident that the answer is yes.

I wouldn't even own crampons if not for Chris. Owning crampons portends traversing some pretty serious terrain. I've used them twice, but it's a safe bet that I won't be using them again. Chris and I don't do stuff that requires wearing crampons, anymore.

It's impossible for me to take a hike and not think of him. I bang my boots against the stump of a solid pine tree, loosening the mud and continuing down the ridgeline opposite from where everyone else hikes. The path to the eternal flame is a popular one these days, so I'll stay on the other side, finding the quiet sounds of nature despite Chris's voice banging around my head, "Jeeesus, they ruined this trail with all those flame markers. Do they really need trail markers with fucking flames?" And then, seeing someone walking toward us on the trail, he'd remind me, "Don't make eye contact." Chris would be proud of me today. I'm staying away from the trail with the *fucking* flame markers.

It's a day so damp, the cold hugs you like a wet towel. There's no beauty in the dreary sky scribbled full of clouds, like the artwork of a four-year-old with a fat number two pencil. So instead, I look at the ground. I almost walk right past it, stomping on it and ruining its beauty. In front of where I stand, embedded in the snow, leaves are arranged in the pattern of a heart. *How cool! Someone had to have made that; they couldn't have just fallen that way.* I find it amazing that an earlier hiker had taken the time to do that, with only a whisker of hope that someone else might appreciate their natural art.

To my right, the creek cascades over terraced waterfalls. There's a fresh skid mark near the water's edge from a fat-tire bike. The rider must have fallen hard. *Don't look where you don't want to go.* White snow frames the indentation of splattered mud on the ground like a crime scene chalk-line. Chris would've loved seeing that, laughing his big laugh. Instead, I only hear the wet-kiss of my boots pulling free from the slop.

I'm coming to the end of the downhill section on the blue trail. I won't attempt a creek crossing at my usual spot, trail marker number 65. Today the creek rushes with the swirling slickness of a waterslide at Splash Lagoon. So I walk further, to where, in warmer weather, we cross on our mountain bikes. The water is slower here, but my effort to build a rock bridge is futile. The water is too deep. There's no way I am hiking back up the same trail I just came down. Chris would never endorse that. No way. That's as bad as asking for directions. I contemplate taking off my boots and socks, pulling up my leggings and wind pants to my knees, and wading into the chill with bare feet. I get a vision of my future. Slipping, smashing my elbow, and completely jacking up my shoulder. I could handle that. But what's the point without Chris to bear witness, laughing hysterically as he drags me from the icy water, twisting my bum shoulder completely out of the socket. *A lot like fun—only different.* I decide not to cross; there has to be another way.

Climbing up an embankment, completely off the trail, I search for shallow water and find it. Kind of. I don't hesitate, hop-scotching my way across rocks partially submerged in the rushing current. I imagine Chris watching me, smiling, proud of my effort. Not so much for the creek-crossing, but because I hadn't turned back and hiked on the trail I'd just come down.

The woods are dotted with dead leaves covering the snow like freckles. Glassy-green water rushes around tangled deadfall and rounded boulders, filling the woods with nature's music, a gurgling sound, like a drain-plug had been pulled open. If Chris was with me I'd tell him, "Hold up. Let me get a picture of you by that little waterfall." And he'd complain, but I wouldn't care. Thoughts of Chris fill my head; he's here, with me. The woods love Chris.

At the end of my hike, I get in my car, but I don't start the engine. I sit there, staring straight ahead, thinking of my friend. He should have been out here with me today. I don't hesitate any further. Warming my dead phone over the front window defroster, it comes to life and I call Jennifer. She doesn't answer, so I leave a message. The Sabres are playing tonight and I ask if Chris is available to go down to Wallenwein's to grab a pizza and watch the game. I drive home without receiving a call back and pull into my garage.

There's a text message on my phone: He's home and available, would be great.

I text back: Ok, I'll plan on picking him up at 5:30.

I'll be flying solo tonight. Nobody else is available. I'll be able to handle things on my own. What could go wrong? This is Chris, my friend. I pause. Doubts creep over me, concerns of him wandering around Wallenwein's while I watch the game, and Chris disappearing out the side door. But it's too late for excuses. I've made a commitment.

A few hours later I pull down Chris's long winding driveway. My headlights shine on the front entrance. Chris stands behind the floor-length window next to the front door, cupping his hands to the side of his face, looking out. He's waiting.

He opens the front door.

"Were you waiting for *me*?" I ask, laughing.

"Yeah." Chris laughs.

I step inside and see his wife, Jennifer. Frustration coats her face, and she tells me, "There's been a change in plans."

"Oh?"

Chris laughs.

"He's not going."

"He's not going?" I repeat, trying to figure out the situation. *Why isn't he going? Did something better come up?* Maybe he's being surprised by an out-of-town visitor, his son, Troy, or maybe his daughter, Marla.

I look at Chris and ask him, "You're not going?"

"Yeah."

"*Yeah*, you're not going, or *yeah*, you are going?"

"He's *not* going." Jennifer explains, "He stinks and won't take a shower. He's been walking around with the same underwear all day. You can smell his poop."

175

"Chris, come on." I spread my arms and look at him. "Take a shower. You smell like shit."

He walks away from me, toward the front door, pausing, looking back at me, "Come on. Let's go."

"You're not going anywhere until you clean yourself up!" Jennifer snaps. I don't know how she's handling this. I can't fathom how she endures the daily frustration and sadness. Jennifer is tough.

I try again, "Come on, Chris. It'll take 15 minutes. I'll wait."

Standing at the front door, he pleads, "Come on. Let's go." His smile evaporates.

"You're not going anywhere!" Jennifer hollers, "Unless you clean yourself up!"

Chris slaps his hands against his jeans. It's a catchy little tune . . . for a while. *Rat-ta-tat-tat-rat-ta-tat-tat.*

"I'll even let you do this." I attempt to copy his beat. *Rat-ta-ta-ta-a-tat-ta-tat.* "If you get yourself cleaned up first. Come on."

"Don't encourage him," Jennifer says to me. Apparently, she's had her fill of Chris's percussion solos.

So I stop. Chris continues. *Rat-ta-tat-tat-a-rat-ta-tat-tat.*

There's a picture of Chris from our high school days pinned to a corkboard in the kitchen. "You know who he looks like in this one?" I tap the 3x5 glossy. "Judge Reinhold. You know, from *Fast Times at Ridgemont High*. Remember? He was Brad Hamilton."

"Who?" Jennifer asks. "I'm terrible with movies."

I Google a picture of Brad Hamilton on my phone and hold it next to the picture of Chris. *How had I never noticed the similarity?*

"Yeah, he kind of does," Jennifer says, but I don't think she's completely sold.

The *rat-ta-tat-tat-a-rat-ta-tat-tat* has stopped. Chris paces on the oriental rugs in the front hall, consistently following a pattern only he can see. Some steps are long, some are short. *Step on a crack, break your mother's back.*

He stops pacing and, once again, stands by the front door looking at me. "Come on. Let's go." He opens the door and walks outside.

"Is your car locked?" Jennifer asks frantically. "He'll get in your car and you won't be able to get him out."

I'm sure that I'd locked the car, but I press the key fob to be sure. *Beep, beep.* "It's locked."

Chris comes back inside and resumes pacing. He turns the lights off in the hall. Jennifer turns them back on. For a minute, we're all in the kitchen, looking at each other without words. And then, Chris is gone again. "You know he's pacing?" says Jennifer, as if I hadn't noticed.

"Yeah, I know. He's been doing that quite a bit lately."

"Did you see his fingernails? I couldn't get him to cut his fingernails. And he's rubbed them smooth."

"Smooth?"

Chris walks past us. "Show Jack your fingernails." Chris holds out his hand and Jennifer tells me, "Feel how smooth they are." It's official. We have reached a level of madness yet to be labeled with Latin medical terminology. It's a level of madness that includes me rubbing Chris's fingernails.

"Wow! They *are* smooth."

"He rubs them all day," Jennifer explains.

Chris holds up his hands so I can get another look. His nails are long and well manicured. Iridescent. Polished like the inside of an abalone shell.

"Very nice, Chris."

He heads back down the hall, following his patterned trail, before stopping at the light switch. He flicks it off.

Jennifer is right behind him. "Keep the lights on!" she hollers, looking up into his eyes.

Jennifer and I talk in the kitchen. We talk about happier times, but she's anxious for me to make a clean getaway. Chris lingers at the end of the hall.

"Go," she whispers to me. "Now, before he sees you."

I don't say goodbye. I rush out through the garage, get in my car, lock the doors, and start the engine. As I back away from the house my headlights shine on the front door. Chris is watching. I worry that he'll burst from the door and try to jump on my car. But he doesn't. He just stares. I feel guilty driving away, leaving my friend without so much as a, *see you later*. I drive home in silence. When I walk in the door, Mar asks me, "What happened? Why are you home already?"

"There was a change in plans," I tell her. I give her a brief explanation before heading upstairs to watch the Sabres, but I turn off the game after a few minutes. I don't feel like watching.

Puddles, Alex, me, the Geek, and Chris near Alexander, NY - 2008

No Brokeback Mountain Biking

Mac and the Geek are meeting me at Chris's house today. I've organized a bunch of photos from our past that will be fun to look at, but I'm realistic about how interested Chris will be in the "slideshow" on my computer. Despite the reality of Chris's condition, I allow myself heartwarming delusions, wherein seeing a particular picture from our past, Chris reclaims a piece of his memory that's been stolen by the disease. And he strings together the words from a go-to. I know it probably won't happen, but I don't lose hope.

I'm almost there, turning off North Davis Road and down his long driveway. Mature trees hide the view of Chris's house from the road. That's the way he likes it. Deer lie on the wet grass in the field a few feet from my car. This particular species of deer are known to Chris as, the *fucking deer,* treating his hostas like their own personal salad bar. A rut in front of his garage is swollen with ankle deep water the color of tea. It's been raining since last night; the Gray Dome has descended upon Western New York. We won't be hiking today. In the past, a rainy day wouldn't have stopped us; Chris wouldn't have let an inconsequential thing like that get in the way of our good time. I can hear his voice from the past, filling my head like a train whistle warning me of a fast approaching locomotive.

"We're riding tomorrow at Sprague Brook. Eight o'clock. Don't be late."

"Chris, it's going to rain all day," I'd protest.

"Jaaack, Jaaack, come on, it's going to be great!"

"Chris, it's going to be a mess," I'd try to reason. "I don't know, Chris. I might have some other stuff to do in the morning. Is the Geek going?"

"Yeees, the Geek's going."

"What about Alex?"

"Yes, Alex is going. Come on, Jack, life is short."

"Okay, maybe," I'd tell him, knowing a *maybe* was as good as a *yes* in Chris's book. Why did I let him talk me into such foolishness so often? I knew the answer. Because so many times he'd been right, it *was* great. Chris made it great. He'd never let an opportunity for adventure flip us the bird as it passed us by. And so I'd tell him, "I'll let you know in the morning."

Before hanging up, he'd always remind me, "And bring beer."

I'VE PULLED together hundreds of pictures: mountain biking, snowshoeing, canoeing, skiing, hiking, Liverfests, pond hockey, Hockey Night, bicycle croquet, and sailing. We've done a lot of stuff together. While assembling the pictures, I couldn't help but notice the ubiquitous blue can of Labatt photo-bombing so many of our memories.

It's 10:30 in the morning when I get out of my car. I'm on time and the first to arrive. Chris won't comment on my punctuality, not that he ever did, but I know he appreciates it. He used to get so mad waiting for the Geek to show up, and other times I was the culprit. *Where the hell is the Geek? Call him and see where he is.* Chris is always on time, except when he's early, which happens frequently. I grab the laptop from my car and head up the walkway next to his garage, almost taking a "header" on the slimy leaves coating the wet concrete. I extended my arm on the side of the garage to save myself. Chris would've had a good laugh if he'd seen me do the old slip-on-the-banana-peel shtick, sending my laptop flying and smashing into pieces.

His wife, Jennifer, is out of town overnight with friends at a concert in Cleveland, so we're spending some time with Chris until she gets home later today. She'd warned me that I might have to get him out of bed and after that had texted me to make sure he takes his pills marked "Saturday."

She further instructed me: They're in the clear case on top of the microwave, and make sure to go in through the garage—the back door is open.

Chris never locks his doors, even while on vacation. I remember questioning him about his rationale. "Aren't you worried that someone's going to steal your stuff?" Chris figured that if someone wanted to get in his house to rob his shit, they'd get in whether he had a lock on the door or not. And he didn't want the *fucking assholes* prying open a door with a crowbar and wrecking his craftsman quality wood trim he had worked so hard on. Again, as with many things Chris said, it kind of made sense, but also it kind of didn't.

I open the door inside his garage that leads directly into the kitchen, mentally preparing myself to roust him from bed and the other responsibilities that it might entail. But, he's there, standing in front of me at the door, smiling. I'm surprised that he's dressed, ready for the day, but I'm not surprised that he greets me laughing, the *big* laugh.

"Hey, buddy. How've you been?"

"Good," he says, still smiling and laughing.

Chris no longer spouts rhapsodically about his plans for the day—adventures involving daring maneuvers that are ripe with potential incidents. These days, his plans are made for him. Still, he greets me every time with a big smile, the big laugh, and a hug. And although the disease is stealing his rapturous zest for life, if you were meeting him for the first time, for a few minutes you might think, what a fun guy, he sure is happy today.

We try to engage him, include him in our conversation, but our initial interactions are followed by yes or no answers, there's nothing but the laugh. When someone encounters us on the trail or in a public place, I watch their response to Chris's unnecessary and untimely laughs. I look at their puzzled face, wondering what they might be thinking about my friend. How long does it take them to realize that something's not right? I want to pull them aside and explain things, tell them what is going on, but I don't. Early in the diagnosis, I'd heard that his wife, Jennifer had business sized-cards printed explaining Chris's condition. I imagine her handing one to an unsuspecting restaurant patron who had just had an onion-ring pilfered from the top of their New York strip steak by a wandering Chris. We don't hike with the cards; maybe I should put some in my pocket for next time.

"You didn't expect *me* at the back door did you?" I ask him.

"Nooo."

Jennifer can't tell him in advance that we're coming, or he'd be waiting by the door at 5:00 in the morning like a four-year-old that's been told his best friend is coming over to play. For Chris, time is an eroding concept, so it seems. He laughs as I slide the computer bag off my shoulder like I had done something hilarious, like I *had* slipped on that "banana peel." I shake his hand, bringing him in for a hug.

"It's good to see you, buddy. Guess who else is stopping over?"

He doesn't say anything at first; it's like my words are coming from far away. Is he going to guess? No, he's not going to guess. He asks, "Who?"

"Mac and the Geek are coming." I pat him on the shoulder. There's another pause and I wonder if he remembers. I tell him again and this time he laughs.

"I brought a bunch of pictures," I point at my computer case. "From all the crazy stuff we've done. I've even got some from our first 24-hour race in West Virginia. Remember Belt Man?!" It's a catchphrase from the trip, reminding us of our never-say-die approach to something that tested all of us. Chris doesn't respond. "You want to see the pictures?" *Of course he does.*

"Nooo."

Now *I* laugh, at least it sounds like a laugh, but inside it's something else. This is my friend *now*, I want the friend in the pictures from *then*.

"Did you have your breakfast yet?"

"No."

So far, "No" answers have a substantial lead over "Yes" answers. Without further discussion about breakfast, Chris mounds his bowl so full with Cheerios that some spill on the counter. He plucks them one-by-one and eats them before pouring his milk.

"Oh, your pills. You're supposed to take these." I pop open the compartment labeled "Saturday" and see four pills. How has it come to this? In what was to be the prime of our leisure years, I'm making sure my friend, Chris, is taking his meds. I sit with him, wondering what to talk about next. He turns on the TV and sits back down in front of his cereal bowl, watching a kid's sitcom. *TV?* Good God, Chris had rarely ever watched TV except for the *Andy Griffith Show*. He loved Barney Fife. That was *then*, this is *now*.

"How's your little grandson, Wyatt?"

"Good." Chris answers without looking at me.

Thankfully, Mac and the Geek arrive. Chris greets them with the big laugh and they both ask him how he's doing.

"Good," he answers, not moving from his seat.

The Geek tries for more, "So what have you been up to, Chris?"

"Nothing."

I place my laptop on his kitchen island countertop. It's time to look at the pictures. The first one is a motley post-ride crew of eight riders in the parking lot at Sprague Brook Park. In the picture, Mac grimaces, holding Caz's leg aloft, displaying ripped pants and a bloody kneecap. In front, kneeling on the ground is Sam the Chinaman, looking at something in the distance, maybe wondering how long it would take him to get back to his home country if he started running real fast. Chris is in the middle wearing his rabbit-fur hat (flaps down) with a firm grip on his can of Labatt. Next to him is Jobe Wheeler, a guy who worked with Chris and reminded us when riding near the steep ridges of Sprague Brook Park, "Don't look where you don't want to go." Fragments of snow ring the fringe of the parking lot where the hatch of the Geek's van and Chris's truck bed cover yawn open. We're surrounded by a variety of six-packs and a Labatt 12-pack beckons from an open Igloo cooler. Our bikes cover the macadam, helter-skelter, like they'd been dropped from a helicopter.

In the next picture, Chris perches on his bike's saddle, brows furrowed, and a red toque covering his head instead of a helmet. Evidently, this was pre-punctured lung days. He rides through a rocky downhill channel of watershed. I press the arrow on my computer for the next picture.

"What the hell is that?!" Mac asks. He bursts out in a hearty laugh. Mac has a good laugh.

"Oh, yeah, that." The Geek and I look at each other. It's a picture that warrants explaining.

It HAD been quite a few years since my first mountain bike ride, during which I suspected the Geek and Chris had plotted to let me take my own life and leave my carcass for the E-Ville turkey vultures. It seemed Arty had been in on it, too. I'd bloodied both shins within five minutes of our ascent up a lung-busting bushwack of undergrowth near Mutton Hollow Road in Ellicottville. And the bike Arty had recently sold me in a sweetheart deal wasn't working worth a damn. I couldn't shift the gears without my feet slipping off the BMX pedals, sending them spinning, and the little metal pins on the pedals punctured bloody patterns into my shins like I was some kind of crazy mountain biker drug addict shooting up below the knee. What I found out later, was that Arty had done a nice thing for me, putting together the bike, but shit, he had put the fucking gear shifters on backwards, causing me to think I was *up*-shifting when I was *down*-shifting, and vice-versa. It was a ride from hell, but at the end we had a couple tree beers and I couldn't wait for the next time.

Since that first ride I had endured muddy places and busted faces, watched Alex slam full speed into a yellow horizontal road barrier, hovered over Chris and his punctured lung, and made it through my own alien birth near the top of McCarty Hill. But this picture on my computer screen, the one that Mac's finger hovers over, was something beyond all of that. It's a rickety structure in the middle of the woods somewhere near Alexander, NY.

Puddles (trail name, King—may he rest in peace), had been there, maintaining his distance, not sure what to make of our latest brainstorm. Sam the Chinaman had been there too, and up until that point, he'd been having a pretty typical ride for him, often asking, "Chris, where is trail? I can't see trail."

"Hey, look at that," I said pointing at an open-air shed clad with rusted corrugated metal-siding and an angled roof of the same material. I took out my camera to capture the rustic structure, tucked into the middle of nowhere, standing 15 feet high, and with similar dimensions wide and deep. It would be a cool picture. I framed the shed from the best angle, to catch it just right, ready to snap a picture before I lost the good lighting. Crossing the boundary of my viewfinder trotted Chris — shirtless, on that raw thirty-degree day.

"Chris, get out of there!" I yelled. "I'm trying to take a picture."

"Hold on; this will be perfect."

I lowered my camera and watched as Alex followed Chris, also shirtless, stepping into a weather-beaten galvanized water trough that was roughly eight foot long and two foot deep. *What the hell?*

"I'm not taking a picture of that!" Grown men were sitting shirtless on the ground inside the rusting animal water trough. Against better judgment, the Geek and I did as the Romans, stripping to the waist, and I handed my camera to Sam, instructing him, "Sam, take one of all of us. Just press this."

The Geek and I joined Alex and Chris. We sat in the trough, shirtless, waving, smiling, as if we were sitting on a parade float. Sam took the picture and we looked at the image on my camera, laughing hysterically.

"Okay, I'm deleting this picture," I said.

"What? No, it's perfect. We can use it for our Christmas card," laughed Chris.

Later that night, I saved the picture to my computer. I looked at it, the four of us sitting in the trough naked as far as anyone else could tell. Long sleeve shirts hung from the shed, clothes were piled on the ground, one bike leaned against the shed, one lay among the leaves, and Puddles was off to the side circling and barking, wondering what the hell was the matter with us.

I showed the picture to my wife, Mar. "Are you guys naked?!" she exclaimed.

"Of course," I strung her along, letting the concept roll around my tongue like a sommelier might savor a wine before spitting it out.

"What is wrong with you guys?"

"It was Chris's idea," I said.

"I'm sure it was."

"You know we're not naked—right?"

She shook her head, "I'm not sure what to believe with you guys."

The next day, in a complete loss of tasteful percipience, I emailed the picture to my mom and dad. They were always interested in what we were up to. They love my friends, telling me I had good judgment in picking my lifelong buddies, but sometimes questioned, "Was that Chris's idea?"

My mom emailed me back immediately, "Oh, no! No Brokeback Mountain Biking."

Okay, Mom. Not politically correct, but no worries, I knew you were just being funny. I get your drift.

Chris, Jennifer Kelley, Cindy Norton, and the Geek on
Toons II on Lake Erie – 2012

Haines, Alaska

CHRIS IS BEHIND me looking at the pictures; his hands rest on my shoulders. It's a good feeling, knowing he's there, looking and laughing along with us, remembering times that seem like just yesterday. It's doubtful we'll return to those times or recapture the zest we had for Chris's adventures. That is, unless we discover a rabbit-hole with access to our own personal space-time continuum. That would be cool! Then we could do all those things—most of them—all over again, and this time we'd be so much smarter. No we wouldn't.

The next picture is of happy times on Chris's sailboat. He looks forward, content to let Jennifer maintain our course with both hands on the stainless-steel tiller wheel and the Geek and Cindy sit comfortably on the other side of the boat. Everyone is all smiles in front of a sky filled with thrilling streaks of orange braided with purplish clouds reflecting off the calm evening waters of Lake Erie. Mar and I were there, too, out of the camera's eye. It's a rare picture of Chris. Despite having a mind stripped of pretense, one that favored mischief and can-do, in this picture he's sitting still, letting his first mate "do the work." Thankfully, we weren't crashing any waves that night, which happened plenty of times on choppy Lake Erie. Chris relished the challenge of slugging it out in epic heavyweight fights—he and his 31-foot sailboat, *Toons II*, against feisty Lake Erie.

I had warned him, "Chris, if you ever want to see Mar on your sailboat again, you need to stay in the harbor. She loves the water; but remember, she doesn't know how to swim, so you can't be slamming around beyond the break wall." And then I'd asked, "You have lifejackets on the boat, right?"

Chris had answered in typical unfiltered fashion, laughing, "She'll be fine, Jack. What's she worried about? She's got those built-in floatation cushions on her chest."

I'll be sure to pass along the information, Chris.

And then, of course, there was the lake freighter incident. I wasn't on the boat that night, and it was actually the Geek's fault. *He was doing it all wrong.* A lake freighter occupies the space of a city block, and if you're floating on the water in a comparatively dinky sailboat they appear to loom over you like a series of down-town office buildings. The point is they aren't noted for their ability to creep, to silently sneak up on their prey. Somehow, that night, it happened. The Geek told me about that evening when he and Chris went for a sail after work, taking advantage of a crystal clear early evening. It'd been one of those nights on Lake Erie that come in short supply and for that reason I suppose they hadn't given much thought to making it back to the dock before the night tarred over its pretty sunset with pitch. They found themselves navigating toward the harbor, guided by buoy lights and the city's beacon glow. As they got closer to the Buffalo River, Chris stood on the foredeck, gripping the braided guy-wires, preparing to lower the sails, while the Geek kept them on course at the tiller.

"There were too many lights," the Geek recalled to me. "It appeared we were sailing directly into a lit parking lot. I couldn't process what I was seeing. Every-thing looked so different at night."

Yes, Geek, the night sure has a way of making it hard to see. Since when had there been a parking lot in the Buffalo River, he wondered? And at this point, the lit parking lot, later dubbed the "Stealth Lake Freighter," turned off its cloaking device and sidled up to the Geek and Chris, illuminating them with a gajillion-watt spotlight and blaring its horn so loud it could have been warning of a nuclear disaster. "Where did that come from?" the Geek exclaimed. Chris yelled for him to rudder hard right, to get the fuck out of freighter's path before his nice little sailboat was squashed into a pile of fiberglass pick-up-sticks and they were spring-boarded into the Lake Erie chop. The Geek must have pulled it off, because they survived, and the sailboat wasn't sucked into the freighter's swell, where it would have bobbed like the discarded cork from a wine bottle. It was *a lot like fun—only different.*

In the next picture, a bunch of us stand at the base of Holiday Valley's Tannen-baum chairlift in Ellicottville. It's a good group; eight of us were skiing that day, another rarity. So many times during the last years of Chris's skiing days, it was just the two of us. We'd crank off run after run without stopping, making sure we got full value out of Chris's free lift ticket, until we'd reach the point where he'd say, "Jack, my legs are fried." We'd stuff a couple tree beers in our ski jackets and ride up the Yodeler lift. At the top of the Champagne trail we'd drag a couple of plastic chairs from the deck of the warming hut. Chris would sit facing the sun and I'd have my back to it, drinking our Labatts, and Chris would laugh at the sight of anyone wearing a colorful ski jacket. *It's a clown suit, Jack.* And we'd tell our stories so we'd never forget, and when we were done for the day we'd put those memories away safely so they'd be there the next time we needed them.

Typically, Chris would be halfway into his second can of beer before I'd come close to finishing my first. He'd scold me, "Jack, come on. You're nursing that thing."

I'd tell him, "I'm in my happy place, Chris. Don't rush me."

"Beers up, beers in," he'd say and we'd clank our cans.

We'd sit there together, watching skiers pause at the top of Champagne before pointing their skis downward. Sometimes they'd look at us, sitting comfortably, slamming back our beers, and they'd say, "That looks good. Got one for us?"

Chris would laugh and say, "Nooo."

It was our special little corner of the world, a place to enjoy each other's company; I looked forward to it, but I'd pay for it later with a dull headache that would remind me, until I went to bed, what a great time we'd had that day. I'd tell Chris, "This beer is going to my head." It was another of our catchphrases that frequently spilled out of us when the situation dictated. The catchphrase started with Caz's wife, Mary. That was back in the days when we'd meet for night skiing, have a few runs, head into the Tannenbaum Lodge to mooch what Mary and Caz had brought in their crock-pot, and wash it down with a couple tree beers.

Mary, always responsible, must have been extra thirsty on this particular evening, saying to us, "This wine is going to my head."

Chris responded with a combination of comic timing and Einstein's mind for all things relative, "That's where it's supposed to go."

There were other times when Chris and I were night skiing, just the two of us. On one particular evening I'd convinced him we should take a break from the cold and get something to eat in the Yodeler Lodge. I ordered a bulging turkey wrap complemented with a crunchy pile of homemade potato chips. "Aren't you getting anything, Chris?"

"No."

"No?"

"Yeah. I don't want to break this twenty."

What the hell! You gotta be kidding me! The disease was in the batter's box, but as I look back with the knowledge I have now, I realized it wasn't the disease's first time at the plate. It had been taking its swings for quite a while. I headed off to get some napkins and came back to observe Chris's claw hand off loading gobs of chips from my plate with the efficiency of a front loader. "Chris, why the hell don't you get something to eat?"

"Do you think they'll just give me some of these chips?" he wondered.

"I'm sure they will. If you give them some of your money, they'll probably give you whatever you want." Chris didn't buy any chips. We skied some more, and when we were done, we popped off our skis and walked in our boots, *ka-clunk ka-clunk* into the lower level changing room of the Yodeler Lodge. We pulled off our ski boots, packed up our stuff, and I headed off to the bathroom. When I came back, Chris was licking his fingers, holding a plastic Ziploc bag of potato chips crumbs.

"Where'd you get that?"

"It was on the table," Chris laughed. "Someone just left it."

I was speechless. His filters were eroding, like the loose soil beneath sluicing winter run-off on the Ego Alley run. We still had fun, and we'd do it again. We would do it as long as we were physically able, which for Chris, I assumed, would be forever. I could have never seen this thing coming, this horrible disease. We'd joked often, that neither of us wanted to die from cancer. I'd tell Chris, "I don't want to go that way." Hell, nobody does, but even if that happened to me, I had a plan. I told Chris, "Chris, if I get cancer. I want you to take me up to Haines, Alaska."

"Haines, Alaska?"

"Yeah. I want to go heli-skiing like in one of those *Teton Gravity Research* movies. I'll drop in off a cornice of drifted snow at the top and ski a steep vertical full of jagged rocks while you take pictures of me. So when people say to you, 'I heard Jack died. Didn't he have cancer?' And you'll be able to reply, 'He had cancer, but that's not how he died.' And then they'll ask, 'So how did he die?' And you'll be able to tell them, 'He was heli-skiing in Haines, Alaska. He got some big air off this crazy ridgeline, but he didn't stick the landing.' And they'll say, 'Really?! Wow, what a way to go.'"

"Okay, I'll do it," Chris laughed. "I'll take you up to Haines."

And then I paused before saying, "On second thought, I'm having the Geek do it. You suck with cameras!" And then we'd both laugh, thinking there'd be so many more times before either of us would be heading to Haines, Alaska.

Me and the Geek at the Genesee Road Forestry Preserve - 2008

The Forestry Preserve

THE WIND THROWS rain at Chris's kitchen windows, sounding like frozen peas pinging the glass. Today, there's not a chance we'll be romping through the elements, counter punching against Mother Nature. We continue scrolling through the pictures on my computer. In the next one, Chris wears his blue mountain biking helmet, time-stamping the picture as "post-punctured lung." He sits with his arms resting across bent knees on a steep shale cliff in Letchworth Park, his heels dug into the loose sedimentary rock braking him from a potential slide to his death, or worse. That's the way he liked things, at the edge. I remember that day; it was "The Letchworth ride from Hell," twenty-miles up and down soggy ravines that carried run-off to the Genesee River in the deep gorge below. At the end of that slog we stood at the top, in a parking lot, grilling Italian sausages. And they were *so* good; no doubt they were yellow tagged.

I ask Chris, "You remember *that* day?" But he doesn't answer. His hands are gone from my shoulders.

He's nowhere in sight. I ask Mac and the Geek, "Did you see where he went?" I turn to look for him, to see if he's pacing on his invisible trail down the hall.

"I think he went to the bathroom," Mac answers, craning his neck to check on Chris's whereabouts.

"Oh."

We look at the pictures and laugh, but it's not the same without Chris punctuating our memories with his rollicking guffaw. He's been in the bathroom for quite a while, but now he's back, standing behind me, resting his hands on my shoulders. I ask, "Hey, Chris, can we turn off the TV?" but he doesn't answer. The Geek walks to the television and clicks it off. Once again the hands leave my shoulders and Chris paces about the kitchen, down the hall, disappearing for a minute, then back in the hall, before returning to the kitchen.

"You okay, Chris?" asks Mac.

"Yeah," he answers.

Off he goes, a panther in his cage, following the same route, cruising by us in the kitchen, pausing only if I insist, "Chris, you gotta see this one. Remember this day? Puddles almost froze his balls off!"

He pauses to look, but nothing registers. We flip through a collection of cross-country skiing pictures of Chris, the Geek, and me at the Genesee Road Forestry Preserve in East Concord. The images seem to indicate that they were taken on different days, except they weren't. We stand with our poles, skis buried in the snow, in a glorious gallimaufry of weather conditions, a mixed bag, if you prefer. As I recall that day, there was nothing we would label as "epic." Others might have thought it extreme when we couldn't see five feet in front of us and weren't sure where we were. I bet the Geek's dog Puddles thought it was extreme, with snow dangling from his undercarriage, almost losing his jibblies to the ravages of frostbite. For us, it really wasn't that big a deal; we did this stuff pretty much every weekend.

IT HAD been a beautiful ride down Genesee Road. The previous night's snow had frosted the tips of tall pines against a primary blue sky. I was coming from the opposite direction, meeting the Geek and Chris for an afternoon of cross-country skiing, taking advantage of the fresh snow.

"What a day, huh!" the Geek exclaimed as he opened the door of his van.

"Gorgeous. The snow is going to be great." The Geek and I leisurely exchanged pleasantries while Chris pulled their skis and poles from the back of the Geek's van, laying them side-by-side, pointed toward the trail, with the poles stabbed into the snow on either side of the skis. He clicked into his bindings.

"Did you want to go across the road, or ski along the creek?" The Geek asked.

"Doesn't matter to me," I answered.

"We're skiing on this side," Chris pointed with his pole, deciding without a vote that we'd be executing our kicks and glides on the creek side of the park.

We glided with minimal resistance on neatly carved tracks that were unfettered by snowshoe tromping. Blue blazes guided us through the long shadows of stately pines, clothed in a feathery veil of last night's snow, until without warning Chris declared, "Let's go here."

Why Chris? Why? Why do we always have to go off the trail? It's so much easier and way more fun to cruise along this beautifully carved trail. I kept my thoughts to myself, while Chris commenced bushwhacking. He sliced his skis through a fresh canvas of virgin powder. In Chris's view of the world, it wasn't as much fun to do what everyone else was doing, to go where everyone else was going. It wasn't you take the high road and I'll take the low road; most times it wasn't even the "the road less traveled by." It was "our road," the road that wasn't even a road. That's the way we found things, saw things, heard things, that others didn't. Chris took us off-trail. Of course with that, came the aforementioned afflictions, and during this particular outing, it was Puddles who bore the worst of it.

We were entering the "punishment" portion of the day: plowing through knee-deep powder, ducking scraggly tree branches, and snaking through the sharp teeth of angry briars that bit into our nylon pants like coyotes guarding their territory. My enthusiasm for Chris's bushwhacking maneuvers waned, and I could no longer keep my thoughts within. "Can't we get back on the trail?" I carped. "I thought we were going to ski along the creek."

"Jack, quit your whining. We're not going on the trail. That's where everyone else is skiing!"

To Chris's ears, my grousing must have sounded like a bleating goat, but I'd had my fill of losing my balance in our ill-defined tracks and falling like a feeble-rooted sapling into the deep snow. The flakes found their way to my bare skin, entering at my neck, melting there, before running down my back. *Come on, Chris, I've had enough of this shit.* What a fem I was that day.

And so it was that we carried on, Chris breaking trail, the Geek tamping down Chris's tracks and me in the rear, having a difficult time keeping up despite the benefit of a freshly carved trail. We climbed what appeared to be a snow-covered brontosaurus, stair-stepping our way up its tail, pausing at the crown of its back, and surveying the steep incline off its side. The brontosaurus was frozen in time, its long neck drooping to the ground, head buried under the snow as it appeared to sip from the creek.

"Let's go down through there," Chris pointed with his ski pole before probing the brontosaurus's rib cage, checking the snow pack, jabbing it like you might stir a dying fire.

"No way," I said.

"You'll love it, Jack. It'll be great," Chris said laughing.

"Just start over there and switchback to the bottom," The Geek encouraged me.

There were three strict rules in Chris's loosely documented "Cross-Country Skiing Code of Conduct," of which the first two were:

> Rule 1- When heading downhill toward a tree, keep both skis
> on one side of said tree.
>
> Rule 2 – Don't cross your tips.

The trees loomed below, spaced like the spindles on a pachinko board, ready to test my resolve. This was not a good spot to start breaking rules one and two. In addition to the rules there were basic guidelines, such as the forbearance of eye-contact if we were to come upon other skiers. Chris didn't want our time together in the woods interrupted by mundane conversation such as, in his words, *useless talk about the fucking weather.*

I considered the chance of breaking both rules on the descent off the side of the brontosaurus. A *two-fer.* There was nothing complicated about the calculation. I figured the probability to be 100%. So it was at that point that I swallowed my pride and made a prudent decision to avoid a potential short-term stay at "Buff" General. I braced myself for the abuse, knowing cautious decisions rankled Chris. Taking a deep breath, I mentally prepared myself to break rule number three.

"Jack, *what* are you doing?!" Chris squawked.

I pushed the tip of my ski pole to release my boot bindings and shamefully stepped out of my skis. Standing off the packed trail, I sunk into the deep snow. Inside—my soul sank even deeper, looking for cover in the nook of my marrow. But a soul couldn't hide from Chris.

> Rule 3 – Never—ever—take off your skis—until you're done
> for the day.

"Jaaack, Jaaack, put your skis back on," he scolded me.

We were in the middle of the Genesee Road Forestry Preserve, and so it was plain to see, I was not done for the day. "*Jeeesus*, Jack!" Chris abhorred my choice. I had forgone the opportunity for an incident, depriving the Geek and him of the opportunity to see me go over the edge, trying not to fall, but inevitably going down at the base of a cherry tree like a jumble of coat hangers. So complete was his disappointment in me, that he didn't say another word. Instead, he shot me his goofy wide-eyed smirky-smile and pointed his tips downward.

"Okay, I guess we'll see you at the bottom," the Geek said and glided through Chris's tracks, shouting back at me, "Fem!"

I watched, amazed, as the Geek and Chris snaked their way through the trees, avoiding stumps and fallen pines, managing to stay upright as their momentum slowed at the bottom. My interminable walk-of-shame began, plodding with my head down, hangdog, with one ski and one pole in each hand. The Geek and Chris stood at the bottom of the gulch, looking up at me, laughing and shouting for me to put my skis back on. I post-holed my way toward them, wearing my coat of humiliation.

"We're back on the trail, Jack. Are you *happy*?" Laughter cloaked Chris's rhetorical question.

"Yes!" I shot back.

We kicked and glided on the well-packed trail along the creek. It was a welcome change of pace, enabling an appreciation of nature's artwork. Snow coated tree branches like powdered sugar and fluffy flakes capped creek boulders like mushrooms.

"Hey, Geek, hold up, let me get a picture of you guys."

"Jack and his fucking pictures," Chris bellyached, but stopped long enough for me to take one of him and the Geek standing next to the creek. In the background, open water churned around natural obstacles like an anaconda slithering just below the surface.

I caught up to where they were standing, and in my haste I broke rule number two, going down in spectacular fashion. Rip-roaring laughter accompanied my futile attempts to get vertical. It's easy to fall on cross-country skis, tipping over comes quite naturally to the inexperienced skier; it's the *getting up* that requires some training. Chris took sympathy on me, extending an arm to pull me to my feet. I latched onto his hand. He yanked me upward, and then without warning, released me like a trout that was below the legal size. I flopped onto my side, floundering in the deep flakes, tethered to my skis, making a sitzmark in the snow, bearing evidence that there'd been a mild incident. I'm sure I was quite the spectacle.

The sitzmark, in this case, a large indentation in the tracks garnished with traces of thrashing, created by a fallen skier, should be filled in; it's proper trail etiquette. And so I did just that, not for the sake of decorum, but out of embarrassment. *Oh, my God, look at that. That guy must have had quite a go trying to get upright.*

Finally on my feet, I emptied the snow from my hood and sloughed the loose flakes from my neck. Chris immediately realigned my senses, slamming his shoulder into me, sending me back into the snow.

"Chris! What the fuck?!" I yelled.

He stood over me, laughing. I fired off a few more f-bombs and then realized what I needed to do, to get myself out of this predicament. Chris was trying to help me in the only way he knew how, providing his sage perspective of things that really weren't all that *serious.* And in so doing, he made sure none of us ever took ourselves too seriously.

So I laughed.

We came upon the cabin. We'd seen it before, on other trips through these woods, but for whatever reason had ignored its weathered charms. This time it beckoned. As the sun tucked in for the day behind fast moving clouds, I handed the Geek my camera, "Here, take a picture of Chris and me in the cabin."

The quaint structure had long ago surrendered to the elements. Its windows were stripped of their glass, a punky-planked floor was home to dented empties, and it wore its green clapboard exterior like a moth-eaten tweed jacket. Chris and I leaned on the snow-covered windowsills, arms across our chest, as the Geek told us, "Smile." I did as commanded and then looked skyward, feeling the increasing wind velocity that announced a brewing storm. Tiny flakes floated about us as we clicked back into our ski bindings and continued on the trail. The wind intensified, blowing snow sideways, but Chris saw no reason to start moving in the direction of our parked cars; to him that was why we were out here, for fresh snow. We skied in a snow globe while Puddles tried his best to keep up, channeling his way through the mounting flakes. When we stopped, he tried to shake free from snow pellets the size of pearl onions frozen to his black curly fur. He was the reverse image of a snow leopard.

The further we got from the trailhead, the harder it snowed, and the more our *snow leopard* shook. Horizontal snow darts stung our faces, as we skied hunched forward into the wind. Despite skiing and hiking the Forestry Preserve many times, I'd lost my bearings. I sure as hell hoped Chris and the Geek knew where we were. My gloves were soaking wet and as a result my hands were numb.

"Geek, how far are we from the parking lot?"

"A ways."

Shit! I'd been down this "path" before.

Chris stood at the edge of an open field. The snow whipped around him, rising like white dust, and from where I stood he was a ghostly image. The gale blew Puddle's tail up in the air from its normal downward position, making him look like a skunk preparing to spray. He barked at the wind, or maybe at Chris, telling him to get moving. Chris must have understood; Puddles had made his point. We continued on. What choice did we have? Flakes the size of confetti cloaked all that was once familiar in a shroud of white mystery. We were seemingly in the middle of nowhere. I followed the tracks laid down by Chris, head down, hoping that every time I looked up I would see the Geek's van. The snow was now up to our knees and up to Puddles's tender flesh.

When we arrived in the parking lot Chris hollered, "Geek, get your van started." Chris slid the side door open and Puddles jumped inside. "Crank the heat. Puddles is freezing his balls off."

Our poor *snow leopard*, jiggling like a bowl of Jell-O, allowed us to pluck frozen snowballs from his fur. Chris laughed at Puddles's forlorn face, looking up at us as if to say, "What the hell?!"

I feel your pain, Puddles.

When we were certain we weren't going to lose our fearless mascot, we got out of the van, and each of us cracked open a Labatt. Puddles stared at us from the van's open side-door, knowing for sure that yes, indeed, dogs really are smarter than humans.

"Chris, here," I handed him my camera. "Take one of the Geek and me over there." I motioned to the park's warming hut. On the building an official sign advised: "This Park is Officially Closed." The horizontal snow looked like Morse code against the brown wood of the building, *dot dash dot dash*. He pulled it off. Chris actually took a picture that was in focus; you can see us covered in snow, holding our beers with our bare hands. And Puddles, not missing the opportunity to prove he was there, rushed into the picture at the last second, huddling behind us.

Later I emailed the picture to Mom, keeping her up to date on what crazy stuff I was doing back in Western New York. She emailed me back, wondering why we were drinking beer in a closed park while the snow shot by us sideways. "And why aren't you wearing your gloves?"

How did I explain any of this?

I replied, "It was a *Chris* thing."

The starting line in Snowshoe, WV - 2004

Snowshoe, West Virginia – 24 Hours

"Oh, my God!" the Geek exclaims at the next picture on my computer. He's seen this one before, but apparently it's been a while. It's as if this picture has improved with age. It sat patiently all these years, waiting to remind us how we were back then: resilient, determined and, most of all, ridiculous. The credit for this one goes to Caz and Chris; they're the ones who got us back on the road.

I holler for Chris to take a look at the picture, "Hey, Chris, you gotta check this one out." He's coming down the hall, walking on the stone tiles in the curious way he does, playing his version of step-on-a-crack, break-your-mother's-back. "Chris, get over here," I wave in a hurried fashion, as if the picture was about to float away like a helium balloon. He stops and looks at me. It's a blank look. I try again, "Come on; you gotta see this. It's from our trip to West Virginia."

He makes his way to the kitchen counter. The Geek points at the screen, explaining why this picture means so much to us; filling in the details, explaining to Mac all that had transpired up until this point. Our buddy, Mac (to others, Colonel James McCready of the United States Air Force) wasn't around in the early 2000s. He was off in faraway places like Guam, Egypt, Saudi Arabia, France, Turkey, and Oman, protecting our freedom while we were *enjoying* our freedom.

There's not a quick explanation as to how Chris came to be standing in front of a 1976 GMC Vandura Midas RV with its engine compartment propped open, proudly displaying a broken alternator belt. He holds the belt with both hands, like he's caught a venomous snake. Caz stands next to him with a smile plastered across his face, holding a jug of antifreeze. They look like a couple of hillbillies triumphantly displaying the winning mega-millions jackpot ticket.

Chris joins the laughter. I hope he remembers. The Geek and I know the story well, but we never tire of retelling it. We stick to the highlights, which in many cases are also the lowlights, and paint the hilarity of our adventures with coarse brushstrokes. "They should make a movie out of this," I say. At the very least it would qualify for an episode on *Jackass*. In the next picture, Chris, Caz, the

Geek, and I stand together in front of the RV with our goofy smiles and rag-tag clothes like an outtake from the movie *Dumb and Dumber*.

"JACK, WE'RE doing a 24-hour race," he told me in early spring of 2004. I was in the midst of putting on my helmet and gloves, preparing for our Saturday ride at Sibley Road. The race might have been the Geek's idea, but no matter its genesis, I was wary. When Chris locked onto a plan, I proceeded with caution, evaluating the potential risks and "punishment," comparing them to any possibility for fun and reward. It sounded like Chris had lashed this idea to the forefront of his "things to do" list, without the frills of deep thinking.

There was one time when this lack of deep thinking went too far for all of us. Chris hatched a plan to buy an SUV in Shanghai, China, drive it across two continents to London, England, sell the SUV there, and fly home. He had connections on that side of the world as a result of his business travels. These guys would be our "escorts" for some of the edgier territory we'd be driving through. The Geek and I made a verbal pact with Chris that we were going to do it; there'd be no backing out. Somehow I concluded this would be a reasonable and safe adventure. It was with great enthusiasm that I told Mar about our latest plan whereupon she immediately blasted me for being certifiably insane. At the time I was hurt. What would I tell the Geek and Chris? I'd be labeled a fem for sure. If you have a minute, pull up the directions for Shanghai to London, check out the countries we would have been driving through or around—that is if we wanted to avoid the Taliban and Al-Qaeda. What the hell had I been thinking? Needless to say, that's a trip we didn't take.

And so I was mindful of my words, "What do you mean a 24-hour race?"

"Jeeesus, Jaaack. It's a race—you ride your mountain bike—on a trail, and it lasts for 24 hours," he explained. And then he blasted me, with the big laugh. Looking back, it was a stupid question. I should have asked, "Why in the hell would we want to do that? We haven't even done a one-hour race yet." I know the easiest thing would have been to answer with an affirmative, "Okay, I'll do it." But I didn't. Instead, I delayed the inevitable and allowed Chris to apply his full-nelson mindfuck to me until I cried uncle, or said, "Okay, I'll do it."

I pressed on with my questions, "Where is it?"

"West Virginia."

"West Virginia?" I volleyed another question, "When?"

"June."

"When in June?"

The tower of Jenga blocks tumbled, "I don't know the fuckin' date!" He looked up from oiling his chain. "Geek, what's the fuckin' date? Jaaack needs to know the date." Chris's eyes widened with aggravation.

"The 26th and 27th. It's the last weekend in June," the Geek politely informed me. "We're entering as a four-man team."

So it appeared the Geek was in. Peer pressure mounted. "Who else is riding?" I asked.

Chris gave me the same sing-song delivery as before, "Me—Geek—you."

"Who else?" I asked.

The Geek jumped back into the conversation, "We don't know yet."

"What about Caz?"

"Caaaz? Caz isn't gonna fuckin' ride any 24-hour race. Jeeesus, Jack!" Chris found my suggestion unfounded in deep thinking — and hilarious. I liked my suggestion for all of the following reasons: Caz is our friend, we needed a fourth rider, and he owned a bike.

There *was* one issue. Caz had just started riding that year.

More questions popped into my head, "What do you do when it gets dark?"

"You ride in the fucking dark. It's 24 hours, Jack. Jeeesus." Chris blasted.

"Does the course have lights?"

"Lights? No—there aren't any lights on the course. It's in the fucking woods." I believe Chris loved this. I was like a bug crawling across the sidewalk as he aimed a prism of sun through his magnifying glass, frying me to a crisp. "We'll have headlights on our bike," he explained.

Oh, that sounds safe. This seemed insane, even for us. I needed some time to think so I asked a few more questions, ones that really didn't matter for shit. "Where in West Virginia?"

"Snowshoe. It's a ski resort," said the Geek.

Perfect, that sounds easy. We'd ridden the trails at Tamarack, the little private ski hill in Colden, but I was fairly certain most of the topography in West Virginia featured steeper elevations and more rugged terrain than quaint little Tamarack. Even with lights I couldn't imagine careening down rocky, single-track trails on a ski slope in West Virginia—in the dark.

Like the town drunk saying yes to another shot of "Jack," I blurted, "Okay, I'm in." He'd done it to me again. There was no turning back.

Later that night, I Googled 24-hour race in Snowshoe, West Virginia. It had a full-blown website. *This was going to be serious.* I read the description of the race.

> Now in its 13th year, The 2004 24 Hours of Snowshoe (formerly the 24 Hours of Canaan) draws as many as 500 teams, 50 solo riders and more than 10,000 spectators. Sometimes referred to as "Woodstock on Wheels," it's one of the largest mountain bike events East of the Mississippi and has been listed as one of the top three mountain bike events in the U.S. by Mountain Bike and Mountain Bike Action magazines.
>
> Three years of rain soaked courses (add water, makes its own sauce!) combined with the extreme terrain of West Virginia's fifth highest mountain have made this event one of the gnarliest and most infamous races in the world, the arena of the hardest of the hard core mountain bikers.
>
> The race takes place on June 26-27, 2004 at The Silver Creek Lodge at Snowshoe Mountain Resort near Marlinton, West Virginia. Racing is a blast, but you can also have fun as a spectator, volunteer, or as support crew for one of the teams.
>
> Get all the info you need, and register, at: GrannyGear.com

What had I gotten myself into?

Chris, Arty, the Geek, and me after our second 24-Hour race in Naples, NY - 2007

Snowshoe, West Virginia – Angry Tuna

W E SPENT ANOTHER hour looking at our past before I shut down the computer. It was time to head to Wally's for a pizza and a couple tree beers. When referring to Wally's, it has nothing to do with Paul Sugnet, whom we also refer to as Wally. In this case, it's the Wallenwein's Hotel, which we affectionately refer to as Wally's. Oh, and it's not really a hotel, at least I don't think it is. Wally's is an old-fashioned bar serving amazing pizza, wings, and a surprisingly tasty fish dinner every Friday. And another thing, it used to be a bowling alley, but rumor has it that the insurance premiums made it too costly to operate. So they pulled out the lanes and replaced them with indoor horseshoes. Yes, indoor horseshoes. Wally's took the necessary safety precautions to avoid the danger of an errant horseshoe galloping, out of control, into an unsuspecting patron's shins. The only things not given adequate consideration were the calculus of Wally's ceiling height when compared with the approximate loft of a properly hurled horseshoe and the pit's ability to generate positive cash flow. Before long, they were ripped out and replaced with the opulent "Grand Ballroom." The wall paneling from the '70s has been replaced by painted walls adorned with artwork illuminated by display lights. Rectangular tables function both as dining surfaces or strung together as a serving line. The hardwood floor is tidy and clean, in contrast to the barroom's floor which can be sticky, or slippery, or both, but you really don't know what you are stepping into since the ambient mood lighting keeps such house secrets a mystery.

Before we head off to Wally's, I use Chris's bathroom. There's a hand written sign on top of the water closet that reads: "Flush Me." Evidently, Chris has been forgetting. I lift the lid to pee and see a girthy turd at the bottom. I guess Chris didn't see the sign.

Like the old days, we pile into the Geek's van. Chris sits quietly in the front passenger seat, staring forward, not joining our conversation with even so much as a yes or a no. In the past he would criticize the Geek's driving—most certainly he wasn't going fast enough, and for sure Chris would have cut Mac's family

211

update short. He had no tolerance for lengthy conversation, or a joke he thought took forever to get to a bad punchline. A good joke in his book went something like this: Why did Chris cross the road? Because there was a cold case of Labatt Blue on the other side. During the ride, Mac updates us on his son, Spencer, who recently had brain surgery, while Chris stares forward, slapping his thighs *rat-ta-tat-tat-rat-ta-tat-tat*.

It's not long before we pull into the Wallenwein's parking lot. Chris opens the van door and walks across the pavement. I watch him while the Geek and I stay in our seats listening to Mac finish telling us about Spencer. He's doing well now, but needless to say it's been a very difficult time for the McCready family.

"I guess he's getting us a table," I nod toward Chris opening the side door of Wally's. He'd always been the one in the lead, taking charge, and we followed. These days it's something different. It didn't seem like that long ago when he was leading us in a different way. He'd push us, pull us, drag us, whatever it took to get us to join his adventures. In the case of Caz, it probably took all of the above for Chris to get him to commit to joining us on our trip to West Virginia.

Now THAT Caz was in, we had our four-man team for our first 24-hour mountain bike race. We had a few months to train, but I wasn't sure what that would entail, or the rigors that Chris would insist upon. We also needed to acquire bike lights, figure out how we would get to West Virginia, and there was an entrance fee to pay. I checked off the last item, doing that the day after Caz committed. I'm sure Chris had told Caz, as he did the Geek and me, "You'll love it. It'll be great." And now we had money invested in this adventure, or at least I did. I wasn't worried about the Geek and Caz paying me back, but there was no telling when I'd see the money from Chris. As it turned out, he squared up with me two years later after a ride at Sprague Brook Park whereby he produced a rumpled check from his pocket that was dated five months prior. "Here," he said, "I forgot to give you this." *Golly gee whiz, thanks, Chris.*

We diligently rode together every weekend. Sometimes I'd even go out for a ride by myself when I had a day off from work. I didn't discuss my concerns about surviving the race without a major injury. I was scared shitless, fearing that I'd gotten into something over my head. I certainly didn't broach the topic with Chris. Good God, he would've had a field day with me. *Jeeesus, Jack, quit your whining.* So without pomp, I went about my own auxiliary training, doing my extra rides, extra running on the treadmill, and watching what I ate. The race had been a great motivator to get me into the best shape since high school.

Chris and the Geek researched bike lights. We all bought the same setup, two lights that mounted on our handlebars, one big one and one small one. I thought the race website had indicated that we were also supposed to have another light on our helmet, but Chris told us, "We don't need another fucking light." I wanted as many "fucking lights" as we were allowed. I would've strapped a light from the Ralph (Ralph Wilson Stadium, now named Bills Stadium, where the Buffalo Bills play) to my head if I had thought my neck could support the weight. There was no further discussion about the lights. We weren't getting any more "fucking lights."

Surprisingly, the lights did a pretty good job on our trial night rides — that is when fully charged. When not fully charged, they did a shitty job, and you'd best hope for a full moon. I found that I liked riding at night, hearing Chris's advice ricochet between my ears, *Jack, don't sweat the small stuff.* That was easier to do when you couldn't *see* the small stuff. So it seemed we were good on bike lights and night riding.

Next Chris told us, "We're using Don's RV." Don is Chris's second stepfather, but Chris never referred to him as such. He's always been just Don. The RV was a 1976 GMC Vandura Midas and it was a beaut. Where do I begin? Do I tell you about its dingy white exterior the color of an old undershirt? Do I tell you about the vertical gray stains from years of grimy run-off (maybe Don parked it under a grove of sappy maples), or perhaps I should tell you about the dings and dangs on the fenders and around the wheel wells, like armpit stains on that old undershirt? Do I tell you about the little curtains that hung across the ripped window screens that had been laced back together with thread? It appeared that Don hadn't put a ton of buckaroos into the old GMC's general upkeep; who could blame him, the RV was 28 years old. But the engine, oh, it purred like a WWII Sherman tank. And Don had told Chris to not expect very high gas mileage on the old Vandura.

Based on my calculations, I figured we'd be stopping every 100 miles to gas up the hulking RV. It was time to pray: Good Lord watch over this old relic, the class of '76 needs to get to the race on time. Apparently, God was tied up with more important stuff when I fired off that intercession to the heavens.

We'd checked off all the boxes. Team Angry Tuna was ready to ride. *Angry Tuna?* Yup, that was our name. And, of course, a story goes with the name. Maybe you can get the Geek or Caz to tell you about it someday. I'm not touching it.

*The Geek, me, Caz, and Chris in front of the GMC Vandura
somewhere in WV - 2004*

Snowshoe, West Virginia – Belt Man

W<small>E WALK THROUGH</small> a sea of tables in the dining room that adjoins the Wallenwein's "Grand Ballroom." Authentic Naugahyde chairs, made from wild "Naugas" hunted in the Canadian woods, are arranged in tidy fashion. The sturdy seats, dyed homey Grey Poupon yellow, wait for regulars to settle in for a Saturday afternoon basket of wings and a couple of brewskis. There's not much going on yet; it's early. Chris has scored us seats in the barroom at one of the euchre tables. Folklore has it, while playing the game, there was to be nothing on top of the table except your cards. Everything else, your smokes, your beers, the keys to the sedan, and your lucky skunk's foot was to be concealed in the cubbyholes beneath the table's surface. Communicating with one's euchre partner to influence their play (cross-boarding) is considered cheating, so verbal cues and the visual hints from foreign objects in the line of sight are strictly prohibited. The cubbyholes aren't necessary today; *everything* will be on the table. I'm careful not to pull in my chair too fast. Those unaware or forgetful can do a real number on their kneecaps when making eye-watering contact with the vertical table struts.

The Quick Draw game looms on the wall behind Chris. Too bad Schuppy isn't with us today; he usually manages to do a good job "quick picking" us to free pizza and wings, compliments of the New York State Lottery. I'm not interested in Quick Draw today, other than to occasionally watch the mesmerizing flashes of light that illuminate the winning numbers, one by one. Chris would enjoy watching, but his back is to the game.

We're ready to order our beers and for Chris a Coke (I don't think he's supposed to be drinking alcohol any more), but before we can say, "We'll take a pitcher of Labatt," the waitress sets a tall draft in front of Chris.

She turns to us asking, "And what can I get for you guys?"

What just happened?

"Chris, are you supposed to be drinking beer?" I asked after we placed our drink order.

"Yeees," he stretches out his response, as has always been his way when emphasizing a point.

He gives me a look. There's no more to be said on the topic of Chris's beer, but I worry that the alcohol might mess something up with his medications. I contemplate the pros and cons of texting his wife, Jennifer. This isn't funny and *this could be serious*. I think of Chris mocking me while I searched for my glasses on the banks of the Battenkill. But it's too late for any kind of corrective action; he's already drinking his beer. I look at the Geek and Mac with wide questioning eyes. They shrug their shoulders. Oh, what the hell, we'll keep an eye on things. What harm can come from one frosty beer at good old Wally's? I don't message Jen.

"What do you want to eat, Chris? Do you want pizza? Wings?" The Geek is polite, but it sounds to me like he is talking to someone in elementary school. Maybe it can't be helped.

"Wings," says Chris.

"Just wings, Chris? What about some pizza?"

"Yeah," answers Chris.

Yes, just wings, or yes, you want pizza, too?

The Geek has no further questions. We order both.

As we wait for the wings to crisp and the pepperoni to curl into little grease cups, the Geek and I recount Angry Tuna's journey to West Virginia back in 2004.

WE MET at Chris's house on a Thursday afternoon. This should've allowed plenty of time to get to West Virginia by evening, set up our "base camp" for the next three days, and get some rest. The plan gave us all day Friday to leisurely pre-ride the course, charge the batteries on our bike lights, and make any mechanical adjustments before the race started at noon on Saturday. It was a good plan. Too bad the whole thing would fly out the windows of the Vandura, scattered like ashes in the Allegheny mountain range. Maybe we should have driven something more roadworthy than Don's GMC relic, but then we would have missed opportunities for "incidents."

Filled with naïve bravado, unconcerned with what pitfalls might lay ahead, we stowed our bikes and gear in the back of the RV. A jangled architecture of metal, backpacks, beer, a nylon 10'x10' canopy tent, and its aluminum skeleton were rammed into the bowels of the Vandura. And away we went. Caz and I rode in the back seats, because the Geek had bogarted the front passenger seat. Chris was driving. I prepared myself for eight hours of glorious motion sickness. *Eyes on the horizon, eyes on the horizon, eyes on the horizon.* We weren't a mile from Chris's driveway, and already we were careening down the steep winding incline on Willardshire Road. It felt like he had the RV up on two wheels. The bikes rattled a warning from their position in the rear. I curled into a protective cocoon as the entire clot of our stuff slid forward. Within seconds the mass slammed back in place when the RV bottomed out at the bridge over Cazenovia Creek. The Vandura chuffed on the uphill.

"Aren't there any seat belts back here?" I asked.

"Does it look like there's any fucking seatbelts back there?!" hollered Chris.

I checked again. Chris was correct; there were no "fucking seatbelts" for the back seats. Thank God, now Caz and I would be able to freely dodge the shifting pile of our stuff while we smacked our heads against the hard edges inside the Vandura. It was indeed, shaping up to be *a lot like fun—only different.*

A map was sprawled across the Geek's lap. His finger traced a route through Pennsylvania that was highlighted in green. Nobody had considered the advantages of a Garmin. Chris wouldn't have been down for that (he still had a flip phone as late as 2017). Instead we navigated like our forefathers, following the tangled web of multi-colored lines that varied in thickness. Then, confident that we knew where we were heading for the next hundred miles, we'd attempt to fold the map back to its original state. I wasn't worried about our route; I was more concerned about not getting bludgeoned by the shit rolling around the inside of the RV. There was that, and my apprehension about riding the single-tracks of the Allegheny Mountains in West Virginia. I wanted to do my part for our team, Angry Tuna, and no way did I want to let Chris down.

It was still light out when we left Pennsylvania in our rearview mirror. Everything was going according to plan. The big guy upstairs was answering my prayers.

"How much longer, Geek?" I asked like a kid on the family vacation. *Are we there yet?*

"We got about three more hours."

I wondered if that accounted for our average speed of 40mph ascending the twisty mountain climbs. Of course Chris balanced things out by consistently slamming the accelerator through the floorboards on the downhill. Everything rattled in the Vandura at 75mph. I felt like a can of paint in that shaker thing at Valu Hardware.

We pulled off the highway. "Didn't we just get gas?" I asked.

"We aren't stopping for fucking gas!" Chris clarified that yes, we had recently refueled.

Oh.

He muttered something to the Geek, and then for the benefit of all passengers on board, shouted, "This fucking piece of shit!" It appeared we'd be pulling into the pits, so our crack mechanical team could determine the reason why "this fucking piece of shit engine" wasn't working.

It was determined that the battery was the issue, or maybe it was the alternator, or maybe it was the "Knutzen valve." I had no idea what Chris and Caz were doing. I'm not the mechanical type. We went into an auto parts store which had what we needed, or so we thought. *Shazam.* The Vandura returned to action like a grizzled hockey player who'd left the ice for "repairs." After losing an hour screwing around in pit row, we rambled on, rambled on, dazed and confused, dazed and confused, for so long until the Vandura broke down again. It appeared that Caz and Chris hadn't properly diagnosed the problem.

"This fucking piece of shit!" Chris, once again, announced that we'd be taking an unscheduled stop in the pits. The problem was, it was dark and the pits were closed. There were no guys in colorful jumpsuits, no big hose jammed into our fuel tank, no *ziiiit, ziiiit, ziiiit* sounds of air wrenches on the lug nuts of our wheels. It was just us, the Vandura, and an occasional *whoosh* of a vehicle passing us as we sat in the concrete parking lot of a gas station in East Bum Fuck, West Virginia. This particular gas station appeared to have been closed since the last mullet flowed from beneath an NHL hockey helmet. *They're coming back. Did you notice?*

Chris and Caz popped open the stubby hood of the Vandura and poked around.

They said "shit" often and Caz might have burned his forearm on something hot. I stayed out of the way and talked to the Geek.

"Well, this sucks," I said as we watched Chris and Caz tinker.

"Yeah," the corners of the Geek's mouth twisted downwards.

We'd given it the never-say-die, class of '76 try. Go Blue Devils! But it looked like we were fucked. Unable to watch any longer, I opened the side door of the RV, unfolded my sleeping bag, and laid it on the plywood bunk. The Geek followed me inside. We listened to Caz and Chris swear, bang things, and repeat. It appeared we wouldn't be up and running anytime soon.

IT WAS quiet. I lay awake with my eyes closed. Did you ever have a moment where you wondered where you were, if you are alive or dead, if you were dreaming or just thinking? If you have, then you understand. For a few seconds I felt like I was lying in my bed at home, thinking about getting up, a bit thankful that this whole crazy adventure was nothing but a bad dream. Then I opened my eyes, unable to make sense of the shadowy shapes inside the Vandura.

"Geek? Are you up?"

A few feet away he flailed inside his sleeping bag trying to find comfort. I guess it isn't easy jamming a six-foot four-inch boney frame into an insulated nylon mummy bag.

"Yeah," he answered. It sounded like he had a mouthful of rags.

"Where's Chris and Caz?"

"I don't know. Maybe they're outside."

We got out of our sleeping bags and opened the door of the Vandura. *Good morning, West Virginia.* Chris and Caz leaned against the RV. Had they been waiting for us?

"Well, I'm glad *someone* got some fucking sleep last night," Chris said to us, dispensing with traditions of a proper morning greeting. "Geek, you're driving. Let's go."

"It's fixed?" I questioned, pointing at the hood propped open by what looked like a bent crab leg.

"Yeah, it's fucking fixed."

Caz started to fill us in on the most amazing tale of good fortune, but Chris cut him off, "Let's go! Life is short! Let's get on the fucking road; you can tell your story later."

We were the luckiest guys in the world. While there must be people who could say they broke down in the middle of nowhere, weren't sure what needed to be fixed, finally determined that it was merely a frayed belt that had been slipping, keeping the generator from charging, and that only a new belt separated them from being back on the road, but how many of those could say that their problems were solved by a mysterious, unseen "Belt Man?" We could. The Geek and I could only guess how all this happened since we were sleeping, but we imagined that Chris and Caz might have had a conversation that went something like this:

"Hey, Caz, what's that over there?"

"Would you look at that? It's an abandoned box truck, Chris. I wonder what's in there, and I wonder if it's unlocked? I betcha it's a truck full of replacement belts."

"Well, golly Cheese Whiz and eureka, Caz you're right. Indeed it *is* a box truck chock full of auto parts!" Chris replied.

"I think this is the one we need," said Caz to Chris, pulling the magical belt from its wooden dowel. And then the two of them, like elves in the night, working by the light of our new bike lights, fixed the Vandura.

Later we postulated that an industrious fellow had started a business selling belts out of that box truck. The business hadn't gone so well, and rather than liquidate his remaining inventory, he parked his truck, unlocked, because someday, some fools traveling from Western New York to Snowshoe, West Virginia, might just happen to break down and need a new belt for their 1976 GMC Vandura Midas.

We stood in front of the hulking Vandura, arms on each other's shoulders, Chris leaning on the side panel of hood, not ready to let go of a jug of antifreeze that he held (apparently there were other issues with the radiator that I would learn about later). We were all smiles as we solicited a favor from a stranger, to take our picture, capturing forever the unbridled joy smeared across our faces.

It was Friday morning. We still had time to get to Snowshoe, set up our canopy tent, register for the race, take our pre-ride, and hydrate (Chris style.) *Beers up, beers in.* And it was all possible because of the forward thinking of a Samaritan we'd never know.

"Thank you, Belt Man!" we shouted from the windows of the Vandura as we careened down the highway.

Chris on course in Snowshoe, WV (Team #140 – Angry Tuna) – 2004

Snowshoe, West Virginia – The Ride

WHILE WAITING FOR our pizza and wings, we talk about the Sabres, what our kids are up to, and the challenges of caring for our aging parents and in-laws. Mac has us howling, as he tells us about his 92-year-old father-in-law's pancake eating prowess. We all know Bill Braun. The long-time East Aurora resident and retired dentist is a legitimate character. Last Sunday, Mac and his wife, Heidi, drove Bill and the missus down to the Arcade Center Farm Pancake House, arriving shortly after 1:00 PM, only to find that they'd just closed for the day. After a few minutes of tense negotiations, Mac pushed Bill's wheelchair inside and the staff worked overtime, bringing him platter after platter of his favorite breakfast food. Bill liberally dolloped syrup on 32 fluffy pancakes (unofficial count), devouring each one as Mac and Heidi watched from a safe distance. "Bill loves his pancakes," Mac tells us, and we laugh.

Chris might be listening, but it's hard to tell. He sips his beer and stares at the TV hanging behind the bar. Our food arrives. Apparently Chris has made up his mind on the pizza. He grabs the crust and pulls a slab off the pedestal tray. I hope he remembers that the mozzarella on a Wally's pizza, straight from the oven, takes on the characteristics of lava. If you rush to take a bite, without allowing it to cool, you'll be peeling the skin off the roof of your mouth in a few hours. Chris peers around the silver pizza platter searching for the wings. There's nothing wrong with his appetite *today*.

Two people stop by to say hi to Chris. I don't know who they are. I'm not sure if Chris does either, but he greets them with his signature laugh and a smile before taking a bite of pizza. The pizza is great (it always is at Wally's), the wings are hot, and the beer is cold.

We talk about fun times, we talk about the Sabres' latest winning streak (a rarity—they'll crash and burn later in the season), and we enjoy being with each other. After we empty our beer glasses and all that remains are two wings (flats), it's decided that we'll head back to Chris's house for a while.

On the way out of Wally's, the Geek smacks his forehead on a low door frame. "When the hell did they lower that?" the Geek looks back, rubbing his head in agony. Too bad Chris is already in the parking lot. He would have laughed hysterically at the minor incident. After all, he would have informed us that the Geek had incurred no "spinal damage," and therefore we had permission to laugh.

When we get back to Chris's house, he tells us, "Let's go in the basement." It's the longest sentence I can remember him saying in over a year. Downstairs, Chris turns on the TV, pushes back in his recliner, and stares at the movie in progress as we continue our conversation.

I ask him, "What's the movie, Chris?" He doesn't answer. I ask again, "Chris, what movie is this?" Why do I ask him the same thing twice as if by repeating the question in a slightly different format, he'll be able to respond with an answer? I'm not doing him any favors asking him about things he can't answer. Maybe it's my feeble attempt to sharpen what little ability he has left to communicate. I long to hear his biting sarcasm; to hear him tell me *I'm doing it all wrong.*

Chris starts to doze off in his recliner. We realize it's probably time for us to get going. I give him a hug, knowing that we'll be leaving him alone, but that Jennifer will be home soon. We say, "See you later, buddy," and he laughs. The Geek, Mac, and I head our separate ways, in separate cars. It's still raining. I feel like the day—damp and gray. I push those feelings aside and think of us standing in front of the 1976 GMC Vandura Midas. What a wild three days that was.

THANKS TO Belt Man we were in high spirits and back on the road. The Vandura sported its new belt proudly, and we confidently chugged along the interstate. By early Friday afternoon we pulled into Snowshoe Mountain Resort where the race was being held. None of us said much as we coasted by hundreds of camp-sites. Riders in race team uniforms whizzed by the Vandura, testing their rides, and others had their bikes up on stands checking the mechanicals. *This looked serious.* Chris had resumed driving at our last stop and so it was him we listened to as we looped up and down row after row of campers, tents, and RVs. "There's no fucking place to park," he groused. "Geek, get out and make sure nothing's behind us. I'm backing in right over there." Chris nodded toward an opening in the mass of campers.

"Chris, you can't put it there. It's going to block the whole row from getting out," cautioned the Geek.

"Fuck it. Where the hell do you want me to park?"

"Let's go around another time," suggested the Geek.

The other vehicles appeared to have landed comfortably quite some time ago and their passengers had been offloaded. Meanwhile we circled the runway in our battered 1976 GMC Vandura Midas. Chris wasn't one to wait for clearance from the tower, but for some reason, on this occasion, he listened to the Geek. We took another lap.

"That spot looks available," said Caz, pointing to an opening wide enough to accommodate our lovable white hulk. Flanking the opening on one side was a glossy black RV with a small pull-behind trailer that advertised Cannondale bikes and the Avondale Gear Shop. On the other side were three glitzy canopy tents blazoned with more sponsor advertising. A dozen riders and their support crew appeared to be enjoying a catered party. Aluminum trays of food were arranged in tidy order on large folding tables and ice buckets held beer, water, and energy drinks. We should have asked Wallenwein's Hotel to sponsor us. I bet they would have thrown in a case of beer and a pizza.

I noticed the reason the spot was still open. There was a swale running through the middle that looked like a dry creek bed. We didn't care. We had made it, the sun was shining, we needed a spot, and—*there was cold beer waiting.* We'd make this our home for the next couple of days. Our new neighbors gawked at the Vandura as we slid into our spot. Our incongruous appearance on the scene rivaled the Clampetts pulling their jalopy into Beverly Hills. Some pointed subtly with *bent* elbows, while others *bent* at the knees, laughing.

Without preamble we set up our 10'x10' white canopy tent (no advertising), erected two metal-legged folding card tables, *foomp, click, foomp, click, foomp, click, foomp, click,* and plugged our fancy orange-cased halogen lights into the RV's outlet. Initially, our new neighbors just peered at us from a distance, as if we were an ancient tribe not yet discovered by modern man. Eventually, they stopped by and introduced themselves, wanting to know where we were from.

"East Aurora. South of Buffalo," the Geek boasted.

Our new neighbors, in multi-colored racing togs pointed at our battered RV. "You drove all the way from Buffalo in that?" I felt bad for the Vandura, like it was a friend of ours getting picked on.

"Yeeesss, we drove all the way in that," Chris answered, wearing his goofy grin, the grin that implied, *yeah, we drove all the way from fucking Buffalo! And I bet it was a whole lot more fun and exciting than your ride.*

The Geek engaged in banter as the rest of us continued hauling our stuff out of the RV. It was like trying to unpack a tackle box of tangled lures with dangling barbed hooks. We grabbed some food (no warming trays for us, we had packed sandwiches), hydrated, (we followed Chris's lead with a beer—carb loading for the big race), and made plans for our afternoon pre-ride to familiarize ourselves with the course. I went into the RV to change. Caz, the Geek, and I had bought colorful jerseys, gloves, and biking shorts for the race, intent on looking like we knew what we're doing. Chris lost it when we exited the RV wearing our new racing duds, blasting us with full-throated laughter.

"Jeeesus, you guys look like you're wearing clown suits."

In the words of Thad Rice's kayaking friend on the Battenkill, Chris was "taken aback" at our skin-tight multi-colored racing shirts. The Geek's was the best of our triumvirate of color, a bold statement of blazing orange and yellow with a happy sun on the front. Chris wanted no part of what he deemed to be our fashion shenanigans.

We waved to our new neighbors and headed off on our leisurely reconnaissance ride. The loop was approximately ten miles long through gnarly terrain. Rocks, like sharks teeth, lined steep descents and six miles into the course we were faced with a lung-busting climb that wound uphill. They called it "The Wall." It took over ten-minutes just to *walk up.* "The Wall" was followed by a technical rock garden that challenged the tensile strength of our wheel rims, and the course ended with a series of swerving high speed s-curves before the finish line. When we finished the pre-ride I was spent. I couldn't imagine how tomorrow, starting at noon, I would endure the next 24 hours of misery. Chris, on the other hand, looked refreshed, propelled by an energy force that was beyond my capacity to understand. He loved the punishment.

The next morning I was awoken by a fusillade of two, perhaps three, slapping wet farts, finely curried with the aroma of raw sewage. Complementing these percussion sounds was the pitter-patter of rain drops on the RV's hardtop. We opened the side door. *Screech.* The depression of our once dry creek bed looked like a hearty lentil soup. The pitter-patter was soon replaced with the sound of marbles drumming the roof. By mid-morning the rain subsided and was replaced with damp mist that cloaked the slop we'd be riding through. As we made our way to the registration area the sun broke through the gloom. We were in the Men's Masters 45+ division. Team number 140—Angry Tuna, stood out in the list that contained other jinky monikers like, "Four Sticks and a Beaver," a cleverly named, four-man, one-woman team.

We sized up the other riders that were wearing actual uniforms near the start/finish line. For Christ sakes, bike shorts had been a major upgrade for Chris who usually wore a pair of frayed shorts with the crotch blown out. The other riders tinkered with their bikes, downed energy drinks, and without exception, looked *fit* as a fiddle as compared to us that *fit* in a riddle. What had eight legs, half a brain, and was black and white and red all over? Team Angry Tuna (our pasty legs would be covered with soupy mud and bloody abrasions, the result of a *couple tree* falls on the course).

We were given our electronic race baton, the size and shape of a lipstick tube. It was the means of keeping track of how many race loops we'd completed, our lap times and, I supposed, our location, if we were to die on the course. It was all about safety and keeping the lane clear for the next rider.

Back at camp we hydrated ourselves, made sure our lights were charging, and fiddled with our bikes. It was okay that I really only knew how to change a tire tube and lube the chain. If anything major happened to my bike, I'd be walking it to the finish line.

"Make sure your pee is clear." Chris advised.

I was drinking so much water I was scooting off to the porta potties every ten minutes. We couldn't use the bathroom in the RV, because Chris said so. Maybe Don had told him it didn't work. After a while I grew tired of running up to the "blue cubes" and instead, followed Chris's lead, and peed in full view next to the Vandura.

We established our riding order, Chris, the Geek, me, and then Caz. The race would begin with a Le Mans start; an uphill run, followed by a loop across a ridge and a return down the same hill, where everyone would mount bikes and head back up the initial short, but steep climb. A mass of runners, soon to be riders, jostled for position, ready to burst from the starting gate. We searched for Chris, our uber athlete, expecting to see him elbowing for position at the front of the pack, but he was hidden amongst a sea of colorful clownfish. I had my camera ready to take a picture of our buddy as he flashed by us. But where was he, we wondered? Did we miss him, hidden within the surging clownfish? Finally we saw him, second to last in a field of over 200 teams, trudging steadily uphill. He gave us his smirky-smile and waved like he was on a float in the Macy's Day Parade.

"What's wrong with Chris?" Caz looked at me for an answer.

"I don't know," I replied, wondering if there had been an "incident." What had happened to our super-competitive leader? He was trotting along as if the goal was to finish in last place?! Yes, there had to have been an incident. Maybe there had been a disagreement with an official over Chris's brazen flouting of the race rules, or maybe there had been an altercation with another rider, the result of a careless snicker or an inappropriately pointed finger. I was sure there'd be a story told later.

I snapped another picture as he made the initial climb on his bike. Chris and his battered blue Nishiki hard-tail, with no front shocks, and caliper brakes, had broken from the pack of clownfish riding on their fancy-schmancy bikes equipped with full suspension shocks and hydraulic disc brakes. There was no wave from Chris this time. He was up on the pedals, forearms bulging, bare hands gripping the handlebars, grinding past the competition with a grizzled face. The helmet he wore (as mandated by race regulations) was twisted askew. Chris's head and the borrowed helmet appeared to resist each other like two north-ended magnets.

Amazingly, after his second-from-the-last-place-position at the start, Chris came across the finish line in the middle of the pack. We had registered our first official lap! Later he explained his strategy at the start, "I wasn't going to waste my energy fighting through all that bullshit." *Good plan, Chris.* We watched the Geek disappear into the woods after the initial climb and then we walked back to the Vandura. Chris regaled Caz and me with his single-track passing strategy. "One asshole wiped out and left his bike lying in the middle of the trail."

"You mean he just left it there? Did you see him crash?" I didn't understand. It sounded as if the rider might have been injured and had left their bike in search of assistance.

"He was standing on the side of the fucking trail like an idiot!"

Oh.

"So I ran over his bike."

Nice.

I made a mental note. There could be at least one team looking to exact some form of race revenge upon us. Good thing we didn't have matching team jerseys. I looked at the time. Considering that Chris had to do the run and the Geek didn't, I figured he'd be finishing soon. I told Caz and Chris, "I better get up to the starting line. Are you guys coming?"

We yelled for the Geek as we saw him gliding downhill through the s-turns. His face and the yellow-orange bike shirt were splattered with mud. "Way to go Geek! Hit it hard!" The Geek looked spent as he handed me the baton. Off I went. I wanted just one ride, as fast as I could possibly go, not saving anything for later. Maybe I could beat Chris's time (I didn't.) The course was now a mess. It was like riding in peanut butter and my caliper brakes clogged with mud that required frequent stops to free the wheel rims from the sticky sludge. I gained ground on a rider in front of me, grinding forward, my thighs screaming at me, begging me to take a break, telling me, *there's no sense killing yourself.* I didn't listen to my thighs. I had to catch the guy in front of me. I heard a spectator cheer for me, "Go get 'em, old-timer." *Hey, hey, wait a minute. Old-timer?* I passed the guy. I didn't ride over anyone's bike, but I passed a few more riders, gaining further ground in our race standing.

Halfway up The Wall, my lungs gave out. I got off my bike, deciding not to waste energy, and walked to the top. I didn't feel so bad, when I found out later, that even Chris didn't ride to the top of The Wall. Team Angry Tuna cheered for me as I came through the spectators lining the orange fencing surrounding the s-curves. Chris was yelling for me to ride faster. It made me feel good that I'd done my part. I palmed the baton to Caz—now it was his turn.

"Good riding, Jack." Chris slapped me on the back and laughed.

"Nice work," the Geek chimed in.

"Thanks."

I looked at the race clock. It was a little before four o'clock, only 20 hours to go.

Caz surprised all of us with a brisk loop. We got to the start/finish line just in time to see him come across.

"Way to go, Caz!" I hollered.

"Nice job!" the Geek added.

"Gimme the fucking baton, Caz." Chris snatched the baton from his hand and jammed it under his racing shorts.

The Geek and I were amazed at how well Caz had done. I asked him, "You didn't pull a Rosie Ruiz, did you Caz?"

He didn't know what I was talking about. The Geek explained to Caz, "She took a shortcut in the Boston Marathon." In 1980 Rosie Ruiz won the Boston Marathon. A week later she was disqualified when it was determined she hadn't run the full course. It wasn't the first time Ruiz "found" a shortcut. In the New York Marathon she'd boarded the subway.

"No way, man. I rode the whole thing," Caz replied defensively. His feelings were hurt.

"Okay, Caz, okay. We believe you."

Caz was a bubbling fountain, spouting details of every rock, root, and ridge he crossed. *Yeah, Caz, we know. We just rode the same course, remember?* He told us of his slip-sliding trip down a tough downhill portion that was lined with boulders the size of campers. Spectators were perched on the rocks, cheering on the riders.

"They were yelling for me, Jack. I was going to walk it down, but I had to ride it with all those people there." *Good going, Caz. We would have called you a fem if you didn't.* As I let him talk, the words surged out of him. Caz told us, "One guy yelled out, 'Ride it like ya stole it' and I just busted it to the bottom."

The Geek patted him on the back, "Nice work, Caz. Maybe you better get your bike cleaned up." His brand new Jamis Dakar Sport was no longer gleaming silver. It looked like he'd been riding through gravy. The rear cassette was caked with dried mud.

"Yeah, I better," Caz lowered his head and pushed his bike in search of the water hoses. I was certain we hadn't heard the end of his race details, but that was okay. Caz is a good guy. We were glad he was part of our team. It had taken a lot of convincing to get him to join us.

"Are your lights charged?" the Geek asked Caz while he walked away from us. Without turning toward us Caz yelled, "Yeah, they're charged."

I sure as hell hoped so. I'd already done the math. Based upon our current riding pace, he'd be the first to take a complete lap in the dark. *Good luck, buddy.*

Chris finished in just a few minutes over an hour. Amazing! His second lap was faster than his first. He must have run over *four* bikes this time. The Geek and I finished our laps in the last of the daylight when I handed off the baton to Caz. He left the starting line as the sun tucked in behind the treetops on the surrounding ridges. It would be over an hour and a half before we saw him again. The bike lights flickered in the woods like fireflies on a hot summer night—within minutes it was black as tar.

We waited in the halogen lights near the finish line, watching bike after bike swerve down the s-curves. It was cool to watch in the dark. A couple of times we mistook another rider for Caz. Chris voiced his concern for our friend, "Where the fuck is Caz?!" And no sooner had Chris wondered about Caz, he appeared. Evidently, things had not gone well with lap number two. Caz's face was covered in mud and green leaves stuck out of the holes in his helmet. He looked like a Navy SEAL in training.

"What happened, Mike?" I pointed to the smeared mud mixed with crusted blood on his shins. His legs looked like burnt scalloped potatoes.

"My fucking lights went out halfway through the course. I had to ride the rocky section in the dark." *Well, I don't think you had to "ride" in the dark, Caz. You could have "walked" the bike. What I think, Caz, is that those guys cheering you on earlier were hoping, like the spectators at Indy, for a spectacular crash.*

I knelt next to his bike, inspecting his mangled rear-derailleur. "You rode your bike like that?"

"Yeah, I rode it like *that!*" Caz was unsettled, the way you might be for example, after slicing your leg open with the oily teeth of a chainsaw. He stared at the limp derailleur. "I guess that's why I had to stay in one gear."

"Bummer, Caz." I consoled him, "Your next lap will be better."

"I'm done!" he informed us.

"What do you mean, you're done?"

"I'm done. I'm not riding anymore."

Done? We're a four-man team. The Geek and I tried to talk Caz down from his personal "rocky ledge." He was angry. We backed off. *Well, wasn't this just great!*

Chris would be back soon and the Geek was getting a bit of rest before going back out in the dark. I lay in silence on top of my sleeping bag, staring into the inky blackness of the RV. It was quiet outside except for the occasional rider coming back in the dark of night to camp, like a soldier returning from the front lines.

"Geek?" He didn't answer. Caz was snoring in the back. I tried again, "Geek?" He answered with a muffled, "Yeah?"

"Don't you think you should be getting up to the finish line? Chris is going to be back any minute."

"Shit!"

Apparently, he'd lost track of time. A giraffe leg from the top bunk searched for the floor.

Yooowww, oooooo, whoooooa! It sounded as if the Geek had stepped on a porcupine. He wailed and grabbed his thigh, hopping around on one leg. I'd seen this dance before. The Geek's muscle cramps were legendary. "Don't even think about it, Geek. No way am I going out there now." I wasn't mentally or physically ready to do another lap, my lights were still charging, and well, I just wasn't doing it. It was the Geek's turn. He rubbed his thigh as I practically pushed him from the Vandura. "You better get going. Chris is probably almost done." *And he's going to be fucking pissed if you're not waiting for the baton exchange.*

Into the dark he went. I checked to make sure my lights were charging before heading back into the Vandura. Maybe I could get half an hour of sleep before I had to jump back on the merry-go-round and do it again. *What the fuck?!* Caz was in my sleeping bag. Why? I turned on the little light by the sink.

"Caz, what the hell?!" I shook him. "Why are you in *my* sleeping bag?" He mumbled something and crawled out. He was covered in dry flaky mud. *Beautiful.* I turned off the light, and lay on the top of my sleeping bag. We had over twelve hours of riding left. Instead of sleeping I ran the calculations in my head. It was easy math—three riders (Mike was definitely done), twelve hours, 720 minutes, at our average lap rate of around 80 minutes that came out to three more laps for each of us. *Yippee.* I made a silent vow—never again.

Chris, the Geek, and I ground out the rest of the race while Caz recuperated. At first I was pissed at him—we all kind of were; we were supposed to be a four-man team. After my initial anger I started to feel bad for our buddy. We had badgered the shit out of him to suck it up and get back on his bike and ride. Shit, it was our fault; we had talked him into the ride. Caz is gritty, he wouldn't milk an injury. He'd done a real number on his leg, and his bike was messed up. As the night threw off its covers and stretched its long shadowed limbs in early dawn, I looked for Caz, to say something consoling. He was slumped in a camp chair outside the RV, sleeping in clothes he might have borrowed from the Grim Reaper, black nylon wind pants and a black windbreaker with the hood draped over the top of his head.

"Mike, you awake?"

"Yeah," he mumbled underneath his cocoon of black nylon.

"Are you okay?"

"Yeah. I let you guys down. I should ... never ... maybe I ... I don't ..." His muttered words were an incoherent stew of disappointment.

"It's okay, Mike. Next time buddy. How's your leg?"

"I don't know. It doesn't feel that great. I just never ... I wasn't ... ready for this."

"Don't worry about it." I patted Caz on the shoulder. "I got to get ready for the next lap."

My last lap started at 9:43 AM. I planned to enjoy the trail, take in the scenery of the craggy mountains of West Virginia with the understanding that this was to be my last 24-hour race. I didn't have to kill myself to complete the loop. Chris would have plenty of time after me to get in his final lap, and the Geek had already told me he was done. So this would be it for all of us except Chris. Maybe he'd try to pound out his last lap and be done before noon so he could keep going and do a "double."

I waited for the Geek at the start/finish line. Others gathered there as well, getting ready for their last rides. One young guy stood out from the rest because he was wearing nothing other than a thong Speedo. I'm exaggerating because that wasn't entirely true. He was also wearing clip-in bike shoes, socks, and a helmet. It appeared someone had lost a bet.

The Geek handed me the baton and collapsed to the ground like the marathon-ers do at the finish. I left the team, and Speedo Guy, as I headed upwards into the humid West Virginia woods. I settled into my ride, savoring the last moments through a tight section of the course when I sensed someone behind me.

"On your left."

I moved over. And, what to my wondering eyes should appear, but Speedo Guy in his thong, tiny and sheer. I averted my eyes from his jouncing butt cheeks perched upon a slim bike saddle. There was absolutely no way I wanted this visual in front of me while I rode my last lap. I pondered getting off my bike to repair an imaginary mechanical issue, but it wasn't necessary. Speedo Guy was a great rider. In no time he sliced through a narrow section of single-track, disappearing from my sight. I finished the loop without further incident and handed Chris the baton for the last time.

He looked fresh, eager for another helping of agony. How did he do it? In the end he completed six laps of treacherous riding—over 60 miles. Astonishingly, his last lap was our team's fastest. We moved up in the standings, assisted in some cases by attrition, and perhaps Chris may have bent a *couple tree* bike rims riding over racers that lingered carelessly after a crash. The final results had our team completing 18 laps, finishing 55th overall, and fifth in our class.

What we endured wasn't remotely close to the journey an expectant mother takes on the way to giving birth, but I couldn't help thinking, maybe I now had a sliver of understanding of their emotions. When the race was over my feelings were mixed, thrilled with the end result and happy we'd survived, but like some moms have explained to me, it elicited a never-again attitude. Over time, like those moms, I started to think, that wasn't so bad. Maybe we should have another. Our mother of a friend, Chris, convinced us to do two more rides.

The following year we even finished first in our class at the Hardcore 24 in Naples, NY. (There was one other team in our class.) If that wasn't enough, Chris decided it would be *a lot like fun—only different* to ride a 24-hour race as a one-man team. Sadly, he didn't finish the race. It wasn't his fault. The race officials thought it best to stop the competition after a rider had a heart attack and died on the course.

However, our West Virginia odyssey was far from finished. We still had to get back home.

Chris in Letchworth State Park after our ride from hell and before we grilled yellow-tag sausages – 2009

Snowshoe, West Virginia – A Circuitous Way Home

As I PULL OUT of Chris's driveway and onto North Davis Road, I think of him in his house, all alone, and hope that he'll be all right until Jennifer gets back. What does he do when no one is around? How can we be sure he won't get into things that he shouldn't? I can't imagine Jennifer's responsibilities, watching over Chris every day. It certainly involves a lot more than hiding the cookies so he won't eat them all. It must be mentally and physically draining, except for when Chris sleeps, which he does a lot these days. But she's strong, a can-do lady, a softer version of her husband. At times, she chuckles about her *new normal*, but I can't comprehend how, beneath those surface emotions, she must wrestle with the challenges of taking care of a husband who always took pride in taking care of himself.

An attic of memories fraternizes with my present concerns for Chris's well being. Some of those memories are in full view, like your wife's wedding dress that's preserved in a hermetically sealed box with a see-through plastic cover. You don't keep it for any practical reason; your daughters will never wear the out-of-style garment. You keep it, I suppose, to remember. And discarding it might feel like part of you has died. Other memories are hidden deeper, in boxes shoved behind the knee walls of the attic, forgotten until, one day, while looking for something else, you discover them. You pull them out, examine the objects of your past and run downstairs holding them like a winning lottery ticket. And you say, "Do you remember this, Honey? Remember when Junior used to play with this?" And then after remembering, you put it back where you found it, until someday you might open that box again while searching for something entirely different. That's how it is with my memories of the things that I've done with Chris. My thoughts start down one path and they lead me past something else. I let them float to the top, maybe talk about them with my friends to see if they can add to the memory, and sometimes I keep them for myself, a little thing that means something only to me.

In this moment, I continue to think about the 24-hour race in West Virginia, realizing it was Chris's fortitude that pushed us forward. He was the glue that bonded us so we could accomplish what we did. At the time we took pride in our race results, but now, they don't seem as important. What stays with me is the adventure and our bond as friends with a common goal. Even if Chris's approach, riding over anyone in his way, was a bit different than ours. I think back to Caz, how we joked with him about pulling a Rosie Ruiz, and how pissed he got when he crashed and burned during his second lap. We knew Caz would never have knowingly taken a shortcut; he's an honest and honorable guy.

Chris wouldn't have either; that wasn't his style. Once he determined a goal, a prank, a project, a responsibility, an educational degree, a race, or a challenge to be worthy of his time, based upon his unique criteria that we never fully understood, there was only one way he approached it—the Chris Kelley way. It was a way devoid of cushioned bumpers, airbags, paved paths, evening pleasantries, fashionably late arrivals, VIP parking, or anything else that made things easier. He felt a powerful desire for physical punishment. For Christ sakes, if he'd had it his way, we would have all been riding without brakes, without helmets, without lights, and without our granny gears to climb the steeps. He was far too disciplined to cheat in order to meet a challenge.

Everything that got in the way he deemed to be *bullshit*, things like attending classes in high school. He enjoyed EAHS more than most of us; it was just those "ridiculous" class schedules filled with subjects he determined to not be worth his time. Speed limits, speed enforcement, or for that matter anything that slowed him down, were also *bullshit*. To that end, he spent a lifetime trying to push boundaries without getting caught—most of the time.

There's a big difference between meeting a goal and pulling off a prank. For young Chris, the two often became one and the same. While some of us were devoting our time to passing AP English, Algebra II, and chemistry, he was busy plotting his next prank. Some were minor, like crashing the group pictures in our high school yearbook with Dickie Moritz; these days it's called photo-bombing. Somehow the two of them must have gotten hold of the schedule of when clubs and groups would have their pictures taken. Chris and Dickie were captured for posterity, credited for things they hadn't come close to being involved in: the Key 76 Club, the National Honor Society, and maybe the Science Club. Some of Chris's pranks were epic—The Smoke Bomb Incident. I'll get to that later.

My memories turn back to our trip home from West Virginia. It wouldn't be enough to have ridden the race, packed up our shit, and coasted for home. What fun would that have been?

THERE WAS an awards ceremony for the winning teams. We weren't one of them, but we watched. The end was anticlimactic. Except for Chris, our bodies drooped with a combination of exhaustion and relief. It didn't stop us from mustering the energy for a celebratory beer.

"Beers up, beers in," declared Chris with his typical vim.

We clinked our cans together and watched another team hoist their trophy into the afternoon sun before we shuffled back to the RV. I got the feeling that we'd be hanging out for a while, taking time to savor our accomplishment, and resting our battered bodies before the long trip home. I figured it was a good time to broach a delicate topic. *It wasn't.*

"How long were we planning on hanging out?" I asked.

"I don't know. What's your fucking rush, Jack?" Chris wondered.

I looked at the Geek, "You remember, I told you guys I have to catch a plane to California at 6:30 tomorrow morning—for work. *Or maybe ... did I forgot to mention this little detail. Come to think of it ... maybe I didn't tell you guys. Sorry. Anywho ... so we kind of need to get going soon.*

"What?" Chris exclaimed.

Caz took a few steps back from a potentially explosive confluence of priorities.

"I've got a plane to catch at 6:30 tomorrow morning. I told you guys a long time ago." I repeated.

"What the fuck, Jack?!" Chris exploded. "Why—the—hell did you schedule a plane trip for Monday morning?!"

"I didn't have a choice. I have to be there. It's an important opportunity," I tried to explain with the same flimsy conviction of a ne'er-do-well teenager telling his English teacher that his pet iguana had eaten his book report. An eight-hour joyride loomed ahead of us in the "trusty" 1976 GMC Vandura Midas. I hadn't slept since Friday night. Chris couldn't believe it. There was a nimbus of grumbling as we packed up camp, stowed our bikes in the rear of the RV, and climbed aboard the Vandura. Chris continued to let me have it, and I let him give it to me. I deserved it.

"What a fucking idiot." His assessment of my mental amplitude was spot on. I had let everyone down, especially Chris. We left Snowshoe Mountain Resort, our home since Friday, bouncing through the dips and gopher holes of the parking lot. It was 2:30 Sunday afternoon and all was quiet inside the Vandura when we hit the paved road. If all went well, I would've made it home before midnight, giving me time for a short rest before heading off to the airport.

The Geek took the wheel after a while and I sat next to him in the navigator's seat. The night was black as we passed through the "badlands" of Western Pennsylvania. I kept looking at the time and leaned toward the driver's seat to check how fast the Geek was going. We were a little behind schedule. My eyelids drooped, I wanted to sleep, but the RV bounced me back to consciousness. And it started to rain. That wasn't going to help getting us home any faster. *Shit.*

"Geek, turn on the wipers." *How can he see through that rain?*

He yelled something to Chris, but I was confused. In my sleepy fugue I didn't understand. The rain was green and it wasn't falling from the sky—it was squirting upward.

"Pull over, pull over!" Chris hollered as he crawled between us in the front seat. The needle on the speedometer plummeted to 10 mph, and the engine light glowed a menacing red.

We rumbled onto the shoulder as steam curled from under the hood. Now I understood why the rain was green. It wasn't rain; it was antifreeze! Chris and Caz burst out of the side door in a flash and yelled for the Geek to pop the hood. A billowing cloud shrouded the RV. Once again, we were fucked.

In a hushed voice I said to the Geek, "I've got to figure out a way to get home." He gave me a look—it was sympathetic—but his darting eyes conveyed a different message. *Don't let Chris hear you talking about that, or he'll use whatever brains you have left to plug the pinholes in the RV's leaking radiator.*

I listened as the Geek came up with an idea that sounded like it could work. "My sister-in-law lives in Erie. I could call her. And maybe she could pick us up and drive us back part of the way."

"Then what?"

"Do you think Mar would be able to come and pick us up in Erie?"

Oh, yeah, no problem, sure she will. She's probably waiting by the phone, ready to spring into action. She'll love the adventure of swinging down and picking us up.

My call woke Mar. She asked, "You're where?"

"Pennsylvania."

"What happened?"

After giving her a brief an explanation, I asked her for the "favor" and braced myself. Mar has done lots of "favors" for me over the years, bringing me spare sets of keys when I locked myself out of my car and Alex wasn't there to wedge his car antenna in my window, taking care of me when I busted my lip, mashed my face, and jacked up my shoulder. Now she was being asked to provide an unexpected courtesy shuttle to the airport. One of these days I might use up all my "favors."

"You want me to pick you up where?!"

"In Erie, Pennsylvania. We'll meet you at the exit. Drive through the toll booth."

There was a brief silence followed by quiet negotiations, after which we settled on a pickup point in Fredonia, NY. Operation Rescue commenced.

"Good luck with your *plane trip*, Jack." Chris sarcastically wished me well. "Thanks for the *fucking* help."

A few hours later the Geek and I said goodbye to Chris and Caz and climbed into his sister-in-law's car with our essentials. She greeted us with questions and a general disbelief of our tales. *How could we make this up, and why?* We were idiots. Check that, *I* was the idiot.

When we arrived in Fredonia, Mar was waiting. I didn't say much more than thanks. I knew better. We drove to Chris's house, dropped off the Geek, and picked up my car. Gratefully, Mar had packed my clothes that I needed for the week in California. It was 3:45 in the morning when my head hit the pillow.

Plenty of time to recharge before I have to get up in 45 minutes, drive to the airport, and catch my plane. Sure it was.

By noon, Pacific Time, I was at work on the West Coast. Somehow I pushed through the rest of the day despite the worst sinus infection of my life. Mucus flowed from my nose like Jell-O shots. It was 6:00 Monday evening when I got to my hotel room and climbed on the bed in my dress clothes. My phone rang. It was Caz.

"Hey, Jack, I was just checking on you, buddy. Did you make it?"

"Yeah. How about you guys?"

He laughed, "I just got home."

It was 9:00 p.m. Eastern Time. I wanted to hear the details about what happened after the Geek and I had abandoned Chris and Caz, but I didn't have the energy to listen.

"Thanks for the call, Caz. I'll call you tomorrow, buddy."

Months later we'd talk about our adventure and invariably we'd get to the part where Chris would remind everyone listening, "And then Jack made us pack up our shit and drive home because he had to get to the fucking airport! He left Caz and me in Pennsylvania to fix the fucking RV. Thanks, Jack!" But after he was finished, he would laugh. That's the way it was with Chris—he wasn't one to hold a grudge, but if you fucked up, he loved keeping the story at the ready, pulling it out when it suited his purposes. And you took it, because you knew you deserved it. I'm not sure if I ever told him I was sorry, so I will now. Sorry, Chris.

Chris, Arty, Jennifer, John Hitchings, and Alex brewing at the
Five Cow Sugar Shanty – 2008

Maple Porter Night

I'M HEADING TO Chris's house tonight to watch the Sabres' game. I called a few friends to see if they wanted to join; everyone, except Caz, had previous commitments. It's a bit of a drive from his home in the Northtowns and a noble commitment on his part to spend a Saturday night with our friend. It's a testament to both Chris and his family that so many have pitched in to spend time with him when he's not under the watchful eyes of Jennifer or the fine folks at Aurora Adult Day Services. Paul (Wally) Sugnet has gone above and beyond, driving from his home in Rochester, New York, every other Thursday to take Chris for hikes, out to lunch, or to the movie theater. Paul told me Chris loves to slouch back in the comfy recliners.

I've invited other friends to visit Chris and to do stuff with him. And when our class of '76 friends, Peter Diebolt, Don Reidy, and Kenny Walker have been in from out of town, I've taken them to visit Chris. Those who haven't seen him for a while will wonder what to expect, asking in subdued tones, "How's he doing?"

I attempt to balance my optimism with realism, replying, "It's not great, but he's doing okay. He doesn't say much these days, but he's still laughing."

Some have asked, "Will he know who I am? Will he know my name?"

And I answer, "Yeah, he'll know who you are." But I'm not so sure. I know he won't say, "Hey, Deebs," or "Great to see you, Head," to Kenny Walker, or "Don—where the hell have you been since graduation?" To avoid an awkward situation, I'll start by saying, "Hey, Chris, you remember this guy don't you? It's Peter Diebolt, remember—Deebs?" or, "Didn't you and Head play in the band together?"

To which Chris will answer, "Yeah," and he'll laugh. And then the two friends will hug or shake hands. Most give him a hug.

I'm looking forward to spending time with my friend tonight. While wondering how the evening will play out, irrational thoughts creep into my subconscious—those of hope that Chris can beat this ruthless disease, that a cure awaits, or that it's all been another one of his pranks. I should know better by now. Implausible musings about this disease without a cure might give me a momentary pipe dream of optimism, but I've been through that before. In the end it's a waste of time and energy. It's a better use of our time together to enjoy what we still have. So I'm pulling down Chris's driveway with three beers I took from my fridge (one a Labatt Blue), and bags of chips and pretzels (Tops Supermarket brand) that I bought on sale—BOGO. Chris loved the cost savings of the supermarket brands and to get them BOGO would have been a thing to talk about. If only I had brought "yellow tag" Italian sausage.

"Chris?!" I holler as I take off my boots in his kitchen. The lights are dim. It's as quiet as if I'd snuck into the Aurora Public Library after hours. I look for notes on the island countertop; perhaps Jennifer has left a message about something: that Chris is sleeping in his room, or that he's decided he doesn't want to watch the game, or maybe he's refused, once again, to change his underwear. There's no note. I holler again, a bit louder this time, "Chris?!" I slip off my coat and hang it on the back of a chair.

I'm about to leave the kitchen and a memory hits me hard. I place the palms of my hands on the countertop and flashback to a night I try to keep hidden. Maple Porter Night. I remember Chris in the kitchen cooking us dinner. We were laughing; it had been a great day up to that point, just Chris and me, Chris leading and me following. That's the middle of a story that I wish had a better ending. It was a low point for me; a night that remains bloated with personal regret. Sure it provided a lot of laughs for the group back then, and did for years to come, but it's a night I'd rather forget.

I could tell you about another memory, like Chris's short-lived ATC (Aurora Tubing Club) where we snuck onto the ski slopes of Kissing Bridge and Emery Park, walked halfway up the hill, and slid down. We spun out of control and there were crashes. It came to an end when one classmate broke his arm at KB and another her leg at Emery. Chris would tell me, "Jaaack, Jaaack, just tell the fucking story. Maaaple Porter, Jaaack." And so, as in the past, Chris pushes me, against what I consider to be my better judgment, to tell you about that night.

To the best of my recollection, Maple Porter Night didn't become Maple Porter Night, until the incident, or better said, the incidents. It fell into the category of things I wished Chris hadn't talked me into. Why do I tell you this story? On the surface it's more about others than about me, or Chris. I tell you, because Chris would be so pissed at me if I left it out. I'd never hear the end of it. It started with a simple, "Hey, Jack. Watcha doing, Jack?"

"I'm relaxing on my deck watching the birds . . . and talking to you." Apparently, this was a good joke. Chris laughed.

"Are you coming to the sugar shanty tomorrow night? Alex is breaking out his new beer."

"Which one is that?" I asked, even though I knew. Alex is into home brewing and regularly brought a few of his creations, in recycled beer bottles, for post-mountain biking hydration. The beers are delicious, but should come with a warning label. Most start at a minimum of 12 % alcohol content, a fact hidden in their ability to smoothly slide over one's palette. My favorite was the Strawberry Blonde, which also happens to be the color of Courtney's hair. Courtney is Alex's wife. I'm not sure which came first, the beer or Courtney. I'm guessing it was Courtney.

"Maple Porter," Chris bellowed. "So are you coming or what?"

"I don't know, Chris. I'll have to check with Mar and see what we have going on."

"Come on, Jaaack; there's beer with maaaple syrup in it." *Thanks Chris, for your in-depth explanation about the science behind ingredient infusion in the brewing process.*

The beer sounded tasty. I loved porters and who doesn't like the sugary goodness of maple syrup? Chris's brother-in-law, Arty Aungst, and our friend John Hitchings make the syrup from scratch in a shack on the hill across the street from John's house outside of town on Olean Road. Rick Ohler came up with a name for the shack after hearing John extol the virtues of another of his schemes that involved livestock. "You should call this the Five Cow Sugar Shack," said Rick, who is always quick with a clever moniker. It sounded official and you might think: working farm, multi-level board and batten structure, factory-grade stain-less steel sugaring equipment, and perhaps at least one person wearing a uniform with a logo-patch replete with grazing cows. It's none of that.

The casual observer might question John and Arty's sagaciousness, but this stuff was important to them. The hoses are laced together from tree to tree as if a giant had woven a web of complex snares to protect this piece of land from other giants. I'd have to do more research to see how this all comes together, but what I do know is the tree sap somehow gets into a bulbous cauldron and it's boiled over a wood fire evaporating the water until it becomes syrup. It takes a minimum of 40 gallons of sap to produce one gallon of syrup. But Maple Porter Night was not about sugaring; that was done in early spring. This night was about John's and Arty's efforts with the sugar water that was turned into maple syrup that Alex turned into beer, which Chris and others organized into a night to share with friends.

"So are you coming?" Chris disguised his command as a question. Grammati-cally it *was* a question, but it wasn't as it sounded. I didn't have a choice. Unless, that is, I wanted to be called a fem. The only choice I really had was when I'd show up.

I answered Chris, "Yeah, I guess I'll probably be there. I'll let you know later. What time are you going? Is the Geek going?"

"Yes, the Geek is going. Everyone is going, even Caz."

Chris threw out another option. "You want to ride before we go?"

"I guess we could ride. What time?"

"Meet me at my house at two. We'll ride Hunter's Creek. Bring some extra clothes. You can shower at my house and then we'll head over." He'd done it again, luring me into a night of his shenanigans.

"Okay, I guess I'll see you tomorrow."

Chris didn't answer. He'd hung up after giving me my instructions.

I MET Chris at his house the following afternoon. It was hot and humid and hadn't rained in over a week. As a result, the trails were dry and fast. We rode without incident (rare) and finished sweaty and thirsty, but we didn't sit on the weathered picnic bench under the mangy white pine, as was tradition, to enjoy a post-ride beer. Instead we loaded our bikes and headed back to Chris's house.

He'd told me we'd have dinner at his place before heading to the sugar shack. That was a first. I would've expected dinner from the Geek, but Chris? Food? Dinner?

"What do you want? Beef or chicken?" Chris held frost-covered cardboard boxes labeled Swanson.

"Pot pies? That's what we're having for dinner?" *You don't have any yellow-tag Italian sausages.*

"These are great. You're gonna love them."

"I've had them, Chris—when I was back in college!" *When the loose change in my pockets constituted my savings account.*

"Which one do you want?"

"I guess I'll take the beef."

Chris put the pot pies in the oven, following the baking directions. In 35 minutes he served us tins of molten gravy and rubbery bits of meat that, in the case of the beef, reminded me of Jujubes.

After we ate our pot pies, he asked, "You want another one?"

"I'll pass, Chris," I told him as I spit the last "meat Jujube" into the garbage and washed the taste from my mouth with a swig of Labatt.

Maybe the dinners were old; evidence of freezer burn was clear. Maybe Chris didn't cook them right. Maybe it was neither. Sorry Swanson. Later, in order to validate the technical facts of this story, I looked up a review online:

(7 ounces, one 370-calorie serving, $0.89) It cost 89 cents. The crust was thin, rubbery, and meaningless, the gravy was mostly salt and modified food starch, the super-salty chicken cubes felt like glued-together lunchmeat, the potatoes seemed reconstituted, and the peas were sour. Carrots were nice, though.

Thank God I had picked the beef!

The sun rested in the treetops when we arrived at Five Cow. Chris parked in Hitchy's driveway and we crossed the road before making our way up the hill with our beer mugs extended in front of us like panhandlers holding tin cups. The climb up the hill to Five Cow isn't excessively steep, but after mountain biking for the last couple of hours I stopped half-way up to catch my breath. "Come on, Jack. There's cold beer waiting," Chris reminded me.

A spiral of smoke rose lazily above the treetops. As we crested the final hill we saw them,the denizens of the Five Cow Sugar Shack. John, Arty, Alex, the Geek, Caz, Arty's son Judd, some wives, Babette, Linda, the Geek's brother, Lance—a sequoia of a man—and a few others I didn't know gathered near a fully-engaged bonfire. Beer flowed, fresh brushstrokes were put on old stories, backs were slapped, and laughter was our medicine. What a great summer night it was. *This maple porter is delicious.* It wasn't a "summer beer," but we weren't about to let a superficial detail like that stop a good time. It's a heavy beer meant to be sipped, savored; maybe it would go well with pancakes.

I sat in a low-to-the-ground beach chair that may have been provided by the Five Cow hospitality crew. Sitting low was the way to go. There's a steep ravine near the sugar shack, a sparking fire was in front of me, and I continued drinking the potent maple porter. An incident laden evening was in the making.

Caz became the first casualty. He walked a jagged line toward the ravine. Once there he stood with his back to us preparing to pee off the edge. It didn't go well. He wobbled, stumbled, and finished it off with flailing arms and an awkward somersault over the embankment. Caz emerged from his fall looking like Yukon Cornelius returning from the abyss. When it was clear that he'd avoided "spinal damage" Chris commenced with howling laughter.[2]

"Where'd you go, Caz?"

"Real fucking funny, Chris!" Caz shot back.

You should know better, Caz; that's only going to make things worse for yourself. You're trying to douse an inferno with gasoline.

We all laughed. It *was* real fucking funny. *What did you expect, Caz? That we'd all rush over to see if you were okay? Seriously?*

It became a spectator sport, watching each participant approach the steep gradient with a combination of trepidation and purpose. I watched the absurdity in

---

[2] Recently, while talking with Caz about that night he told me, "You know Chris warned me."
"He warned you about what?"
"About how steep the ravine was. I should have known better."
We all should have known better, Caz.

front of me from my low vantage point and then quietly headed off in the darkness to find level ground so I could pee with dignity. When I returned, I made a commitment to stop drinking for the night. It had been fun watching the others make fools of themselves, but no way was Chris talking me into another beer. I sat down in the beach chair.

I wanted to get up, to join the Geek and Chris. They were laughing about something, but I couldn't tell what they were saying. Everyone sounded like they were talking underwater and the ground wobbled. I was the steel marble on the tilting maze game, Labyrinth, banging against the wooden sides, attempting to roll along the twisty-line, not wanting to drop through the hole in front of me. If you've never played the game, look it up on Amazon and buy it. It'd be worth the 24 bucks to play the tabletop game made by Brio so that you could safely experience the oscillating condition of my failing equilibrium. I puked the Jujube beef pellets, the gravy, and the foamy coffee-colored maple porter beer. Chris whooped it up. His is a contagious laugh, and soon he was joined by the rest. They pointed at me as I lay on the ground, "paralyzed" by my own stupidity. Puddles lapped the barf surrounding my head that now felt as heavy as a bowling ball. And there wasn't a fucking thing I could do about it.

"Come on Jack, it's time to go. You gotta get up. Come on," the Geek attempted to coax me to get on my feet.

"I can't move." I replied.

"Come on, you can do it. We're just walking down the hill." He reached down. Chris was with him. They pulled me up, hooking the crooks of their arms under my armpits. I was standing, but my legs provided no more support than if I had two earthworms attached to my hips. Chris and the Geek guided me, slowly, a step at a time down Five Cow hill.

Jennifer picked us up at the bottom of the hill and drove us back to Chris's house. It was probably sometime around two in the morning by the time we all sprawled on the floor of their house. I give her a lot of credit for putting up with this sort of thing, more times than I'll ever know.

The next morning, I found out that Alex had called Mar on my phone to advise her I was doing the prudent thing by not driving home and sleeping over at

Chris's. A week later, when Mar had resumed communication with me, I found out the call went something like this. "Ahh, this is Alex. You don't know me that well, but umm, I'm Chris's nephew, remember? And umm, yeah, Jack's really messed up, so umm, yeah, he's sleeping it off at Chris's. Bye." And not a word was slurred. *Sure.*

Now, years later, I know how this all looks. It's not great. Maybe I'm rationalizing, making excuses for Chris's misguided attention to the details of cold beer and my willingness to follow his orders of, "Beers up, beers in," but I think there was more to it. I think, whether he realized it or not, Chris was like the best man at a wedding who'd beseech us to raise our glasses to toast the good times of the past and to even greater times in the future. In Chris's case he never wanted those times to end.

In the case of Maple Porter Night, we were there as friends, to celebrate the making of the beer and to stay connected with each other. What happened—just happened.

For years, I'd receive a call from Chris, reminding me, "Maple Porter night, Jack. You're coming, right?"

"No."

He'd drag the words out, saying them slowly for emphasis, "Maaaple Pooorter. Come on, Jack. It'll be great." Then he'd pause before reminding me, "Puddles will be there."

So there, I told the story, Chris. I hope this makes you happy. Now everyone knows about Maple Porter Night. I hear Chris's laughter, and so I know it's okay.

Chris and me in an abandoned cabin at the
Genesee Road Forestry Preserve – 2008

Third Floor Demo

I TAKE A few steps toward the front hall in Chris's house and shout his name once again, "Chris?!" I wonder if maybe signals got crossed, or I screwed up on the time. His bedroom door is ajar a few inches. I push it open, look at the bed and quietly inquire, "Chris?" The bed is empty. I back out of the room, close the door, and walk to the top of the stairs that lead to the TV room below.

"Chris?"

"Yeah."

He's awake. *Good.* I head downstairs, excited to see my friend and watch the Sabres game together.

"Hey, Chris." He's stretched out in his comfy recliner. "Good to see you, buddy." He doesn't get out of the chair. We do an awkward handshake-hug thing as he leans back like he's waiting for the dentist to examine him for cavities. He laughs.

I ask him, "Did Jen tell you I was coming over?"

"Yeah."

I look at the TV and ask, "We're going to watch the hockey game, right? Is this the right channel?" He's watching a college basketball game.

"Yeah."

"Where's the remote?" He doesn't answer. I look to see if it's shoehorned between Chris and the recliner, but I don't attempt to dig around in there. God only knows what might be wedged in the depths. I look around and see it on the table behind him. I press the button for the channel guide and change the station to the Sabres game. Ice skaters slamming into each other as they chase a hockey puck replace young men in shorts dribbling and shooting a basketball. Chris stares at the sudden change with the same indifference you might have if your wife was to ask your opinion on which pair of shoes she should wear to a party.

"They're both nice."

"But which one do you like the best?"

"The black ones."

"They're both black!"

"Oh."

The game doesn't seem to matter to Chris. We're together, that's what matters to me. I hope he understands that much. I open the BOGO chips and pour some in a bowl.

"You want some?" I extend the bowl toward the recliner. Chris doesn't hear me, or ignores me (that wouldn't be anything new). "Chris! You want some chips?" He studies the bowl, shakes his head, and turns his attention toward the TV.

"Chris? Jack?" Caz thumps down the stairs.

I get up and give him a hug. "Great to see you, Mike. It's been too long, buddy. How've you been?" Sometimes I *think* Caz, but I *say* Mike, except when I call him Caz. It's not that complicated. There's no reason. It just is.

Caz tells me he's well and thanks me for inviting him. He turns his attention to Chris, who is firmly in the grip of the recliner. Caz hovers over him and gives him a little kiss on the cheek. I didn't expect to see that. *That was a nice thing you did there.* Caz sits next to me on the couch and we catch up on many months of new family developments. The Sabres score to take the lead and we watch the replay before returning to our conversation. Every so often I slide a relevant topic toward Chris, teeing it up in such a way so as to position him for success.

"How is Danielle doing?" I ask him.

"Good," Chris answers.

Caz tries, "Hey, Chris, what's Troy up to? Where's he living now? What kind of engineer is he again?"

I look at Caz, giving him a little headshake with wide eyes. I hope he understands. That's *too* many questions, Caz. *Too* much detail. Chris is done with multiple choice exams and Caz is administering essay questions. *Let's stick to true/false.*

I demonstrate once again for the benefit of Caz. "Troy's out in Colorado isn't he, Chris?"

"Yeah."

"He's an engineer isn't he?"

"Yeah."

Caz tries one, "Who does he work for? What's the company's name?"

Chris appears frustrated. He's trying, but there's nothing. He shakes his head. That's okay, Caz. You'll get the hang of it, eventually.

Caz talks to me as if Chris can't hear us. His intentions are pure, but it's making me uncomfortable. There's nothing wrong with Chris's hearing.

Caz asks me, "Do you think he knows who I am?"

I whisper with my head turned from Chris, "He knows, Mike. He knows you; he just might not remember your name." I answer with conviction, although I'm not sure.

And then Caz surprises me by asking Chris, "Hey, Chris. Have you seen Caz lately?"

Chris pauses, gives us a glance, and shakes his head from side to side.

Geez, Caz. Why did you do that? That isn't helpful. I hope Chris is fucking with you. I know Caz didn't mean any harm. I look at him but don't want to make a thing of it, so I shrug my shoulders and change the subject.

"Hey, Mike, did you know Chris did all of this woodwork down here?" I nod toward the detailed finish of the Arts and Crafts style oak wainscoting and door-frames.

"You did all of this, Chris?"

"Yeah."

There you go, Caz. Nicely done. Now you're getting the hang of it.

Talking about Chris's woodworking brought to mind the time Chris assisted me with phase-one of my third-floor remodeling project. I was in the process of converting half of my third-floor attic space from a spare bedroom/junk room to a home office. Step one was demo. It was going to cost $2,000. I looked at the estimate on a yellow sheet of paper, did some calculations in my head, and then crumpled the paper into a ball and tossed it in the trash. No way was I paying someone $2,000 to just rip apart half of my attic.

The next day I was having one of my typical 30-second phone calls with Chris, who was trying to set up a ride. "Sorry, Chris, I can't make it. I'm tied up the next few weekends."

"Tied up? Doing what?" Chris's tone suggested that he couldn't imagine what it was that could be so important to take me away from our weekend mountain bike rides.

"I'm remodeling half of my attic into an office."

"*You're* doing the work?" Chris laughed at the thought of me working with my hands.

Fair enough. I knew the basis of his thoughts. Anytime we were riding and I'd have a mechanical issue, a chain break, or a flat tire on a rear wheel requiring its removal from the bike, simple things that I could fix myself, I'd never move fast enough for Chris. He'd practically shove me to the side after watching me, then laugh and say, "Jeeesus, Jack, life is short; we don't have all day." He'd make quick work of the repair and off we'd go. It got to a point where, subconsciously, I'd take my time, making sure he noticed, so that I could eventually stand back and watch Chris fix my bike for me.

"Yeah, I'm doing the work," I shot back, "some of it."

There was more laughter.

"What is it you need done?"

"I have to tear down the existing walls, there's a wall heater I have to disconnect and remove, the floor needs to be ripped up, and ..."

Chris heard me say "tear down" and "ripped up" and I realize now how my choice of words must have incited him, like telling a pyrotechnist you had a trunk full of Chinese sky candy you planned to send toward the heavens just as soon as it got dark.

He didn't hesitate, cutting me off in mid-sentence, "I'll help you. I've got nothing else to do." At this point in Chris's career he was out of work again. Since he'd left Derrick Manufacturing there had been quite a few jobs. He routinely chided the "idiots" he had to work with and each time he moved to the next job he'd provide us with an insightful explanation of why he was no longer working at his last job, "Those fucking engineers don't have a clue what they're doing. Everything they design is crap." *Yeah, it was damn lucky that they had someone like you, Chris. What with your patient ways and all, to calmly steer them away from their foolish schemes.*

I knew I'd have to endure him telling me, as he did so often, "You know, Jack, you can't solve everything with a spreadsheet." *Yeah, yeah, Chris. But you know it's a damn handy thing when you're doing math stuff.*

Early on I'd try a rebuttal, but after a while I learned it was best just to say, "Yeah, I know, Chris," then laugh, and he'd laugh, and that would be the end of it. Chris liked doing things with his brawny hands. And he was damn good at what he did. What you needed to know going in, was any way other than Chris's way was "bullshit," and he wouldn't hold back from telling you what you were *doing all wrong.*

I considered his proposition. On one hand, I'd have free labor (it'd probably cost me a six-pack of Labatt) and a tireless work force rivaling the Egyptian pyramid builders. But on the other hand, it'd be like letting a Brahman bull loose in our house.

"Okay," I said, throwing caution out my third floor window. "Are you available tomorrow?"

"What time?" Chris asked.

"How about right after dinner? Can you get here by 7:00?" I figured we'd put a decent dent into the project if we worked until around 10:00. I'd see how things went and then reevaluate the pros versus the mayhem. I knew I'd have to endure doing it "Chris's way" so I made a promise to myself that I'd be more *open*-minded to his *closed*-mindedness. I figured if he hadn't punctured a hole in the roof or blown out an exterior wall, maybe I'd invite the Brahman bull back for phase two of the project.

Chris reported for duty on time. No surprise there. Actually, he was early. I finished my dinner as Chris sniffed around the kitchen looking for leftovers.

"Did you want a piece of chicken, Chris," Mar offered to make him up a plate.

I wished Mar wouldn't have asked him about eating; I mean it was a nice thing for her to offer, it was the least we could do, but I wanted to get started upstairs. Chris grabbed a chicken breast from the plate on the counter and wolfed it down. I was used to the peculiar jaw-clicking noise he makes while eating, but I suppose Mar was hearing it for the first time. She looked at me, but didn't say a word. *Yeah, that's the way he eats. You offered. Don't worry, he'll be done in a minute.*

I was in the midst of telling Chris to take off his shit kickers and carry them to the third floor instead of tromping through the house, but it was too late, he was already halfway up the stairs. Oh, what the hell, I had bigger fish to pan sear.

Chris had brought his own crowbar. It banged off the railing at the top of the stairs on the second floor.

"Careful, Chris."

He ignored my persnickety request.

When we reached the third floor, Chris tapped the hardened steel of his crowbar against the wall like a six-year old at a birthday party measuring his baseball bat against a donkey piñata. "Do you have another one of these?" he asked.

"Yeah—it's in the basement."

"Well? Did you want to get it?" As always, Chris strung-out the words for emphasis. He was now unofficially in charge of the project. *Shit!*

I was torn between following his edict, or hollering downstairs for Mar to bring me up the crowbar. But she'd only holler back, "What does it look like?" I thought about the crowbar, but worried about the carnage Chris would inflict upon my defenseless third floor in the time it took me to scurry up and down three flights of stairs. I decided to chance it and told him, "Wait until I get back before you start smashing anything."

"Okay." Chris answered with a sparkle in his eye. Upon my return, I was greeted by the sound of snapping wood and dust filled the air as if something had exploded in the attic.

"Chris! I told you not to do anything until I got back."

"You said not to *smash* anything. I wasn't smashing anything; I was prying and ripping." So now Chris was playing *literal* word games with me. *Good Lord, help me.*

"Chris, I didn't want *everything* ripped out. What the hell?! I wanted to keep the window trim." I pointed at the jagged edge of splintered wood dangling like a loose tooth beneath one of the third-floor windows.

"You don't want that trim. It looks like shit. Do it right, Jack. I'll help you."

He didn't end up helping with the trim. That was the year I learned how to frame the interior of a window. I'm sure I didn't do it up to Chris's standards and

I had probably *done it all wrong*; nonetheless I was proud of my new skill. At that point, I figured what the fuck. Let the bashing begin. "Here, want one of these?" I extended my arm, offering Chris a dust mask.

He laughed, "No, I don't want one of those." As I put on my dust mask, Chris watched with curious interest as the band of the dust mask tangled in my glasses when I pulled it over my head. Laughter burst from him like an opened fire hydrant on a hot summer day. I suppose in his mind, I had validated that indeed, a dust mask was "bullshit." He turned toward the drywall and set about bludgeoning the gypsum like he had a score to settle. After his initial wallop into the wall, it was as if he'd tasted blood, turning him into a savage demo man. Chris pulled, pried, punished, smashed, bashed, and the wall heater crashed. His sinister laugh and powdery white face made him look like the Joker. Within minutes he'd busted a hole through the knee wall, exposing the empty storage space on the other side of the studs and peeled back the wallboard like he was pulling skin off a dead animal. He worked around the pointy screws, splintered wood, and shards of glass from an old window without the benefit of work gloves. Gloves were for fems. I was a fem.

I started to break up fragmented hunks of drywall, preparing them for flight to the driveway below. If anyone was watching from outside they might have been inclined to call the fire department on account of the dusty air billowing from the third floor. I hurled pieces of wallboard and splintered wood out the window, making sure none of it banged against the side of the house. "Look out below!" I hollered to be funny, but was also concerned about someone walking up my driveway in the dark and taking a piece of drywall to the noggin. Hopefully, the Boy Scouts weren't out late trying to sell that popcorn of theirs that's so stale it can crack a molar.

The walls and ceiling were now gone. Just like that. All that remained was a skeleton of studs. Chris poked his head out the window to get some air. I took off my dust mask and did the same out the other window. We were separated by the chimney so I couldn't see him, but I could hear him laughing his giggly-laugh.

"What's so funny?"

"Oh, my God. Look at the size of the ass on that one!"

Below, a girl, bathed in amber streetlight, walked her dog on the sidewalk in front of my house.

"Chris?!"

"What?"

"You can't talk like that."

"Like what?"

"You can't call people fat ass."

"I didn't call her fat ass. I said look at the size of her ass."

If a human's head could swivel, you know spin like a top, mine would have unscrewed from my neck. Then I thought about it. No, I guess he didn't call her fat ass. Somehow I knew he meant no harm. He was more amazed at the size of her ass, like finding a huge boulder in the woods, or maybe a juicy beefsteak tomato growing in his brother's garden. I realize now, Chris couldn't help himself, his thoughts were, in many cases, the same as all of our thoughts, but we know to keep those buried, not verbalizing them until we sanitize them, put a sympathetic spin on them in cases where a comment is necessary. The disease was taking its toll on Chris's brain, and if we had known what was going on we would have had some understanding, as you would have for a grandmother with Tourette's who f-bombs the mail carrier.

We finished dropping the debris into my driveway and I asked Chris, "You want a beer?" A silly question. I knew I could use one, but more importantly I wanted to get him out of the room while the damages had been limited to ripping apart the window frame I had intended to keep. Outside, we popped open a couple of Blues, had a few laughs and I told Chris, "Thanks for giving me a hand."

"Sure."

I saved a few grand, completed a project with the help of a friend, there was no "spinal damage," and no animals were harmed during the making of this episode. Thanks buddy.

Chris waiting for me in his kitchen - 2018

Stepping Stones in the Kitchen

Most years, February in Western New York numbs us with frigid wind chills that cause us to walk like penguins when we venture outside. The snow buries most indoors, except when it's necessary to travel to work, pick up young children from school, or to stock up at the grocery store. We're used to it, but that doesn't mean people from the Town of Aurora to Zoar Valley don't complain about the weather. Not Chris, he loved when the wind howled, coating his beard with snow, and on an especially cold day, froze "snotsicles" to his mustache that looked like miniature stalactites. He lived for those kinds of days. Today isn't one of those days—like Chris, the weather is changing. Winters don't seem to be as severe as they used to.

Melting ice drips from Chris's roof, pinging off the curved J of the downspout on his garage. The woods around his house are covered in snow, but it's less than an inch deep. In four days Chris will be 61 years old, born on Valentine's Day in 1958. Most of my hard-ass friend's life has been diametrically opposed to the day synonymous with flowers, hearts, and romance. But there have been other times when he'd overwhelm you with his caring ways, doing anything for someone in need, especially the underdog. There was that—and his love for chocolates.

I knock on the backdoor, knowing better than to wait for someone to greet me at the Kelley house. It's pretty much an open-door policy.

"Come on in," says Jennifer from inside.

I'm greeted by Chris, standing in front of me, ready to go, with his puffy orange coat zippered to his chin. He smiles at me and laughs as if I'm wearing something ridiculous, or have a piece of this morning's breakfast on my face.

"He's been waiting for you," Jennifer informs me.

I look him in the eye and ask, "You've been waiting for me, buddy?" I shake his hand and give him a good hug. His orange jacket squishes against my black windbreaker. We must look like a poorly fashioned Halloween costume.

"How have *you* been?" I ask Jennifer, as Chris paces out of the kitchen on his imaginary path down the hall.

"I'm doing okay."

I didn't expect her to say anything different. Jennifer is resolute in her ways, as tough as her husband when necessary, but with a softer, more reserved approach to the challenges that face her. I give her a lot of credit for taking such good care of Chris; I'm sure it hasn't always been easy being Mrs. Christopher Kelley.

"How's he doing?" I nod toward the hallway.

"Okay."

What else can she say? It's a stupid question, meant to fill a void in the conversation.

Chris comes back for another pass through the kitchen and I tell him, "We're waiting for Mr. McCready." He looks at me like I just asked him to explain String Theory. "Mac," I say and Chris laughs.

He doesn't pace down the hall, choosing this time to circumnavigate around the kitchen island, striding with purpose. It looks like he could be walking on evenly spaced stepping stones placed in a gurgling stream. The kitchen floor is dry. There are no stones. There is no gurgling stream.

"He's counting the steps," Jennifer tells me.

I follow Chris around the countertop, carefully tracing his footsteps. When I'm halfway around I announce, "Five steps down and three across!" 5-3-5-3, apparently Chris likes the pattern.

"Can you go in reverse?" I ask.

Chris stops in his tracks, studies me; I detect a faint smile, but maybe I imagined it. He turns and walks around the kitchen island in the opposite direction, 5-3-5-3, and repeats.

Mac arrives and receives the same greeting I did—a smile, a laugh, a handshake—and they hug. Wouldn't it be great if everyone greeted each other like that? How can you not love a guy who's always laughing when you see him? Mac and Jennifer exchange routine pleasantries before we head outside. Chris paces inside the garage, staring into the top corners as if he left something up there, something he'd forgotten, something important.

"Get those down," he tells me, pointing to his downhill skis hanging on the garage wall.

"Chris, we're not going skiing; we're going hiking."

He motions with his head, insistent I get his skis down. Jennifer comes out the kitchen door and sees Chris pointing. "Chris, you're not going skiing! Now go. You're going hiking with Mac and Jack—at Hunter's Creek." Chris doesn't want to hear any of it, standing by his skis. "Go!" she implores him. "Mac and Jack are waiting for you. You're *not* going skiing!"

It's sad. We always had so much fun at Holiday Valley Ski Resort, ripping up the hill, having a couple tree beers, and telling our stories. It won't happen again. I miss those days.

Finally, we get Chris into my car and drive to Hunter's Creek. I turn on Sirius Radio Channel 25—Classic Rewind. Chris loves the channel, tapping his personal beat on the top of his well-worn blue jeans. *Rat-ta-tat-tat-rat-ta-tat-tat.*

It's surprising for such a warm day that there's only one car in the parking lot up on Centerline Road. I help Chris out of the car (his legs stiffen up these days) and without any discussion about what trail we'll be taking, he makes a beeline for the woods. Solid ice coats the trail so I stop to put on my Yaktrax. "Chris, hold on for a second." He turns to watch me kneel, stretching the "rubber band" fitted with coiled metal grips over my hiking boot. He doesn't wait for me to finish with the other boot; he's off, down the trail.

"Mac, follow him. I'll catch up." No way do I want him out of our eyesight. I know there will be a stream crossing soon that he'll stop at, but I don't want to take any chances that we'll lose track of him. It happened to his brother Brent and to Walt Lyons. *Not on my watch.* I feel almost as responsible for Chris's well being as I do for my granddaughter's.

I pull a muscle in my back struggling with the Yaktrax. Too bad Chris didn't see me twist like a worm on the end of a hook; he would have loved it. When I'm done pulling on the foot grippers; Chris and Mac aren't in sight. I quicken my pace, skidding on the frozen meringue of footprints from yesterday's hikers. Rounding a corner, I see them at the stream crossing. Mac stands on the other side of the rock bridge; he's talking to Chris and pointing where to step. Chris looks down at the stream coated with ice and then raises his head, looking far into the gray sky, or maybe he's only looking as far as the treetops. He takes a step forward and stops. As I get closer, I hear Mac talking to Chris and tapping his foot on one of the rocks in the stream, "Just step right there, it's easy. There's nothing to it." Recently someone told me, it's not that he's scared to cross the stream (it's only a few inches deep in most places), it's that his brain has forgotten how to do it, to take the necessary steps. I'm not sure if it's true, but I like thinking that's the case, instead of Chris being scared. He's never been scared of anything.

I gather two rocks as I approach the eight-foot long stone bridge and add them to the row of small rocks that vary in size and shape. They're shellacked in ice like someone could have dropped a fruit basket and it froze in place. I show Chris what to do. Literally, step-by-step instructions, "You can do it, Chris. Come on, like this." I walk across the stones several times, but it's not registering. "Chris, I'm going to push you like last time if you don't do it yourself." He laughs at my flimsy threat. I get behind him, "1-2-3-4-5-6-7," I count and then guide him over the rocks in the narrow stream the same way you might help Grandma cross the street. He swats my arms away and proceeds without assistance. "Way to go, Chris. Nice job!" He stares at me. My accolades pass by his ears like the sounds from a dog whistle.

We hike for another hour. Chris wants to keep going, putting more distance between us and the parking lot. "Chris, go this way," I point to a steep climb a few hundred feet from the serpentine banks of Hunter's Creek. He ignores me, instead heading further down the trail. "Chris, we have to go up. That way takes too long. Come on, I have to be home around 4:00." I'm uncertain if Chris has a concept of time; it had always been different from mine anyway. *Life is short, Jack.* I *do* have to get home, but it's not like another half hour is going to be a big deal. The little white lie is still a lie; it doesn't make me feel great. I rationalize that it's in Chris's best interest that we don't go further, but really it's in mine. We all have limits.

I catch up to Chris, getting in front of him, blocking his path, and motioning back to where Mac is already climbing up through the snow. "Come on, Chris. You gotta turn around." Corralling him isn't something I relish doing and with a bum shoulder I don't want to get tangled in an impromptu wrestling match with him. I'd lose. We make our way up the side of the ravine, stopping numerous times while Chris surveys the landscape. I tell him, "Come on, we have to keep moving." I'm above him on the incline, taking a break from ramming my boots into the snow, creating snow stairs so the climb is easier for Chris. I shout down, "I don't want to have to come back down there." He laughs at me.

I look up at Mac waiting at the top; he shrugs his shoulders before hollering down to Chris, "Come on, Chris. You can do it." I could have never seen this coming; the guy who always set a pace we couldn't match is the same guy we now "pull" behind us like a barnacle encrusted anchor of a once great ship. Thankfully, it's only the ascents that give him trouble; he's still setting the pace on the flats. At the top Mac holds our climbing reward, "Here want one?" He holds two freshly peeled clementines. The orange skins lie at his feet, a bright contrast to the white and gray tones of winter.

"Is *that* what you were doing up here? You know — I could've used your help getting our buddy to the top," I joke.

"Hey, hey, hey," Mac feigns hurt feelings. "Did you want them, or not?"

"Yeah, sure, I'll take one." I answer.

"You want one, Chris?" asks Mac.

"No."

"Are you sure? They're *sooo* good." Mac plops the fruit into my hand and exhibits the other in front of Chris, rotating it as if it were a precious gem. Chris shakes his head back and forth.

I've noticed that he's not eating as much these days and wonder if it's because he's having trouble swallowing, or maybe it's his increasing apathy toward all things in general. I've read that swallowing can become an issue as the disease progresses. I don't dwell too much on this shit, but occasionally I'll investigate what the disease has lined up for our friend, hoping that there's something we can do to slow it down. Or at least be prepared.

After Mac and I each eat two clementines, we head back in the direction of the parking lot, leaving the skins for the chipmunks. Chris is in front of me. His legs are thinner. I wonder how much longer we'll be hiking together, enjoying the simple blessing of him on the trail with me, and the big laugh? It would appear it's all a joke to Chris.

IT WAS November of 2013. We were celebrating Mac's retirement from the United States Air Force. He had invited his family, the Geek, Caz, Chris, me, our Class of '76 friend Bob Lippert, and our wives to the formal event at the Niagara Falls Air Force Base. We were all proud of Mac; he'd earned the title of colonel and for a couple of years had been in charge of the Air National Guard at the base. I had been there for the event that recognized his promotion. I was also invited to his swearing-in ceremony when he was promoted to colonel, so it didn't come as a surprise that he'd invited me to his retirement party. What *did* come as a surprise was that he had invited Chris.

Chris was a friend to all of us, but for the past four or five years his relationship with the McCready family had been contentious to say the least. There had been an "incident." One night, liberal-minded Chris had clashed with the conservative-principled McCreadys. It's not like that had never happened, but this time things went too far. The night had started out with lifetime friends and our wives having dinner and enjoying each other's company. Later, we made an impromptu visit to Nowak's Tavern in Sloan, NY. The Geek had suggested the stop. Sloan was, and to some degree still is, a heavily Polish neighborhood. Above Nowak's (formerly, The Corner Tavern) was an apartment where the Geek had lived as a toddler until Mr. and Mrs. Norton (Nadratowski) had decided to head out of the city and settle in the idyllic East Aurora suburbs.

We toasted the Geek's humble beginnings with a couple tree beers and played a few games of shuffle bowling, the one with flashing lights, a sawdust-covered mini-alley, and hanging plastic bowling pins that magically flip up when the sliding steel disc passes below them. The arcade game is a lot of fun and far less strain on your arm than real bowling. Actually, the only things it has in common with real bowling are ten pins, strikes are heavily rewarded, and a couple tree beers makes it more fun. Otherwise it's nothing like real bowling.

The Geek was the designated driver for those heading back to EA and so Mar and I said goodbye to the Nortons, the Kelleys, and the McCreadys as we all headed for home. The next day I gave the Geek a call to revel in what a great night it had been and to make sure everyone made it home safely.

"Yeah, it was a great night, Jack. It was good to see the old stomping grounds."
The Geek paused before continuing. "There was an incident on the way home."

"Oh?"

"Yeah. Chris got into it with Mac and Heidi. Mainly Heidi."

What else is new? Chris was always getting into it with everyone. "About
what?"

"He was kind of bashing the military and then things got political."

"Oh, boy."

What the hell? Chris was barking up the wrong oak tree taking on Heidi. I
imagined a battle roy-yale. *Good Lord! Chris had taken his big knife to the ca-
rotid artery of his friendship with Mac.*

The Geek continued, "Yeah, Mac wasn't saying much, but Heidi and Chris
were really going at it. Jen was telling Chris to shut up, but he wouldn't listen to
anyone."

I imagined Jen and Mac trying to get things under control and then, like two
hockey referees, backing off to let the heavyweight enforcers bash away at each
other until they tired and could be separated. Apparently, they hadn't tired.

Mac told me recently, "Chris called the next morning to apologize, so we were
good." Mac's not one to hold a grudge, but spoken words can't be unspoken.

We didn't know then, and I'm not crusading to make excuses for Chris's behavior, but I believe by that time the disease was hard at work, attacking his ability
to filter what should have remained his private thoughts and opinions. Chris had
always been direct, especially when over-served, but even by his "standards" this
was uncalled for. Mac was our friend, had served to protect the citizens of the
United States, had carried out that duty with dignity, and had been acknowledged
with honors.

All of us have opinions, but if we want to avoid pointless confrontations with
our friends, we keep many of them buried, verbalizing them only when we know
they will be accepted. Chris didn't roll that way, and as a result, he torched a few
bridges. To Mac's credit (maybe Heidi had some influence, too), he had invited
Chris to the event honoring his promotion to Commander of the 107th Airlift

Wing of the New York Air National Guard in January 2011, and to this night celebrating his retirement.

At one point during the retirement dinner Heidi came to our table and asked, "Who wants to get up and say something about Mac? I know all of you guys have some great stories."

I looked at the Geek, at Caz; I looked at Mac sitting behind flowers up at the head table, and I looked at members of the United States Military scattered throughout the room. They were disguised as every-day partygoers, in suits and nice dresses, but they weren't fooling me. It was easy to pick them out and I had a feeling they had their eyes on us. *Yeah, I could tell some stories about Mac, but I don't think they're the type you have in mind, Heidi. That's not to say Mac isn't a straight shooter, but we were all young and stupid once.*

"What about you, Jack? I know you probably have some funny stories."

Oh, yeah! I sure do. You mean like our college road trip to the Outer Banks? "I don't know, Heidi." I looked at the Geek and Caz; they smiled their "secret" closed-mouthed grins. We weren't about to start telling stories about Mac, here at his retirement party, in front of the United States Air Force.

"I'll do it! I've got a story," chimed in Chris.

Oh, no. What the hell is this going to be about and should I leave before they put the base in lockdown?

"Okay, Chris—great," and with that Heidi was off to join Mac and the rest of his family at the head table. *Had she lost her mind?*

I leaned close to Chris and asked in a hushed tone, "What are you going to talk about?"

"The soccer brawl with Lakeshore."

"The soccer brawl?"

"Yeah, the one Mac started in our senior year!"

"Chris? I don't know if that's such a good idea. What are you going to say?"

He answered my question with a smirk.

Then it was time. Heidi introduced Chris, explaining that he was a boyhood friend of Colonel Mac. And then, standing in front of the United States Air Force, visiting dignitaries, Mac's friends and his family, Chris told all of us about the big soccer brawl. He started off by declaring, "We were always raising hell back in high school, Mac and I."

Mac was raising hell? Are you sure you don't mean you were raising hell, and Mac, like the rest of us, stood back at a safe distance? I talked to Mac about this night recently and asked him, "What kind of hell were you and Chris raising back in high school that I didn't know about?"

He told me, "Are you kidding? I steered clear of Chris in high school. I couldn't imagine where he was going after that opening line."

"Weren't you concerned that he was going to ruin your retirement party?"

"Hell, no! I was retiring."

Chris continued, "Mac and I were the goalies on the soccer team. We called ourselves The Inflictors. If anyone came near the goal crease we *inflicted* pain."

This earned Chris a laugh. *Careful Airmen, don't encourage him too much. You're flying into hostile airspace.*

"We were playing Lakeshore; it was our first league game at home. Mac started in goal, but he was playing like shit," explained Chris, pausing for more laughter.

I looked at Mac to gauge his reaction. He smiled a tight-lipped smile, as if preventing a small bird from escaping his mouth, and his eyes locked onto Chris with unwavering attention to his words. Chris continued, "Coach Wagner pulled Mac when we were down 2-0 and put me in goal."

The significance of the game was lost on Chris, but I remembered we were heavy favorites to continue the dominance we had exhibited in our junior year. Also, Chris didn't get into the details, but I wondered how much it must have galled him to be the backup goalie. Mac was an all-star, one of the best goalies in the league, but Chris was a tremendous athlete with his own rugged style. The problem was, there wasn't enough playing time for two goalies.

"We battled back to tie the score at 2-2 near the end of regulation. Coach Wags left me in goal for the rest of the game and threw Mac into the field. We went into overtime and scored with a few minutes left to make the game 3-2, but the game wasn't over. There was no sudden death back in those days, so the game continued. The other team was pissed that we scored. And then ..." Chris smiled in the direction of our table, "near the end of the game, Mac started pounding away at one of the guys from Lakeshore near the middle of the field. They were on the ground going at it and then Thurbee, Wally, and I jumped on top of the pile, pairing off with guys from the other team. The benches emptied and Coach Wags had to be held back from going after someone on the other team. We bashed the shit out of Lakeshore and we won the game in overtime 3-2."

The gathering erupted into laughter, a few uncomfortable smiles, and then a big round of applause. Thank God Chris took this as his queue to end his story, while everyone was still laughing, and before veering into enemy territory. There was no talk about who had scored the winning goal, or miraculous saves Chris had made—that wasn't what was important to him. It was about the melee, which surprisingly hadn't been started by Chris, but instead by one of our country's finest, Colonel James McCready.

Back then, I understood it took someone with kahunas the size of coconuts to get up and tell *that* story in front of *that* gathering. I also understand, *now,* that it might have been another sign that the disease was percolating, breaking down filters, and maybe on this particular night it resulted in Chris reminding us: No matter your rank, your calling in life, where you've come from, or how many buckaroos you've stashed away, don't take yourself too seriously, and—good friends are friends for life.

Later, while having a few beers in the officers club that Mac referred to as the Fuzzy Bison, Chris asked me, "Do we have to pay for any of this?" The invitation had indicated a price per attendee.

"I don't know, Chris? Did you bring any money?"

He looked at me with his googly eyes. I guessed he had the exact amount, stashed in his pocket, nothing more and nothing less. Jennifer had probably made sure of that, but most certainly Chris hoped he wouldn't have to use it on this night, saving it for beer money the next time we got out riding.

The Kelley Family - Marla, Chris, Troy, Jennifer, and Danielle in Singapore - 2000

The Guy Could've Drowned

CHRIS HAD TOLD us on a few occasions that he'd saved a guy's life, but I couldn't remember the details. Where had he been? China? South Africa? Thailand? He'd traveled extensively on business trips while promoting mining equipment for his employer, the Derrick Corporation. In many cases these trips took him to countries where workers' compensation insurance was defined as having another worker ready to step in when there was an injury or death. Chris ate the local fare (eyeballs, testicles, brains, bird's nest soup), assimilated into foreign cultures (I couldn't imagine it had been seamlessly), and brought his own brand of *a lot like fun—only different* to the other side of the globe. I don't think he did any of this just because the job required relationship building; that was merely a happy byproduct. Chris could find a friend anywhere—as long as they weren't into a lot of fancy-schmancy bullshit. I can't imagine anyone being more up for the challenge of new cultures.

There had been so many tales about Chris's work-trips that after a while we became accustomed to his wild stories. That's not to say we still didn't ask, "You *ate* that?" or "Why did you do that?" or "You really said *that* to them?" And like most of Chris's communications, the story about saving the guy's life was short and to the point, void of frilly details. I remembered him telling me and the Geek—Caz had probably heard the story, too, "We were hashing and got caught in a monsoon; another runner got washed down a storm drain. And I got him out." *Washed down a storm drain? How can something like that even happen?* If it hadn't been Chris telling the story, I would have thought it was an exaggerated tall tale. Chris would wrap up his story with a shit-eating grin and roll his eyes, telling us, "The guy could've drowned." He laughed from start to finish; we didn't need to be reminded that this was funny since we had heard nothing about "spinal damage." It was pure Chris, but there had to be more to the story about our friend saving a stranger's life. Did it really happen like he'd told us? Who could I ask? Wally told me I should check with Jennifer.

I texted her: Do you have any details about Chris saving that guy's life in Southeast Asia? I'd like to incorporate it into my collection of stories about Chris.

She texted back: I was there, so yes.

It came back to me. Singapore! That's right! Derrick had sent Chris there to set up a sales office. Looking forward to a new adventure, he sold his house in East Aurora and took his essentials (Jennifer and their three young children) to live, for an undetermined amount of time, on an island off the southern tip of Malaysia. In the end, Singapore had withstood the ravages of Tropical Disturbance Chris. But not before there had been a few incidents.

I set up a time to meet with Jennifer the following Tuesday and prepared by jotting down a few questions, realizing I had no idea how to properly interview someone. I hoped for the best.

"Are we still good to meet tonight?" I asked Jennifer before heading over to their house.

"Oh, are we meeting? I thought maybe we were going to do this over the phone."

"I think we should meet," I answer, trying to sound confident.

"Okay, sure. I'm leaving the grocery store now. I'll be home in 15 minutes."

As I pull down Chris's long driveway, the headlights from another car shine in my rearview mirror. I assume it's Jennifer. The car passes by me and pulls into the garage as I stop and park near the house.

"Can I help you carry any bags?"

"Here, you can take the milk." She hands me a gallon jug and I wonder how much of it's for Chris and how much is for his grandson, Wyatt. Chris loves milk, especially on his mounded Honey Nut Cheerios.

Inside I ask, "Is Chris home?" and before she has time to answer, I say, "Oh, I see you still have the bumpers on the corners of the kitchen counter." They're there to protect little Wyatt from banging his head as he chases Grandpa Chris, circling the island over, and over, and over.

"He's home," she tells me. "He's probably hiding in Troy's room. That's what he does now."

"Maybe I should go see him. Do you think he's awake?"

"I don't know," answers Jennifer. I get the impression she doesn't want me to check. In her situation, maybe it's best to leave a sleeping Chris lie. So I stay in the kitchen.

We talk for a bit. I see a piece of mail, addressed to the Kelleys' son Troy, lying on the counter. "That's cool," I say, "that Troy's moved back to town." Both Troy and his sister Marla, have recently moved back home to help out. I tell Jennifer, as if she doesn't already think of such things, "He's still having an impact, you know. It's because of Chris that everyone is back in town. That's nice."

I proceed with my questions, but quickly abandon the script, letting Jennifer tell the story as she remembers it; the story about Chris saving a guy's life. She tells me they were doing a hash run and it started to rain. The words flow from her; she speaks quickly, only pausing as I interrupt her with questions, "What *is* a hash run, anyway? Is it an acronym for something?"

"I don't know. I don't think so," she tells me and reaches for her phone. "Wikipedia says, 'An event organized by a club is known as a hash, hash run or simply hashing, with participants calling themselves hashers or hares and hounds.'"

"Oh."

She continues, "It says the 'Hash House Harriers: A drinking club with a running problem.'"

It all comes together now.

Weeks after meeting with Jennifer, I do a bit of research, curious about the origins of hash running. I have a silly thought. Maybe there's a reference to Chris; after all, the hash run is like so many of the events he came up with. But I find no mention of Chris. I do find out that hashing originated in 1938 in what is now Malaysia when a group of British colonial officers and expatriates began meeting on Monday evenings to run in a fashion patterned after the traditional British "hare and hounds." The objectives of the Hash House Harriers, as recorded on the club registration card dated 1950, were as follows:

- To promote physical fitness of its members
- To get rid of weekend hangovers
- To acquire a good thirst and to satisfy it in beer
- To persuade the older members that they are not as old as they feel

Rick Ohler, the town wit and author of weekly stories for the *East Aurora Advertiser*, referred me to the bit of first and second hand research he wrote about in *Buffalo Spree* back in May of 2013. He even referenced Chris in this nifty paragraph.

> While hash running might seem like nothing more than a crazy afternoon of running, drinking, laughing and singing, hashers are quick to say that the friendships they develop go deep and last forever. "Whenever I go to a new city," says Nine-One-One, a Buffalo-based international business traveler who got his name after he rescued a hasher from a raging storm sewer in Singapore, "I'll find the local hash. They welcome me, invite me to a run and before I know it, I've made a bunch of new friends."

Running, a couple tree beers, camaraderie—yeah, a hash run was definitely made for Chris. You get the idea that if those British officers hadn't invented hash running, Chris would have. It seemed logical to me that Chris joined up with a hash group in Singapore. Jennifer, an avid runner herself, went along.

According to Jen, they set out on Friday night for that week's hash run with their friends Jim and Meredith White. The course took them through rain forests and urban streets. "And there were beer stops along the way. We ran together, but not side by side, and we were past the deepest part of the jungle."

I asked her about the weather that day.

"It was hot and humid—it was always hot and humid. The wind picked up and it started raining. It was raining hard."

I have never been to Singapore, but from what I remember Chris telling me, you were always wet, and not just when it rained. I imagine the dampness clung to their skin like cellophane wrap. And the rain came in different forms: downpours, heavy downpours, and monsoons. But I knew it would've taken more than a deluge and swirling winds to divert Chris off his running course. Severe weather and Chris had long been rivals with mutual respect for one another. Specifically, it was the wind that Chris sparred with the most. He had duked it out with gale forces on his sailboat in Lake Erie, bashed his way through howling blizzards in the Adirondack High Peaks, and slugged it out with a tornado on the Battenkill River, before pinning its neck to the ground and asking, "Is that all you got?!" I wouldn't think a little thing like a monsoon in Singapore would stop him from the hash run—or the "cold beer that was waiting." Deluges be damned.

Jennifer continued, "It got dark fast. Chris came out of the jungle ahead of me. There was a 30-foot slope that led to the street below and it had become a mudslide. By the time I got there, the other runners and Chris were at the bottom, jabbing at the mud with sticks. I think they were probably yelling someone's name.

"Did you know who they were looking for?"

"No, and there was no answer."

"Chris was on his knees, digging in the ground with his hands as the mud kept coming down the slope."

"I don't understand?"

"They couldn't find the runner. He just slipped down a hole or something. Chris told me that a runner was in the sewer drain and he took off running in the direction of a walkway bordering the street."

I don't want to stop Jen in the middle of this amazing story, but I can't process what she's describing. I ask, "He was below the road?"

"Yes. He was below the road. He was hanging on to the metal *thingy*; you know those things along the road that let water drain into the sewer."

I assumed she meant the grate where the curb butted the sidewalk and the road. "Oh, yeah," I say, "I think I know what you mean. So then what did Chris do? Did he pull him out of the drain?" I wonder. How could that even be possible? The guy would've had to be pretty skinny.

"No, they followed him."

"What do you mean they *followed* him?"

"From one drain to the next, they could hear him down there. And they saw him hanging onto the metal grates."

I envision Chris trailing this guy throughout the city, plunging through a manhole, and swimming through the sewers in search of him. I would find out it didn't happen like that, but I could have seen him doing such a thing. I let Jennifer finish telling the story.

"The underground sewer eventually spilled out into an open drainage ditch. Chris and the rest of the runners had tracked the guy to this point by following the sound of his voice. They finally spotted him at the bottom of a 15-foot embankment."

"How did they get him out?"

"They tried dropping this firehose down there, you know, so maybe he could pull himself up. I remember it was white. But he couldn't do it so they ..."

"Wait. A firehose? Where did they get a firehose?"

"Chris found it across the street. I think it was a construction site."

It's hard to understand, but from Jennifer's description of the events, I pictured Chris dragging a weighty hose to the drainage ditch and letting it drop toward a floating head. I imagined the hose sluicing through the water like an albino water moccasin and Chris hollering for the runner to pull himself up. I couldn't remember what Chris had told me about that time, how they had eventually rescued the guy. Had he dove headfirst into the drainage ditch?

"So how did Chris get the guy out?"

"They got a ladder," explains Jennifer.

"A ladder?" I ask, and then like it matters, "What kind of ladder?"

"A wood one—I guess."

Why didn't they do that in the first place?

"They lowered it down and the guy climbed close enough to the top that they were able to pull him up the rest of the way. He was really in rough shape and bleeding badly from the head," she explains before adding, "He was bald," as if I might have wondered how she could see the blood on his head. *I believe you, Jennifer.*

"They called a hospital. And after a while an ambulance came and took the guy away. I saw him on the stretcher. He was pretty banged up."

"And what was Chris doing while everyone was waiting for the ambulance?" I ask, picturing him commanding the rest of the rescue team and laughing at the absurdity of it all.

"It was very serious," says Jennifer. "No one was in a partying mood after they took the guy away in the ambulance. It was very scary."

"I bet. Did you ever see that guy again?"

"Yes, but not for quite a while."

I pictured Chris, jumping into action, taking charge, ready to risk his own life to save the life of the sewer swimmer—a guy he didn't even know. I assume that's all Jennifer has for me, but she tells me, "And that's how Chris got his hash nickname."

"A nickname?"

"Yeah, every runner gets a nickname. Chris's was Nine-One-One."

I want to be clear; this is too serious to be making up fantastical story endings, so I ask Jennifer, "Would you say if it wasn't for Chris and the others, the guy could've drowned?"

"Yeah, there was a pretty good chance."

It was typical Chris.

"That's all I can really remember. I don't have a very good memory," she tells me after answering my questions about that Friday night in Singapore. *I think her memory is a lot better than she admits.*

I jot a few more notes as she sits silently, I suppose wondering if I'm done asking her questions. When I look up she asks, "So how is anyone going to be able to read about any of this?"

"Because it's going to be in a book," I explain.

"You mean like an actual *published* book?"

"Yeah."

"Uh, huh," she nods, but doesn't seem too confident in my ability to deliver.

I explain to her, "Along with telling about all the crazy times we had, I want to bring some awareness to the disease. Maybe someone reading the book might say, 'Hey, I think Uncle Bob has what this Chris guy has.'" and I ask her, "Wouldn't it have been better if you had known sooner about what was affecting Chris's behavior?"

"Why? Why would anyone want to know about this horrible disease any sooner than they have to?" she answers.

"Because maybe things would be different."

"Like what?"

I'm tested again. *Why is it that nobody thinks it would be better to know?* Maybe she's right. Maybe if she had known sooner, things would have been different, but in a *bad* way. She would have had more time to carry the weight that burdens her now. I don't know what else to say.

Jennifer is strong; she doesn't tear up. I can't imagine how she gets through each day. She goes on to tell me, "We were watching the news the other night. All of these horrible mass shooting deaths, and Chris laughs. It's terrible. I tell him, 'Chris, it's not funny. Why are you laughing?'"

There is no answer to that question.

Abruptly, she changes the subject, asking me, "What about the pig? Have you written anything about Chris's pig?"

Sandra Lee - 1975

Sandra Lee

I SIT ON one of the bar stools at the Kelleys' kitchen counter. I get the impression that Jennifer's starting to embrace my effort to collect stories about Chris. She surprised me by asking about the pig story. I'm just now beginning to realize that Chris's pig might be worth more than a casual reference.

I tell her, "No, I haven't written anything about the pig yet. I was hoping Peter Diebolt would have some details."

Her eyes catch mine while emphasizing, "You should put *that* story in your book."

"Oh, I am—for sure." I answer, as if I've known all along how much the pig meant to the Kelleys.

Jennifer shifts back to the present, sharing a sliver of what she's endured since finding out the harsh reality of Chris's condition. *Your husband has Pick's disease.* "We never had a discussion about the disease, Chris and I. He was in total denial. He didn't want to talk about it. Not that there was anything we could do about it at that point, but ..." she trails off.

"Really, I thought he would have ..." I stop talking. I don't know what it is I want to say so I pretend to look at the notes I've written, a distraction from the awkward silence. After a moment I fill the emptiness with my recollection from that period of time, "Yeah, I remember him telling me, 'Jack, I'm in the worst shape of my life.'" That was back when we were still mountain biking and skiing and stuff like that.

I had never heard of Pick's disease until Chris's nephew, Alex, told me while we stood next to our bikes in the woods at Sprague Brook Park. "I don't know if you've heard yet, but Chris has this thing called Pick's disease ..." His words that followed were noise to me, until he bluntly concluded, "Yeah, he's got like two to ten years to live." That was probably about five years ago. The slide from the top has been rapid considering that prognosis, but of late things seem to be stabilizing into Chris's new normal: single-word sentences, general apathy for everything other than hiking and sweets, and hiding out in his new favorite room — the bathroom. I haven't talked to Chris about the disease, either. I wish I had. So that I could tell him how sorry I am and to let him know that I'll help him as much as possible, to be with him, like always. I guess I could have that conversation now, but it might be weird. I'm afraid I'd prepare seemingly elegant words, start speaking, telling Chris how sorry I was, and then he'd laugh, or maybe stare at me before taking off on a familiar path. He'd leave me looking to the heavens for something—an answer, guidance, a pat on the back. *That's okay, Jack. You tried.*

Instead, I spend time with Chris and hope he understands that I *am* sorry, he's still my friend, and that I'll keep doing stuff with him. And when I have these thoughts, I hear his voice from the past, "Jack, quit your whining. Life is short. Let's ride."

Jennifer abruptly shifts back to happier, crazier times, insisting, "You should ask Chris's mom what she remembers about the pig."

"I will," I promise, but wonder about the best way to get in touch with Chris's 90-year-old mom. *Will she be willing to talk to me about any of this? Maybe it will be too upsetting for her. No, probably not. She's a Kelley. The Kelleys are tough, the Kelleys are resilient, the Kelleys confront things head-on.*

"*Do you* know anything about the pig?" I ask Jennifer.

"Well — I know he named her Sandra Lee."

"Sandra Lee?"

Jennifer hesitates before answering, "That was his *girlfriend* at the time—I guess. Or at least the girl he liked. Sandy Peavy, I think."

"Then he got a boy pig," Jennifer tells me, "but the first one was too big."

I decide not to ask what she means by "too big."

"They made little pigs. There were six of them, I think. That's when the real trouble started. I guess they must have escaped a few times and were eating the neighbor's stuff."

I assume the "neighbor's stuff" were their vegetables.

She reminds me again, "Chris's mom might remember more."

I take her signal that it's time to wrap things up. I'm sure she wants to enjoy some quiet time in her own home, free, for the moment, of her daily responsibilities, so I say goodnight.

A few days later I receive a text message from Chris's brother, Brent:

My mother has written out a narrative about the Sandra Lee affair (aka "Chris's pig"). If you come over this way next Tuesday we can meet at my mom's and you can pick it up. She is quite proud that she remembers so many details.

I guess Jennifer must have been talking with her mother-in-law. This is exciting, blowing the dust off the pages of a story from so many years ago. I set up a time to meet Brent and his mom. Later I receive another text:

My mother wants to invite you for lunch. Could you make it at noon instead of 12:45?

I answer:

That would be great, see you at noon.

As WITH any Kelley house, the doors are unlocked. I knock out of courtesy, but from inside I hear Brent holler, "Come on in."

I greet Chris's mom, "It's great to see you again, Mrs. Kelley." I call her Mrs. Kelley even though she's been Mrs. Donald Damon for around 40 years. She kisses me and gives me a nice hug. She's 90, but could pass for 70.

"I don't know what you and Don have in the water out here, but you both look great. You haven't changed a bit." Don is Mr. Damon. I've never heard Chris or Brent refer to him as their stepdad; he's always been just, Don. He's the guy who, in a lapse of judgment, allowed us to borrow his 1976 GMC Vandura Midas on our trip to Snowshoe, West Virginia, back in 2004.

Don waves a hand in my direction, fanning my praise into a corner of the sunroom, "Oh, I don't know about that," he says, but I think he knows things are well. Don plays golf weekly and moves around the house with the quick steps of someone half his age.

Mrs. Kelley holds pictures from our high school years. She hands me one and I tell her, "He looks like a young Judge Reinhold."

"Who?"

"Judge Reinhold. He was in *Fast Times at Ridgemont High* and a lot of other movies like that."

"Oh, I don't remember that one."

"I guess it's better that you don't," I laugh as I pull up a picture of Judge Reinhold on my phone and tell her how I noticed the resemblance for the first time in a photo of young Chris on his kitchen wall. "I showed Jennifer, too," I explain enthusiastically.

"Well, maybe, I don't know. I guess Chris kind of looks like him." His mom doesn't see it anymore than Jennifer. Picture albums sprawl across the kitchen counter. Brent points at one and says to his mom, "Remember that time."

"Oh, yes — I remember *that time!*" They both laugh. Chris, hearing the laughter, joins in like the guy in the back of the room at an awards ceremony, not paying attention, but upon hearing everyone else laughing, figures he'd better join in.

"I brought some pictures, too," I tell her. "I'm pretty sure you haven't seen any of *these* before," I laugh thinking of the one of Chris, the Geek, Alex, and me sitting naked, from the waste up, in the cow drinking trough. *What else do I have in these pictures? Maybe I should have gone through them before showing her. I remind myself—she's a Kelley, no worries.*

"Please, sit down. We'll have lunch first. Then we can look at your pictures— and talk about Sandra Lee."

Chris and I sit at a round table next to the bow window in the sunroom. He stares at the deer roaming in the backyard before shifting his attention to the red plastic hummingbird feeder stuck to the casement window. Wings whir as a needle beak dips into the little hole, sipping nervously.

"How have you been, buddy?" I ask. He looks at me, startled, as if I'd shaken him by the shoulder, waking him from a trance. "Did you see your grandson, Wyatt, this week?" Chris turns to look back out the window. *Okay, we don't have to talk. I'm okay with that. You look good, though. I think you must've just got a haircut and a beard trim.*

"Is all of this your artwork, Mrs. Kelley?" I stand up and point to the watercolor paintings hanging on the walls.

"Yes." She answers, polite not to correct me, to tell me she's now Mrs. Damon, or to tell me to just call her Diane.

"They're gorgeous. I love the colors on this one!" I take a few steps forward to inspect the abstract splashes of watercolor oranges, blues, a bit of yellow, and shades of green. "I don't know what it is I'm looking at, but I really like it." I appreciate the abstract swooshes of color and I'm relieved she doesn't appear to take my clumsy words the wrong way.

"Yes, everyone likes my colors," she explains. "I've always had a knack for the right color choices."

I look at the other paintings. "Wow, they're all so different!" I check the artist's name subtly brushed near the bottom of each painting, indicating that indeed, the artist is Diane Damon. "This one is amazing!" I point at a western mountain scene that I'd thought was a photograph when I saw it from the other side of the room.

"I painted that one from a picture Brent took in Yosemite." Mist rises through tall pines that skirt iconic Half Dome. "When I saw the picture, I said to Brent, 'I *have* to paint that.'"

"That's really an amazing picture!"

I return to my seat and watch as the table fills with a platter of deli meats, sandwich rolls, grapes, a bowl of potato chips, and pastries. Mrs. Kelley asks me what I want to drink.

"You know, I'll think I'll have a root beer, like Chris. I haven't had one of those in a long time." Root beer is Chris's favorite. It's his new go-to, replacing the blue cans of Labatt.

While Chris's mom gets the drinks, he snatches two pieces of pastry. "Uh, oh," says Brent, "Someone put the sweets too close to Chris." He moves the plate to my side of the table. After devouring the pastry, Chris turns his attention to the chip bowl. He tweezes a single Lay's Classic, with a surgeon's precision, between his thumb and forefinger.

When we're done with lunch, I mention to Brent, "He didn't eat the sandwich you made for him, but at least he was respectful with the chip bowl."

"That's because he thought it was his own *personal* bowl of chips."

I laugh, but I'm not sure Brent was trying to be funny.

It's time to get to the story that I came here for — Chris's pig. I turn to Mrs. Kelley, "So tell me about Sandra Lee."

She gets up from the table. Maybe she didn't hear me; she told me that she has a bit of trouble with her hearing these days. Mrs. Kelley comes back, handing me three pages in beautiful cursive on line paper; the work of an artist, "I wrote what I remembered."

I read her words. The year was 1974.

> In Chris's second year of high school he wanted a pig for a pet. A neighbor's pig had recently had a litter of piglets. He asked his stepfather, Bud Kelley, and me for permission to keep it in our large backyard at 101 Buffalo Road. We told Chris that he would need a permit to keep a farm animal on a village lot and that he would need to appear before the Village Board. He sought out the information to do that. And because the Board had previously granted permission to a young girl to keep a goat in her yard, a precedent had been set. Chris was granted a permit for his pig.

I don't say anything about this, but am amazed that Chris would take the time for such paperwork "bullshit." The Chris I knew *never* asked for permission, and didn't give a damn about being forgiven in cases where he felt he was exercising his rights as a citizen of the *free world*. If Chris wanted something he went for it, in a straight line, bashing through the roadblocks.

> He built a small barn in the rear part of our backyard for the piglet which he named Sandra Lee after a girl of whom he was fond. He was diligent about caring for her. All the neighbor-hood children loved her.

In February of 1975, Bud Kelley died of a heart attack. He was 59.

Recently, I asked Brent about Bud and his relationship with Chris. I told him, "Chris didn't talk about him too much."

"That doesn't come as a surprise," was Brent's unexpected response. "Bud was a hard worker, a regular guy, but he never really connected with any of us, Chris, Daryl, or me."

"Really? From the couple of times Chris talked about Bud, it sounded like they got along fine."

"Oh, they got along *great*. Bud let Chris do what he wanted, which was always the path of least resistance when it came to interacting with Chris." Brent had told me, before explaining the circumstances surrounding Bud's death, "He was a smoker, but I don't think that was the only reason he died. I was too young to understand back then, but later, I learned the employees at Keller Printing, the company he worked for as a lithographer, wanted to unionize. These guys were his friends and now he was at odds with them. Bud was a principled guy, and felt that he'd been treated fairly by the company, so he was against the union idea. I think as a result he became an outsider and maybe feared losing his job."

It sounded to me like Brent could have been talking about Chris.

"The company was also contemplating moving its operations to Gettysburg, Pennsylvania. Bud and my mother went down there, but she told him, 'I don't want to move. All of my friends are here, in East Aurora.' There was a lot going on at that time with the three of us, all teenagers, or older, and my three step-sisters Sally, Nancy, and Diane all around the same age as us. Eight of us under one roof — it was tight quarters. I think Bud was under a lot of stress."

After almost ten years with a stable father figure, the dad Chris and his brothers knew best was gone. A pet pig could never be a replacement for a father, but I wonder if somehow Sandra Lee provided an outlet for Chris, the responsibility to care for her, something to look forward to each day. Chris, of course, would have never admitted to such a thing, probably telling me, "Bacon, Jack. It's about the bacon."

I read further.

> After Bud died I began working in the Dental School at U.B. (University at Buffalo) as the registrar. During that time there were quite a few incidents with Sandra Lee involving irate neighbors, plus quite a few motorists on Buffalo Road, and finding the EA police in our driveway upon arriving home from work.

I look up from her words, laughing, "The police were in your driveway?" That seemed a bit excessive for any "incident" involving a pig.

"Yes," she answers succinctly, as if no further explanation is required.

"This is perfect," I tell her. It's a typical Chris incident. So many of them involved a visit from men and women in blue — or green, or whatever the color uniform the local gendarmes wore. "So what were the police doing in your driveway?"

"There was a lot going on at that time." *Yes, I'm sure there was.* "The neighbors were upset about the damage Sandra Lee was doing to their gardens. They weren't as enamored with Sandra Lee as their children who would stop by to pet her."

I picture a growing pig on the loose, "rototilling" through tidy rows of vegetables, foraging for food and leaving behind trails of destruction.

Mrs. Kelley recounts the episode from the beginning, "One day when I returned from work, a police cruiser was in our driveway. I remember the policeman with a big loop of rope around his shoulder. It was early winter, a bit before the piglets were born. I remember it had snowed the night before. The ground hadn't frozen yet, so it was slippery. And the snow was so deep! I remember walking behind the policeman — in his footprints. He made his way to the back of our lot near Knox Road. And the neighbors' kids came running when they saw what was happening."

"And did he find Sandra Lee? Did he take her?"

"No, for some reason he didn't. Not when he saw her calmly trudging through the deep snow, snout down, searching for things to eat. I suppose he figured it best to leave her be."

"Was Chris there?" I can't wait to hear about this. My thoughts leap forward to Chris giving *it* to one of EAPDs finest. Blasting him, telling him his attempt to catch Sandra Lee was, "bullshit."

"No. Chris wasn't there. He might not have been home from school yet."

School? I'm sure Chris could have been just about anywhere, except school.

"What about the boy pig? Did Chris give him a name?"

"No. He was only there as long as needed. Once Sandra Lee became pregnant Chris took him back to the animal auction. I think it was in Springville."

"How did he get the pig to East Aurora?"

Brent has the answer for this one, "In the Corvair. Another one of Chris's $100 specials."

"The one with the white stripe?"

"Yes, that's the one."

Later I did some checking on the gestation period of pigs, learning the rule of threes: three months, three weeks, and three days. I guesstimate Sandra Lee had her brief tryst around the end of August, just before we returned to school for our senior year.

I continued to read.

> When the time arrived for the piglets' birth Chris rigged up an electrical system so they would be warm, as it was near Christmas.

"What kind of electrical system?"

Brent chuckles at this. "Knowing Chris, it was most likely a succession of extension cords running from the garage."

Mrs. Kelley tells me, "Chris took such good care of the little pigs. Diligently administering their shots and medications. They grew fast."

There were now *seven* pigs to keep track of and the little ones routinely escaped from the small barn and pen that Chris had created for them. Recently, Peter Diebolt had told me, "Being that it was winter, they were easy to track. We just followed their footprints in the snow."

I had asked Deebs, "What was it like that night the pigs were born? Do you remember how Chris handled it? How did you guys have any clue what to do?"

"That's so long ago, it's hard to remember. At the time it didn't seem like such a big deal. Chris was always doing crazy shit."

Anyone who knows Chris has a story to tell. The business with the pig wasn't that big a deal to Deebs, but that didn't stop him from sharing another story. "You got to write about the night we rode through the East Side of Buffalo."

"What happened? I never heard about that one."

"We were in his Corvair. Chris, me, and some others, I don't remember who, but we were yelling stupid stuff out the open windows to anyone walking the streets. It didn't take long before a few 'locals' jumped in their car and started chasing us."

I laugh and tell him, "I can picture that Deebs, but geez, I don't know about putting this in the book."

"Oh, you have to man. It was epic."

Epic. Everything with Chris was epic. Lines needed to be drawn.

"Anyway, Chris floored the Corvair and ran every red light to get some separation from those wackos."

Who are you calling a wacko, Deebs?

"When we finally stopped, I remember looking in the back of the Corvair for some kind of "weapon" and found a chain saw. I started it up and had it ready if the local bad guys happened to catch up to us."

"Yeah, that's typical Chris shit, but I don't know about this one Deebs. If you remember anything more about the pig, let me know." Deebs could only remember that it was night-time, it was cold, and Sandra Lee might have needed a little help.

By the spring of 1976, the neighbors had had enough. In addition to battling rabbits, squirrels, and chipmunks when it came to cultivating that year's plantings, they now waged war against a family of hungry pigs. Sandra Lee and her growing piglets buried their snouts in the soft spring earth looking for anything to eat. They created a muddy mess.

> We received a notice from the village that we were in violation of the "one farm animal per village lot" rule. And because of that, being the property owner, I was summoned to appear in court.

"Jennifer told me about the court date," I said, looking up from her written words, "but she said you didn't end up having to go to court. She said the case was dismissed before you had to appear,"

"Oh, no, we went!"

I could see a bit of Chris in her at this moment, not much, but sweet Mrs.

Kelley wasn't about to be pushed around by the authorities. After receiving the notice, the Kelleys decided it was best that Sandra Lee say goodbye to her adolescent piglets and Chris once again fired up the Corvair, transporting them to the animal auction in Springville.

Prior to the court date, Chris rallied his buddies to attend the proceedings. I wasn't one of those buddies. I hadn't made the cut, hadn't obtained my junior hellion's badge, or maybe it was during the period of our friendship when I had grown enough brain cells to carefully contain my interactions with Chris to the soccer fields.

Mrs. Kelley continues, "We waited our turn before the judge. He thought it was a case involving *dogs* and wondered why we were in court about *dogs*, but the attending policeman corrected him, 'It's about *hogs* — not *dogs*,' he told the judge."

I laugh, thinking it seemed like an episode from the old sitcom, *Night Court*, starring Harry Anderson as the judge. I pictured a very silly scene, with Mrs. Kelley in front of a wedge of Chris and his friends preparing to plead their case to quirky Harry Anderson.

"By this time the six little piglets were gone so we were told we could go. The judge said to us, 'Case dismissed.' On the way out of court I remember the judge leaning over the bench and quietly asking me, 'How did she get pregnant?'"

"Really?" I said. "Oh, my God, that's hilarious. So what did you say to the judge?"

She pauses, collecting her memories from that time and then answers me with a smirk, "Oh, I don't know. I suppose I told him, 'In the usual way.'"

At this we all laugh. Chris, hearing the guffaws, joins in. "That is beautiful, I love it!" I say, thinking about her words, writing them down on my little pad, not wanting them to escape from me. Indeed, it had been in the *usual way*. That's not to say that anything involving Chris was done in the *usual way*.

She continues, her memories fill the room like flood waters, "While Sandra Lee was growing up, we dog sat for a basset hound while his owners went to Florida. The dog was so jealous of the pig. She ate vegetable table scraps that the dog wanted. Beauregard was the dog's name," she adds as if a pig eating table scraps didn't require some explaining.

"The pig was inside the house?"

"Yes, but only on special occasions."

Oh, that explains everything. I picture Chris cleaning up Sandra Lee for dinner.

"We also had a cat that had a batch of kittens and we wouldn't let Beauregard anywhere near Chris's bedroom, which was the birthing room. I have some pictures of Sandra Lee and her piglets, if you want to see them. I don't have many," she apologizes.

"Oh, yeah, definitely. I'd love to see them."

As she hands me the pictures, her joyous memories swell to the brim, "We had lots of activity during the Sandra Lee time of our lives and it's well remembered by the whole family. Chris received many 'pig remembrances' over the years. You know, pig related gifts: pig towels, pig mugs, pig wall decorations, ceramic pigs, and things like that until he finally said, 'No more!'"

I'm guessing *Jennifer* might have been the one that said, "No more." I look at the pictures of Sandra Lee and her piglets, studying them closely, wanting to transport myself back to that simple, crazy time. The six little pigs snuggled together on a straw bed, four facing in one direction and the other two stacked on top, facing in the other. What appears to be a heat lamp looms over them in the corner of the small barn lined with newspaper.

"So what ended up happening to Sandra Lee?"

"Well, since Chris was graduating from high school that June, I told him I would not become Sandra Lee's keeper. Sadly, he took her to be auctioned and we never knew what happened to her."

There is a pause out of respect for Sandra Lee before I ask, "Chris must have gotten money for her. I wonder. What do you think he did with it?"

Without missing a beat, Brent answers, "Probably bought another $100 beater."

"So how was it being Chris's mom back then?"

Mrs. Kelley listens to my question. She doesn't speak right away and I wonder if she heard what I'd said. After a period of silence, she answers, "Chris would listen to me compliantly, but in the end, he was going to do what he was going to do. There was no stopping him. I didn't get into many arguments with him because I knew it wouldn't have been worth it."

"That's why you're 90 and look like you're 70," I tell her.

She continues, "Chris always loved animals. I remember when he was little. I came downstairs one morning and there was a sign on his door, 'Open door slowly and carefully,'" she stretches out the word, "carefully." "So I did. Chris was standing there holding a baby animal he'd found. Oh, what was it?" She looks at Brent for an answer.

"Was it a possum, Mom?"

"No, I don't think so. Oh, what was it?" And then it comes to her. She excitedly tells me, "It was a baby raccoon. Chris said to me, 'Isn't he cute? Can we keep him?' I told him, 'No!' I think Tiny the dogcatcher came and took the raccoon away. Chris was so mad at me. He didn't speak to me for quite some time."

"Remember the time he brought home the baby woodchuck?" Brent says, looking at his mom.

"Oh, yes. I remember."

Brent explains, "That was when he was driving back and forth from that job he had down in Hollidaysburg, Pennsylvania. He found it along the side of the road and brought it back to East Aurora. I think Jen told him that he couldn't keep it at the house, so he took it back down to his apartment in Hollidaysburg."

"He had a woodchuck living in his apartment?!" I ask.

"Yeah. He didn't have much down there. I'm not even sure if he had a bed." Brent tries to get his brother's attention, "Chris, Chris! What was the name of the company you worked for in Hollidaysburg?"

"Yes," Chris answers.

"What was the name, Chris?"

Chris can't find the answer; none of us can. I think back to Chris's phone call to me when he was pulled over for speeding on the 219. That was during the time he was driving to Hollidaysburg on Sunday nights. It was a four-hour ride each way every week. He didn't say anything about a woodchuck in the passenger seat. Maybe the critter was already living at his apartment by that time.

"McLanahan!" shouts Brent. "That was the company. They did mineral processing." He looks at me, "I had heard the employees down there were scared of Chris. Did you ever hear anything about that?"

"No, but I know he could be rough on people who didn't know what they were doing." It's sad. Those people never got to know the Chris I know. The disease had to be in full bloom by that time.

Later that night, I look more closely at the pictures of the pigs; I zoom in on the image now collected on my phone, holding the picture close to my face. Something on the newsprint catches my eye. Directly behind the piglets is an advertisement for Super Sausage and Sliced Bologna. *Jeeesus, Chris! Maybe it was all about the bacon.*

Note: I searched the internet for information on Keller Brothers Printing. It was quick work. A company by the name of Keller Bros. & Miller, Inc., hailing itself as a family-owned, commercial, union printing company founded in 1916, is still alive and well, doing business in downtown Buffalo, New York. I noted that Morris Titanic, (great hockey name) a former 1973 draft pick of the Buffalo Sabres works in the sales department at the company. Could it be that the company that Bud worked for had never left town? I emailed the company, briefly outlining the basis for my inquiry, hoping for a fond remembrance of hard working and loyal employee, Bud Kelley. In a few minutes I receive my answer from the owner:

> The company you are looking for is William J. Keller, entirely different than mine. W.J. Keller has been out of business for decades and although I receive inquiries like this frequently. I have no more information to offer on the company.

It appears the company Bud had worked for must have indeed left town, leaving the Kelley family behind. For this I am grateful—grateful that it gave me the opportunity to experience all that I did with Bud Kelley's stepson, Chris.

Brent Kelley, Diane Damon, Don Damon, and Chris having lunch at his mom's house - 2019

Elko, Nevada

W<small>E FINISH TALKING</small> about Sandra Lee and Chris's love for animals, but no one seems anxious for me to leave. I may have loosened the cap on a jar of memories.

Don had moved to a corner, away from the lunch table, while we discussed Sandra Lee. Hearing us talk about Chris's last job in Hollidaysburg sparks a few memories for him. I only knew him as the guy with the Vandura. He tells me, "You know when Chris applied for the job at Derrick Corporation, they told him, 'What makes you think you can do this job? You don't know a thing about mining equipment?'" Don explains how Chris let them know it would take a lot more than a flimsy roadblock to stop him from anything. "He told them, 'I haven't failed at anything I've tried to do. Give me this job and I'll prove it to you.'"

I picture the interviewer, his head down, scribbling a note on Chris's application; it could have gone either way. Dealing with Chris was an acquired taste, typically sipped before deciding if you wanted the full bottle. He got the job.

Don recalls, "And there was the time when he moved back from Connecticut in the '90s and started working construction. He needed a pickup truck, but didn't have the money so he came to me for a loan. We set it up like a bank, five percent interest with a five-year term. And instead of taking five years, he paid me back in three months. He was someone you could trust to follow through on an agreement."

Yes, I can picture that, but then why did it take him almost two years to pay me back the entrance fee for the West Virginia 24-hour mountain bike race? I hold that thought, answering, "Yeah, Chris is a principled guy."

"Brent, what was your last name before you all became Kelleys?" I ask, shifting to another subject in order to verify a few facts.

"Nimon. Bud adopted all of us after he married my mother. That's when our name was changed to Kelley."

His answer is followed by silence as I write a note.

Brent looks at his mom, "Jack was wondering about some of the details from Elko, Nevada."

"Oh, that's okay," I say to her. "We don't have to talk about any of that. I know it was a difficult time for all of you. That's okay, I understand."

"I helped them pack. It was on a Thursday," she starts, "right before Mother's Day."

It's been over fifty years since Chris and his brothers (ages six, nine, and eleven) were driven across the country on a "vacation." As Mrs. Kelley tells me about this painful time, filled with jagged edges and unspoken wounds, I feel uncomfortable. I feel like I'm intruding on the hidden details of a time that she'd rather forget instead of recounting to me. Is this part of Chris's life that needs to be told, or is this a private matter that should be kept within the family?

Weeks later I discussed this with Brent, "What do you think? Is this part of Chris's story?"

"I guess that's up to you. It's your book. But I would say, yes, it definitely should be in there. It's like you're saying to the reader, 'If you really want to know my friend, Chris, then you need to know this about him. You need to know what he went through when he was in kindergarten, or maybe it was in first grade; I'm really not sure, exactly. We were all quite young. I suppose it might not have been the same for all of us. The impact it had on me might have been quite different from how it affected Chris or Daryl. I've actually never talked to them about that time. There's no doubt this was a very formative event for all of us."

AT THE round dining room table, I listen to Mrs. Kelley, pausing as she collects her memories. "Paul told me he was taking the boys with him overnight."

Overnight? Did you have any idea where he was headed? I have so many questions, but don't want to bombard her like it's an inquisition. I came here to talk about the pig. Sandra Lee. Brent was the one that brought up Elko. I had no idea I'd be stirring the silty bottom of this long tranquil pool from the past.

Brent interjects, "I remember we stayed at the Holiday Inn on Dingens Street. At least it *was* a Holiday Inn back then. I don't even know if it's still there. The only other thing I remember was that we stopped at Mount Rushmore."

I know parts of this story. Chris had told us bits and pieces about his sojourn to a town in Nevada with his biological father, his brothers, his father's girlfriend, and her three boys. Pieces of two families, eight of them in total, irregularly joined together for a two-thousand-mile road trip in one station wagon. The whole thing was always unbelievable to me, but it's not something I ever thought about much. So many things surrounding Chris were unbelievable. But now, sitting in his mom's house, talking about that time, gives me a new perspective.

I make a note before turning back to Mrs. Kelley, "When did you know something wasn't right?"

"I received a letter the following Monday. It was from their father." She looks in the direction of Brent, sitting on the couch. "It said the boys would be well taken care of."

"What did you do then?"

She pauses again, I suppose looking for memories that have been hidden on a back shelf. This was the early 60s. There was no internet, no cell phones, and no 24-hour news. I imagine the process and means to find three kidnapped children was quite a bit different than it would be today. "I remember telling my parents, my sister, Sally, and her husband, John, and of course we contacted the authorities. We hired a private investigator. I had no idea where to begin to look for them."

Brent explains, "Uncle John was married to Mom's sister, Sally. He was the one that eventually found us along with Mom."

"Oh, yeah, I remember Chris telling us about Uncle John. He was the one-armed golfer—right?"

"Yeah, that's him," Brent answers.

"Chris told us he was a great golfer even though he had a hook for a right hand."

"That sounds like Chris all right."

Chris sits in the corner, as if he's a statue of himself, while we talk about his young life. I know he can hear us, but I wonder if he understands or remembers.

I turn back to Mrs. Kelley, "How did you figure out where they were?"

"Well, I remember somehow we tracked them down through school records. They were registered in school out there — in Nevada."

How the hell would you track someone down through school records back in those days? I want to know, but it doesn't seem right to ask about such a detail. The more I find out, the muddier the waters become, and the more questions I have.

"I remember being on a Little League baseball team," chimes in Brent.

"How *long* were you out there?"

Brent looks at his mom, "How long do you figure we were there, Mom?"

"It was about a month. I remember you left the Friday before Mother's Day and we found you around Father's Day."

"Yeah, that sounds about right. I remember we finished school out there. And when we came back, our friends were still *in school*, but we didn't have to go."

I turned back to Mrs. Kelley, "So what did you do when you found out they were in Nevada?"

"John and I flew out there. We staked out the motel they were living in, but wanted to avoid a confrontation."

I think about Mrs. Kelley on a stakeout with her brother-in-law, the one-armed man with a hook. Later, Brent fills me in on Uncle John. He tells me that he received the Purple Heart from the Navy in World War II. He lied about his age, entering the war at 16, and fought in the Pacific theater.

I ask, "How did he lose his arm?" hoping to hear about a heroic war story.

"It was a work accident," explains Brent. "He worked in a factory. I don't know what happened. I just know he lost his right arm from the elbow down."

"Oh."

"And I don't think he could do that job anymore," Brent tells me. "He might have sold cars for a while."

"He's not still alive, is he?"

"Oh, yeah, don't put him in the grave yet. He lives out on Milestrip Road in Orchard Park."

"Really?! How old is he?"

We both do the math and figure he must be around 92. Maybe if I need some more facts about that time back in the early '60s, I'll take a spin over to see Uncle John and thank him for his service; first, for protecting our country and second, for rescuing my friend Chris and his brothers.[3]

I LET Mrs. Kelley finish her story. "We waited until their father left for work. We could see the boys inside. When he left we just went in and got them. And then we all flew home."

Where was Paul Nimon's girlfriend? She must have been in that motel room. What did she do when they came in and got the boys?

Turning to Brent she asks, "You went to Mount Rushmore?"

"Yeah. I thought you knew that."

She looks at me, almost apologizing, "The boys never wanted to talk about it."

It's okay, Mrs. Kelley, I understand.

I look down at my notes, not knowing how to respond. There are so many more questions, but I don't have the will to press forward. As I leave, I tell her, "You've done a worthy job raising three boys."

"Don't put all the blame on her," interjects Brent.

"She's not done with you yet!" I tell him while smiling at Mrs. Kelley.

She nods in agreement.

TWO WEEKS later I stop to return her handwritten notes about the pig, Sandra Lee. I show her a picture of Chris on our recent hike. She stares at the picture and says, "He looks so normal." I feel the pain in her words, for the loss of a son, and I feel my own sorrow, for the loss of a best friend. Before the moment can overcome me, I tell her, "Yeah, he looks great. And I still enjoy getting out with him on our hikes. It's just different." I think—*a lot like fun—only different,* but I don't tell her that.

She holds my hand, "You are a good friend."

"Thanks," I reply awkwardly. I feel like I should be doing more. She doesn't

---

[3] Sadly, Uncle John passed away on December 6, 2019. He was 92.

cry. She's tough, but I can't imagine how difficult this must be for her; losing her son to such a cruel disease.

A FEW more weeks go by. I can't let go of the questions. There has to be more to this story, but I don't feel right asking Mrs. Kelley, so I call Brent. "Do you mind me asking you a few more questions about Elko?"

"Sure, okay. We can talk on our hike today."

I write a list of questions I intend to ask Brent in my blue spiral notebook.

In a few hours I walk through Chris's garage and open the door leading to the kitchen. Brent has Chris pinned into a corner by the kitchen cabinets. Chris is laughing and Brent is not.

"What's going on today?"

"I'm trying to give Chris this pill."

Brent holds it in front of Chris's face, but he keeps his mouth shut tight. He squirms away from Brent and only then resumes laughing.

"What does that pill do?"

"I have no idea," answers Brent before pausing to think. "Wait, yes, I do. It aggravates me every week when I have to give it to him!" (Months later I asked about Chris's pills and found out they are no longer necessary. At least that is what Wally told me.)

Chris has found an extra gear today; Brent and I walk briskly to keep up with him. "I don't know how he does it," I say to Brent. "It doesn't even look like he's walking very fast. I know his stride is longer, but *Jeeesus,* how does he get so far ahead of us on the flats? It's like he's on roller skates."

Sweat beads on my back. The temperature is in the 80s, a warm day for the first of October in Western New York. "I'm impressed! How did you get him to wear short sleeves today?"

When we stop for a break, I recount stories from our past, but Chris sits indifferently as if I'm speaking a foreign language. He peels the shell of an acorn with his long fingernails and puts a piece of the bitter nut in his mouth.

"Chris, Chris," Brent hollers. "You're not eating that are you?"

"Yeah." He gives his brother a bug-eyed smile.

At the end of our hike I ask Brent, "I don't understand how your mom found you guys through school records."

"Well, I think that's something he didn't plan on." The "he" is his biological father, Paul Nimon. "When he registered us in school, he probably needed to have proof of age and information about where we were previously. I suppose they notified our school in West Seneca, Ebenezer Elementary. They probably contacted Mom and she told the private investigator. Once he had that information it wouldn't have been too hard to find out where we were," explains Brent. He pauses before adding, "At least that's what I think might have happened. I'm really not sure."

"Why Elko, Nevada? Why did your father take you there?"

"I guess Nevada was the easiest state to get a quick divorce. At least that's what I've always thought, but I really don't know. There were no plans to stay there for very long."

Brent answers my questions from that time so long ago; his responses come more slowly with each inquiry and I remind myself that he was a little boy back then. Chris has his back to both of us while we talk, looking in the distance. *Does he understand what we are talking about? Does he want to remember?* Brent catches my eye, but then looks away as he continues.

"I seem to recall that our father told each of us separately that we were leaving on a trip and each of us a different story of where we were going and why. I suppose he felt since we were different ages we might react differently."

Brent wants to answer my questions, but it's so long ago that he often responds, "I'm sorry, I just can't remember," but then he shares a random memory from the time. "I got a sliver in my hand. It was a big one and maybe it was infected, but I was told we weren't going to a doctor's office."

I try to understand what it had been like for him. "You guys must have missed your mother very much; I can't imagine how terrible that must have been."

"Yeah, I remember once, I was sitting on my bed, thinking my life is over. I'll never see Mom again, or my grandpa and grandma."

I digest his words, trying to understand how this affected all the Kelley boys, and I see my hard-ass friend, Chris, as a little boy, crying for his mom and perhaps for the first time thinking — life is short.

Brent continues, "I didn't like school very much out there in Nevada. I remember they delivered milk to our classroom and I didn't like that because by the time we drank the milk it was warm." He continues with another memory, "And I was terrified, at first, to ask anyone where the boys' room was."

His halting words ooze from him like the puss from a festering wound. He's a good man, answering all my questions. We could sit here all day with Chris content to stare into the woods, but I don't want to put him through anymore of this. I ask my last questions, "One thing I'm confused about is what actually happened when your Mom and Uncle John came into your motel room and retrieved you. What were you doing when they found you? Wasn't your father's girlfriend there?"

"No. They had a separate room. All of the kids were in one room and my father and his girlfriend were in another. He'd left for work. I remember I was playing with my electric football game. We had all been allowed to bring a toy with us on the trip."

An electric football game? What a peculiar thing to bring on a "vacation."

"I guess she (the girlfriend) might have come into the room when my mom and Uncle John came in. I really don't remember. The whole thing (the *rescue*) might have taken three or four minutes."

"And then you all flew home, right?"

"Yes."

"That must have been your first airplane ride."

"It was." Brent finds his sense of humor, "I guess Chris and I enjoyed the plane ride so much that both of us decided to fly the friendly skies for most of our business careers."

"How did your mom meet Bud anyway?"

"They met in a support group, Parents without Partners. I think it was a couple years after Elko. Bud's wife had died of cancer."

"What ever happened to your biological father? Did you ever see him again?"

"No." Brent's answer is short. I understand. "Chris tried to locate him. He might have been in Phoenix. And he tried to get Daryl and me involved, but I was done with him."

"Did Chris ever find him?"

"No."

Later that night I think about the questions that I asked Brent. Had it been necessary to get the facts to this story at the expense of resurrecting painful memories?

I text him: Thanks for taking the time today to answer so many of my questions. I recognize this as a hurtful memory for you and your family. Your willingness to help with this project, Chris's story, has been indispensable.

He answers: Frankly, it has been tougher than I thought it would be. I suppose we can never truly leave that little boy in us behind. My view is that by helping you, I am also somehow helping my brother, Chris.

Yes Brent, you are helping. Chris is blessed to have you as a brother, my good friend.

Chris at Whiteface Mountain in Lake Placid, NY - 2015

When Did You Know?
The Pickled Brussels Sprouts Caper

It's DIFFICULT TO pinpoint when I first knew something wasn't right with Chris. I know it was before the doctors diagnosed his condition and Alex told me, "I don't know if you've heard yet, but Chris has this thing called Pick's ..." I've wondered about this disease, any disease for that matter. It's not like the day before the diagnosis, you don't have it, and after receiving the bad news, you do. Maybe this thing had been festering inside of Chris for quite some time. I wonder what Brent thinks.

I've gotten to know Brent Kelley quite well over the past year. Prior to our hikes with Chris we'd had only brief conversations. Chris didn't talk much about his brothers. When he did, Chris made it clear they were different—very different. Occasionally someone might ask what Brent was up to these days and Chris would tell us, "Brent loves fly-fishing, Jeeesus." Chris couldn't understand how someone could spend so much time devoted to such an activity.

These days I spend quite a few Tuesday afternoons with Brent and Chris, hiking the park trails of Knox Farm, Chestnut Ridge, and Emery. We didn't pick Tuesdays; Tuesdays found us. It's one of the days Jennifer needs help with Chris, to get him up, to make sure he gets dressed, to make sure he eats his breakfast—all those things most of us do without adult supervision. Like so many others, Brent does a lot to help with his brother's care these days. It's important that you know this. It's also important that I tell you the truth about their relationship; it's been a road filled with potholes and hazard warnings.

Since another commitment will keep me from hiking with Brent and Chris this Tuesday, I give Brent a call to ask about his past relationship with his brother and hear what he has to say about Chris's condition. I wonder when he first suspected something wasn't right. I'm not sure how to begin, so I start by telling him, "I know we talk about a lot of stuff while we're hiking, but I want to make sure I have a few facts straight. I need some information about you. You know, for the story about Chris."

"About *me*?"

"Yeah — you're an important part of the story."

"Well okay, I guess," Brent says, not sounding too enthusiastic.

"You started out in culinary school, right?"

Brent chuckles. It's a "throat clearer" that precedes many of his comments. His words are spoken in a booming voice with a deliberate cadence, buffered by chuckles, a couple more words, and another chuckle. "No, no, I never went to culinary school. I started out at Indiana State—until I ran out of money after my freshman year."

"You were a business major, right?"

"Nooo. Actually, I started out majoring in journalism."

I'm 0-for-2 on Brent facts. He must be wondering if I listen to anything he says while we're hiking.

"After that I was hired to work at the Roycroft (an iconic restaurant in East Aurora, New York) as a busboy. Funny story about that. It didn't last very long. They told me I was too big."

"Too big?"

"Yeah, you know—you need to be a bit nimble in the dining room. I suppose I might've been knocking over a few wine glasses when I was clearing the tables. Anyway, they told me they could use me in the kitchen. I worked under the corporate chef for the owners, the Turgeon Brothers. His name was David Green. He's the one that showed me how to cook. After that, I worked as a chef for both Wanakah and Orchard Park Country Clubs. The board member that got me the job at Wanakah is the one that insisted I go back to school. He brought me the application to go to Buffalo State as a business major."

"I guess you owe him a big thank-you for getting you back into school. What year was it that you graduated from Buff State? That had to be the mid '80s, right?"

Brent chuckles. I feel a story coming; nothing is ever standard operating procedure with the Kelleys. "I went to Buffalo State from 1979 to 1991."

"1979-1991?!" *Had I heard that right?*

"Yeah. Remember, I had a family to support and was working full-time for the country clubs and then Delaware North (a global food service company)."

Following that, Brent went on to teach culinary arts at Alfred State University from 1998 until his retirement in 2017. There's much more to Brent than a career in food service: he's a devoted family man, a catcher of big fish (caught on his hand-tied flies), and a grower of mushrooms and asparagus. How many people do you know that grow mushrooms?

That's all nice, but I have questions about a potentially thorny topic. There isn't a good segue, so I plunge headlong into what I hope doesn't come off sounding like an interrogation. "I need some stuff on your relationship with Chris. I know there was a period of time when you guys didn't get along very well."

"That's putting it kindly." Another chuckle. "Hey, I'll be the first one to admit—there was a lot of tension between the two of us. There were years when we barely spoke a word to each other." Brent pauses, collecting his thoughts. "I'll tell you a story that's typical Chris. It was at my mother's house—not that long ago, maybe ten or fifteen years. I remember it was the year Chris and Jennifer were hosting that exchange student."

"The soccer player?"

"Yeah, that's right. We were playing football and I intercepted a pass Chris threw. Someone had already tackled me—I was on the ground and Chris came in late, piling on top of me. I guess he was pissed off that I'd intercepted his pass."

"Yeah, I could see him doing something like that. Everything was always full contact with Chris."

He would tell us often, "It's all about maximizing angle and velocity." Mind you, Brent is no lightweight, not someone to be messed with. His forearms, as thick as bowling pins, accompany a barrel chest supported by legs as sturdy as the trunk of a mature fruit tree. That wouldn't stop Chris, who feared no one, no matter their size, and he certainly wasn't about to back down from taking a shot at one of his brothers.

Brent continues, "I was mad. I had to go to work the next day. It just wasn't necessary. I guess you might say we had a bit of a rivalry. Chris was the youngest, and in my mother's eyes, he could do no wrong. Our relationship for a long time was contentious, to say the least." He pauses before making sure to tell me, "That's not to say that my boys Jason and Jake didn't think Uncle Chris was cool."

Chris could be very cool, especially in the eyes of his impressionable nieces and nephews. He was the ringleader of "cool stuff," routinely sweeping up anyone and everyone that was bold enough or naive enough to join him in his crazy, insane, death-defying, law-testing, ill-advised plans for that day's epic escapade.

"It's commendable what you're doing for your brother, driving up here every Tuesday to spend the day with him. You know, not everyone would do that." Brent lives an hour south of East Aurora in Belfast, New York. It's even more amazing, knowing how things were for so many years between the two brothers. Maybe it's one of the blessings within the mess this disease has made of my friend's brain, bringing two brothers together, perhaps closer than ever.

Brent deflects my praise, "I guess. There are others that are doing a lot, too,"

I think of the others, the ones that I know of: Paul "Wally" Sugnet driving from Rochester every other Thursday to spend the day with Chris; Bill Shanahan who helps out Wally when he's available; our classmate, Sally Wiesner, née Brown who watches Chris on the opposite Thursdays; Walt and Patty Lyons who provide comfort at Aurora Adult Day Services; his son-in-law Dan and his daughter Danielle who fill in the gaps while at the same time raising a young family; his daughter Marla and her boyfriend Jess, who Chris always reminded us, "is built like a brick shithouse" (another of his go-to descriptions); his son, Troy, who moved back from Colorado to help out; his sisters-in-law, Babette and Darcy, and of course, Jennifer, a rock of toughness who deals with this every day. There are others I have failed to list—you know who you are. I apologize for not mentioning you by name. I'm sure Jennifer appreciates your help.

I tell Brent, "I've enjoyed our time together this past year." I think of the things I've learned about nature from him: how to identify a sassafras leaf, the habits of the green darner dragonfly, how to grow asparagus from seed, the name of the plant with "those cool looking berries"—except I can't remember now if it was baneberry or pokeberry—and the reality that fly-fishing probably requires far more patience than I have.

"You remember when you were tying Chris's shoes last week?"

"Yeah, *that* was a process."

"While you were down on the ground, I was holding his hands. You know, so he wouldn't run off." I could not have imagined a circumstance where Chris and I would be in the woods at Chestnut Ridge Park holding hands, nose-to-nose. "I looked into his eyes and there was nothing, not even that smirky look." The emptiness saddened me. Was any of the "old" Chris still in there? "I wonder, Brent—does he know who I am?"

"He knows. He might not remember all the times you've had together, but he knows you're here as a friend. Sometimes I'll ask him, 'Chris, who am I?' and he answers, 'Brent.' And then I'll ask him, 'Who am I to you?' And most of the time he'll tell me, 'Brother.'"

"Does he see a doctor regularly?"

"I don't think so, maybe every four or five months. There isn't much that can be done, other than what we're currently doing. The pathway's certain. It's only the timeline that we don't know."

Up until that moment, it wasn't something I'd devoted much thought to—Chris not being around us, losing what we have now. I was still coming to grips with what the disease had already robbed from my friend—his words, his can-do, his uncensored humor, and his ability to do what we had done together for so many years. Still, I look forward to our time together in our new normal. Things aren't epic, but they're still worth savoring. They're little things now, some sad, some funny, some just so "Chris." Things like sitting on the bench overlooking a pond at Knox watching the storm clouds gather, or the way he smirks when he comes to that path in Chestnut Ridge Park we don't want him to go up, and then grappling with Brent when he attempts to guide him down. Things like walking up to a stranger and laughing for no reason (or so it seems to the rest of us), or greeting me with a laugh, a smile, and then giving me a hug.

Brent says, "Maybe we'll see you next Tuesday."

"Yeah, for sure." I hang up and realize I forgot to ask him, "When did you know?" I consider calling him back, but decide against it. Between all of my questions about Elko and his past strained relationship with Chris, I'll save that question for another day.

RECENTLY, RICK Ohler asked me, "When did you know that something wasn't right with Chris?" Since my conversation with Brent, I'd given this more thought. I haven't gotten around to asking Brent. We always have so many other things to talk about.

We know the cause of the carrot finger, and the punctured lung, and why they stopped the 24-hour mountain bike race Chris attempted to solo. In each case there had been an incident. This is different. I suppose it's like someone losing his hair, his hearing, some weight. If you're always around him it's hard to notice. You don't see it happening. But one day you say, "Hey Geek, you know you're getting a little thin on top." I was with Chris so much, I suppose it took me a while to realize he was losing a piece of his mind. He repeated stories, our plans for the day, or what toppings we were ordering on our pizza. The big laugh—the one we had always enjoyed, now burst from him at the most inappropriate times. His belligerence reached a level that many no longer wanted to tolerate. Most surprising of all, he was developing an unwillingness to accept physical challenges, to do two fun things in one day, or go off the trail.

I told Rick, "I think it was on my last expedition with Chris in March of 2015. It was on that trip when I suspected something serious was going on with Chris. He wasn't right." Back then my wonder manifested into anger, embarrassment, frustration, and was void of empathy. I didn't understand. I just thought he was being a jerk.

THE GEEK had organized a triathlon of activities for our winter weekend. Day One—cross country skiing at the Olympic track in Lake Placid, Day Two—downhill skiing at Whiteface Mountain, Day Three—snowshoeing to the top of Wright Peak.

Ten of us wedged into the Keene Valley Hostel, an unassuming structure with two floors. The sign near the road contains an amateurish painting of a hiking boot filled with snow leaning against a gray pot with a red ribbon and hand-drawn words that read simply: *the hostel*. Melted snow had frozen in place, curling off the front porch roofline like overgrown fingernails.

Inside, the spartan second floor is outfitted with ten cots, each neatly wrapped with a white sheet and a pillow—ten human envelopes. Downstairs includes the living room, furnished with comfortable well-worn couches and chairs, two bathrooms, and an adequately equipped kitchen. Chris bogarted the barcalounger for most of the weekend, flopping quickly into its reclining comfort as if we'd been playing an adult version of musical chairs.

Day One had gone well. There were no injuries (spinal or otherwise) and beers were flowing. Our group of ten included the Geek; our friend Jim Bebak and his brother Ray; Tim Buchanan, who for three decades counseled and mentored the youth of East Aurora at the Boys and Girls Club and through his hiking and camping club called Trail Camp; Chris; me; and four college-aged members from Tim's Trail Camp group.

I'd be remiss to not include a brief note about Tim. He was a great man who did so much for so many, while we learned years later, at the same time struggling to find his own inner peace. Tim introduced countless young people to what nature has to offer through weekend adventures in the ADK or easy day hikes at Camp Ska-No-Ka-San. For many it was their first taste of the outdoors. He reminded us, "There's so much more in life that you miss when you can't be exactly who you are." Sadly, we lost Tim to pancreatic cancer last year.[4]

Inside the hostel, Chris told all of us what we were doing wrong, what we should be doing that we weren't, and what, in his opinion, was "bullshit." He questioned me, "You're going to take a shower? Now, Jack? There's cold beer to drink!" *Nothing new to me; I'd heard that one before.* Jim's tidy ski boot bag contrasted with Chris's musty smelling equipment jammed haphazardly into a broken-zippered canvas bag. Chris was "gracious" enough to let Jim know how he felt. "Jeeesus, Jim, do you ever *use* that thing; there's not a speck of dirt on it." He belittled a Trail Camper's colorful ski jacket, "You're going to wear *that,* tomorrow? Really?" And then Chris would have another beer, another laugh, and look for his next target. The Campers did well to not be "taken aback" by our

---

[4] For more about Tim watch the film **The Long Trail Out** by Shai Ben-Dor at *www.thelongtrailout. com.* It's the story of a 70-year-old youth counselor and mountaineer. The film takes place on the Presidential Traverse, a challenging 23-mile hike known for its deadly weather, as he chronicles the challenges of his journey coming out of the closet.

friend. Piggybacking on Chris's overbearing presence, they locked onto his thirst to do the unthinkable, the disgusting, to break any and all rules. *Good luck, Trail Camp members, if you think you're going to get the better of our friend Chris.*

Recently, I caught up with Shai Ben-Dor, one of the Trail Campers that was on the trip. I asked him if he had any memories from that time, if he remembered Chris, and if he did, what he remembered the most.

"Oh, yeah, definitely," he told me enthusiastically. "That was my first winter hiking trip. I loved it."

"Did you remember Chris?"

"Oh, for sure. He had a very strong presence. On the snowshoe hike I remember there was a 'fast' group and a 'slower' group. He was always up at the front with the fast group."

"Yeah, that was Chris, always at the front."

"And I remember we were trying to get him to play the 'Odds Game.' We were playing it with Tim and he had to eat a big spoon of parmesan cheese."

"Oh, yeah, I remember that now. And do you remember the powdered cinnamon?"

"Yeah, Tim lost that dare, but I think Chris did it, too. Just for the hell of it."

Yes he did. Chris held back a cough that might have covered the Trail Campers with a cloud of brown dust. He downed it all—no water allowed. *Bravo, Chris, well done!*

I asked Shai, "Do you remember the pickled Brussels sprouts? I think one of you guys must have brought those."

"Yes, because it became a thing we did on other trips. Pickled beets, pickled Brussels sprouts."

"Do you remember Chris drinking the brine?"

"Yeah, that was crazy. I remember him saying, 'Why would I waste my time playing that stupid game? I'll just do it.' I think he drank two jars!"

The sprouts were a big hit and were quickly devoured, leaving only the brine. Chris, spying the jars that were three-quarters full of science-experiment-green liquid, levered the handle on the Barcalounger and reached for one.

"Chris! What the hell!" I watched as he put down his beer and sipped the brine. He gave me his familiar smirk accompanied by wide eyes. "You're going to rot your innards with that shit," I told him. He probably thought, perfect, Jack thinks I shouldn't do this.

"Chug! Chug! Chug!" The campers shouted encouragement to Chris.

He lowered the jar from his lips and swirled it like you might a fine wine. A vortex of sprout detritus circled in the glass looking like turbulent seawater. He held the jar aloft for all to see, savoring his moment in the brine's radiation-green glow. *Watch this, boys.* Inside the hostel, moisture ran down the windows, the smell of dank discarded socks filled the air, and we all watched Chris, like a contestant on *Fear Factor.*

"Chug, chug, chug!"

Brine up, brine in. Chris gulped it all. *Good to the last drop.* When he was done the hostel filled with hoots and hollers. Chris smiled before wiping his lips with his sleeve and slamming the jar on the little wood table next to the barcalounger.

"Chris, what the fuck? Why?"

I'd have done better to direct the question at myself. *Why?* I knew better. *Why?* Because few, if any, would do it. That's why. It was no different than jumping off the covered bridge of the Battenkill, riding the rocks of the Bent Rim Trail in Ellicottville, or suggesting to Rick Ohler they walk into town during a winter travel ban in 2015. The two of them didn't let a brutally cold wind, or the ban, stop them from visiting Rick's octogenarian buddy, Paul Fickenscher, in the "lockup," aka the nursing home.

Next up was skiing Whiteface. We got to the resort early; of course we did. Chris had no patience for stragglers, barking at everyone back at the hostel like we were in a race for our lives, "Let's go! Life is short!"

At Whiteface, the first ten skiers to show up are rewarded with the opportunity for "first tracks," a ride to the top with the Ski Patrol and a screaming run down the mountain before they let the masses on the lifts. Ski Patrol offered our group two spots. Chris and one of the Trail Campers declared they would do it. Inside the lodge we ate a hearty breakfast and leisurely waited for the lifts to open for the commoners. Chris laughed as he watched us eat, as if it was the silliest thing he'd ever seen. *Really, Chris? People eat breakfast you know. What's the deal?*

I asked Chris, "Aren't you supposed to be at the chairlift? You've got like five minutes before they go up."

"I'm not doing it."

"What do you mean you're not doing it?"

"You go."

What the hell? I couldn't believe it. *Chris declining a physical challenge?* At the time I only gave it a passing thought. I was mainly thrilled that it would be *me* skiing first tracks. I took the last bite of my breakfast sandwich, scrambled to get my gear on, and joined the others at the lift. Chris missed an epic ski run. I couldn't believe it.

There was more to come. If only I had known back then what I know now, it might have prepared me to be sympathetic, to understand, to not waste time on confusion and anger toward our friend. The information about Pick's is out there with a simple Google search: inappropriate actions (that had been happening for years, so it was hard to tell), a loss of empathy, diminished interpersonal skills, a lack of judgment and inhibition, a general apathy toward everything, a tendency toward repetitive and compulsive behavior (he hadn't yet found his imaginary stepping stones or his *rat-ta-tat-tat-rat-ta-tat-tat* beat), a decline in personal hygiene, a change in eating habits, a craving for sweets, and an oral exploration and consumption of inedible objects (I believe powdered cinnamon and sprout brine checked that box). And now I think of him trying to peel the hard shell off an acorn at the Ridge this past fall.

It's not like we weren't used to disagreements with Chris. He'd want to do *it* one way and we'd want to do *it* another. After a brief period of negotiation we'd compromise—and do *it* his way. This was different. After the hike to the top of Wright Peak, we poked at Chris. Knowing his disdain for spending money on food when it could be used for beer, we tweaked him, suggesting how nice it would be if he bought the group a couple of the homemade apple pies we'd seen advertised at the corner store in town.

"I'm not buying any fucking pies!"

He didn't get it. We were busting his chops in the same manner he'd done to us in the past when we'd forgotten to bring beer, even though there was always more than enough.

"Come on, Chris," said the Geek. "You told us you wanted some apple pie," egging him on while smiling at me.

"I told you, I'm not buying any fucking pies!" Chris became angry. His outrage was no longer accompanied by the big laugh; a mean spirit crept into the place previously inhabited by the keeper of good times. He seemed to have lost his joy.

The Geek headed into town, bought the group a couple of apple pies and a half gallon of vanilla ice cream. Chris descended on the first piece. "I thought you didn't want any pie?" the Geek declared, feigning a face of consternation while the rest of us watched from a safe distance. Chris scurried back to the barcalounger, cradling his pie and ice cream like a dog with a soup bone. The Trail Campers had fun with the whole thing—I'd had enough and the Geek had had enough, too.

I TOLD Rick, "That was our last attempt at 'epic' together." Perhaps the most telling was his unwillingness to rocket down Whiteface. To go as fast as you could. Chris lived for that type of thing. And his truculence had reached another level. It wasn't balanced with the joy he found in our company. You know, it was like when you guys invited Chris to join your annual fishing trip to Raquette Lake in 2015."

Rick had told me about that trip; a trip they had been doing for over 30 years and that year he asked Chris to come along. Chris should have fit right in; he'd known all the guys for years, went to school with most of them, had been on adventures with them, and hung out at the same parties. But according to Rick, it was a disaster. Chris was somehow "off." In a group where acting inappropriately should have been nearly impossible, he managed to be inappropriate. His humor was too nasty, his tone too combative, his spirit of competition too hard-nosed. He had no filters. Chris just didn't get it. His ways were completely different from the easy-going ways of these guys—LAYYD (Look at yourself, you're disgusting) they called themselves. Nobody could put a finger on it; he was just "off."

The underlying affection he had for all of us, what we had always counted on, was disappearing. Maybe Chris was like oil and vinegar. He had contained a unique, and at times mystifying, quantity of both. We accepted his vinegar because it was counterbalanced by the oil of his encouraging words and his push to make every day worth living. The mixture was becoming bitter; the oil was slipping away so all that was left was the vinegar. And I think about how he is now. He can still be stubborn, like when he wants to go one direction on the trail and we want to go another, but the belligerence is gone. I don't know if it's the result of medication, or just the next phase of the disease. I should probably ask Jennifer, but I haven't, not yet. Maybe it's best I don't know.

OUR LAST trip together to the ADK was almost over. We were north of Utica, on our ride back, when we heard the siren. Lights flashed behind the Geek's van. "Shit!"

"Geek, how fast were you going?" asked Jim Bebak.

"I don't know? I wasn't using the cruise control."

I felt bad for the Geek. He'd be taking the rap on this one and dealing with the crap that comes with a speeding ticket. It could have been any of us. Our minds were in other places; maybe subliminally the Geek was in a hurry to get home, to be done with the weekend. I told Chris, "When the trooper gets to the window, don't say anything. And don't laugh."

"Yeah, I know. Okay, okay."

The trooper stood next to the Geek's van, behind the driver's door, craning his head to get a better look at us. Snickering sounds leaked from Chris. It was subtle, but I believe our hard-nosed trooper friend was momentarily "taken aback," before he asked us the standard question, "Do you know why I pulled you over?"

"I guess I might have been speeding," the Geek gave himself up immediately. He's an honest guy. *Geez, Geek, you could have at least feigned ignorance; we're usually pretty good at that.*

"I had you going 75. The speed limit here is 55."

"It is? I thought it was 65," the Geek responded.

That's better, Geek. We're in a tricky speed trap. Maybe this guy will see we're upstanding citizens and let us off with a stern warning.

There was another snicker.

Shit!

The Geek received his speeding ticket.

"Chris, why did you laugh? I told you not to laugh."

"I didn't."

"Chris, you laughed."

Even for Chris, who has spent a lifetime stretching the rules and boundaries most of us live by and within, this was strange behavior. It called to mind another of Chris's evening phone calls to me, around that time.

"Hey, Jack."

"Hey, Chris. What's going on?"

"Have you seen the weapons those guys at the airport wear? Jeeesus!"

"You mean airport security? TSA?"

"I guess so. You should *see* the weapons they have."

"Yeah?"

Why are we having this conversation? There must have been an incident.

"I was picking up Marla from the airport and I walked by one of the security guys and he hollered for me to stop. He asked me, 'What's so funny?' I told him, 'nothing,' and started walking away. And then he followed me and told me to stand against the wall."

Uh, oh.

"He asked me, 'Why did you look at me and start laughing.'"

"Chris, you were laughing? At airport security?"

"I didn't laugh!" There was a pause in our conversation. I didn't know what to say. Chris continued, "I guess I might have smiled at him."

"Chris, why in the hell do you care what weapons airport security has? I'm *glad* they have guns. Christ, I'd be okay if they had flamethrowers strapped over their shoulders."

The call ended. Something wasn't right.

After the ADK trip, the Geek and I took a "break" from Chris. I look back with regrets because it's time we'll never get back. We could have been doing stuff together, stuff that we can't do now, stuff we'll never do again. Shit, if we could just have a nice little talk, a couple tree beers, I'd be good with that. After all, this isn't a story about the ending, it's about the middle.

I know I can't dwell on those missing months. Instead, my memory is drawn to a day last summer when Chris, Brent and I were hiking at Knox Farm.

Chris sat in Brent's truck clutching his root beer like it was his lucky rabbit's foot. "Come on, Chris, come on, Bud." I'd noticed lately that Brent often calls his brother, Bud. "If you're hiking with us today you're going to have to get out of the truck. Are you joining us or not?" Brent stood next to the open passenger door. Chris didn't budge. Brent pulled him from the truck. It's a game Chris plays with his brother; they're still competing.

Surprisingly Chris poured the remaining root beer on the ground and looked for a trash bin to dump the can into. I watched him from a distance. He lifted the lid on the box containing the park trail maps. *Nope, not there, Chris.* Next he opened the top to the dog poop bin. *Nooo, Chris, not there!* He dropped the pop can into the poop bin. I looked at Brent, we both smiled. *Okey, dokey, let's hike, shall we?*

The temps were in the 90s, but Chris wore a flannel shirt over his tee-shirt. "Aren't you hot, buddy?" I ask. "Why don't you take off one of your shirts?" Brent tried unbuttoning it, and for a moment Chris accepted the intrusion before swatting away his brother's hand. *Well, you never know when the weather's gonna change. It's always good to stay warm.*

We stopped to sit on the bench by one of the ponds. It's a regular stopping point for Chris. We watched dragonflies zip over the water; it's as if we had all the time in the world. I told Brent about the iridescent green dragonflies I saw earlier in the week at the Eternal Flame in Chestnut Ridge Park. "That's the green darner," Brent told me with confidence. The dragonflies zoomed with urgency as we lazily watched from the edge of the pond. A bass broke the water and snatched a dragonfly for lunch.

"Wow, did you see that!"

"Yeah," answers Brent.

When you're a fisherman, you've probably seen a bass eat a dragonfly a ga-

jillion times.

We watched another dragonfly become a fish's lunch and Brent advised me, "You have to Google the video, *Damsels in Distress*."

"What's that?"

"Just do it, you'll love it." I made a mental note.

When we got up from the bench, I convinced Chris to stand by the water with his brother. In the background the bright sky to our left contrasted with dark storm clouds to the right. I took their picture. Later I examined it closely; it's a good picture. Brent had a firm grip on his brother's shoulder so that he didn't scamper away before I captured the memory.

Near the end of our hike Chris motioned for two middle-aged women sitting on another of "his" benches to slide over so he could sit. Brent and I were 50 yards behind him so we were helpless to intervene, to explain that his brother and my friend merely wanted to sit and rest, just as they were. The women got up quickly and walked away. I could see them talking to each other; I wanted to run up to them and explain, but I didn't.

"What did you say to those women, Bud?" Brent asked Chris when we joined him at the bench.

Chris looked up at his brother, like a scolded child, "Nothing."

"I think you said something. What did you say?"

Chris shook his head sideways and looked up into the tree near us.

I felt bad for Chris, so I changed the subject, asking Brent, "Did you ever see the historical pictures they have over there?" I pointed to a building labeled with a sign "The Milk House."

"No, I haven't."

We walked to the Milk House and then took another walk, this time along the trails of childhood memories. Brent pointed to a picture of a Pierce Arrow car, "Do you remember this, Chris? It was on the property." He looked at another picture, "Do you remember this guy?" The Knox Farm information identified him as Lewis Smith, the stable manager of ESS KAY Farms (named for Seymour Knox—S.K.) Brent identified him as, "the guy that got all of us jobs. Do you remember, Chris?" Brent told me how, while working for the Knox brothers (owners of the Buffalo Sabres), he'd often be given a single hockey ticket to a Sabres game and would get others to drive him because the ticket came with a parking pass.

Chris answered, "Yeah," whenever Brent asked him if he remembered, but I'm not sure he did. What a time those teenaged Kelley boys must have had working there. Certainly there had been pranks that led to incidents. I'd love to hear some of those stories, but Chris wandered out of the building, so it was time to wrap things up for the day.

We walked to the parking lot. Chris headed to the barn twenty feet away, peed on the side of the building, zipped up, and glided toward where we stood waiting. "I'm not shaking your hand, Chris, but I'll give you a hug." As we said goodbye, the hatches holding the weather at bay busted open. I pulled my door closed as a deluge gave me a free car wash. The day had been a good one, a lazy July day that made me feel like a kid on summer vacation with a whole world to explore right in front of me. That's the way it has always been, spending time with my friend Chris.

The Kelley Brothers at Knox State Park, Daryl, Chris, and Brent - 2020

Hey, Jack

October 22, 2019—it's a date I don't want to forget, so I've written it down. As time passes it might not prove to be a big deal, but for now it sticks with me. It pleases me like the sweet taste of my mother's pumpkin ice cream pie, its flavor lingering on my tongue.

The weather is gloomy; it's been raining since last night. Prospects for getting out on the trail with Brent and Chris are fifty-fifty.

I text Brent: Any idea about the plans today?

He texts back: Looks like rain will persist. Maybe Knox Park at 1:30?

I haven't seen them in three weeks. The weather will have to step off. I'm not about to let it get in the way of our plans for the day. I hear Chris's voice from the past, *Jaaack, Jaaack, come on, life is short. It's going to be greeeat!*

The weather gives up, realizing it's wasting its energy. As I drive to Knox Farm State Park, a light drizzle hits my windshield. I can work with that.

Even though we've come from different directions, have different drive times, and Brent has to manage unplanned delays with Chris, we arrive at the Knox parking lot at the same time. It happens often. We're a timely group, the three of us. Brent backs his pickup truck into an open area of the almost empty gravel parking lot. I pull into another. A van separates us. I step outside, grab a yellow poncho off the back seat (in case the weather changes its mind), and hang the hood of my black jacket over my head.

"Hey, Jack."

I turn, expecting to see Brent. He's not there. Chris stands behind my car, smiling. He laughs while watching me struggle to get my arms through the sleeves of my jacket.

"Hey, Chris."

Have you ever been in a place by yourself, and you hear a voice? The voice speaks to you. You hear it clearly, or so you think, but then after a while you realize it's all in your head. There is no voice. It's just your mind playing funny tricks on you, replaying a sound bite from the archives in the folds of your brain.

That's what I heard, a memory, *Hey, Jack.*

I ask Chris, "Did you see your mother today?"

"No," he answers, looking at me as if I've asked him the most ridiculous question ever. I guess she and Don must have left for Florida. They head south every year during the winter months.

We start down the trail. "How was your party?" I ask Brent about the family picnic he hosted at his house a couple of weeks ago. He had told me he wanted to get everyone together before his mom and Don left town.

"It was great. A good turnout."

The rain stops and there isn't so much as a wisp of a breeze. The day is tired. It rests on our shoulders as we make our way toward the leafy woods. Brent and I walk side by side as Chris bolts ahead.

"Chris! Chris!" Brent hollers.

Chris ignores him, bounding ahead like Fido off his leash.

Brent steps up the pace. "Hey, Chris, are you going to be hiking with *us* today?"

There's no response. We close the gap as Chris marches forward on the slight downhill before the trail enters the woods.

I ask Brent as we walk, "Hey, did you hear Chris call me by my name? Or was I hearing things?"

"Yeah. That was a surprise. And he recognized your car when we pulled into the parking lot."

Maybe the shit feasting on his brain has taken a break. I'm realistic; I know the medical facts; there is no cure, no chance for recovery. But you never know; miracles happen.

"So I guess your mom left for Florida."

"No, not yet. Chris and I just had lunch with her."

And with that, my thoughts of Chris's brain recovering are gone. We spend the rest of the hike, keeping Chris in our sights. We stop by three buildings that once upon a time were part of a working horse farm. Green doors on a building that might have been a stable are covered with orange and red ivy. "Hey, Chris, wait up. Let's get a picture in front of here." I point at the colorful leaves. He stops, looks at us, and then walks away.

Brent hollers, "Chris! Hey, Chris, hold up! Jack wants to get a picture."

There will be no pictures today. *Jack and his fucking pictures.*

We come to the section of trail near Knox Road. Chris wants to exit the park and walk along Knox. It's something he's been doing often, but only when I'm with Brent. I don't know why.

"This way. We're going this way, Chris."

He smirks, "No, this way."

I point, "This way."

"No, this way."

And so it goes, back and forth, like we're a couple of six-year-olds. *You are. No, you are. You are. No, you are.* This verbal exchange isn't lost on me. It's a surprising amount of words for someone that answers almost every question with a yes or a no, or by walking away. In a small way it reminds me of the many times Chris and I would argue about the most stupid things. This time we went my way.

"Chris, why do you want to go that way?" asks Brent.

"Yes."

"But why? Suppose we go that way. What is it that you want to see?"

"I don't know."

I suspect he remembers walking that way, a familiar way home.. Maybe someday we'll take the road. Not today.

Back at the parking lot we say our goodbyes and I give Chris a hug. As I drive home I think of what happened today. It stays with me.

Hey, Jack.

Chris and Wally in front of the Eternal Flame Falls in Chestnut Ridge Park - 2020

The Smoke Bomb Incident

I<small>T'S A</small> T<small>UESDAY</small>, my standard hiking day with Chris and Brent, but it doesn't look like we'll be hitting the trails. The rainy weather is intent on altering our plans for this early day in May. I call Jennifer to make sure Chris is around. I still want to stop for a visit.

"Oh, I'm sure we'll be here," she tells me in a voice tinged with gallows humor. "I'm home from work today and Brent's here. I'm not sure what *his* plans are for the day."

"Okay, great. I'll see you guys in a little while."

An hour later I walk through their garage and knock on the back door. Jennifer calls from inside, "Come on in."

She sits at the small kitchen table; papers are scattered around her laptop. Life goes on. My eyes focus on the completed jigsaw puzzle on the island countertop. "I see somebody's been busy. That's quite a puzzle for little Wyatt."

Jennifer laughs, "No ... that's a big person's puzzle. Remember—I have a *big* "little" person living here."

"Chris is doing puzzles?"

"Oh, yes. He *loves* doing puzzles. And rubbing his hands over the smoothness when it's done. I think he likes the feel of the pieces when they're all neatly fit together."

I couldn't picture it. It takes patience and time to complete a puzzle. The Chris I had known wouldn't have taken the time to so much as dump the pieces from the box.

"Is he here?"

"Yes. He's downstairs with Brent."

I head downstairs. Chris reclines in his lounge chair. "Hey, buddy. How're you doing?"

"Good," he laughs.

I reach to shake his hand, but don't attempt a hug, afraid I'll fall awkwardly into the crevasse of the recliner. "It doesn't look like we'll be hiking today."

"Nooo." He stretches out his one-word answer before returning his attention to the TV. He holds the remote, scrolling through the movie options: Action, Black Action, Action Comedy, Adventure …

Brent and I talk for a bit before I return my attention to Chris. He's still busy working the remote. "What movie are you looking for, buddy?"

Chris stares straight ahead while Jennifer informs me, "He just likes scrolling. He's keeping the battery companies in business."

While Jennifer finishes giving me the lowdown on Chris's clicker obsession, Brent hollers, "Chris! Chris, are you stuck? The TV is waiting for your response. You have to choose something." Somehow he'd come off the movie category tracks. Jennifer takes the remote from his hand, pointing it at the screen and gets him back on course: Comedy, Comedy Drama, Crime …

"I saw a couple of the bumpers are missing from the kitchen counter."

"Yeah. Wyatt has been chasing Chris around in circles again," Jennifer explains. "Either Chris caught one on his belt or Wyatt bumped his head. Thanks for reminding me. I have to tape those back on."

I turn toward Brent. "Hey, do you know anything about Chris's Smoke Bomb Incident?"

"No, not really," he chuckles. "I was out of the house by then—at college."

"I wish I knew who was involved. I'd like to get the details about that 'incident.' You know, for the book. That's definitely worth a chapter."

"Hey, Chris, Jack wants to know about the smoke bomb. Who else was involved with that?" Chris shakes his head. "I guess he's not going to tell us who his accomplices were."

"I can't imagine how thrilled your mom must have been about that whole thing," I say to Brent.

"Oh, yes!" There's another chuckle before he continues. "Mom was on top of the world. There was significant blowback from that decision."

The word "decision" seems to be an odd choice of words. *Is that what Chris did, made a decision? A poor choice, maybe, or I might say a large scale error in judgment by the scheming mind of a teenager.* What I did know was that Chris planned and carried out said plan to smoke bomb our high school.

Brent and I talk about other things, his plans for fishing the Delaware River later that week and our hopes for better weather the following Tuesday. I look at Chris in his lounge chair; his eyes are closed, "Chris, hey, Chris, I have to get going." I nudge his sock-covered feet and he wakes up for a minute before closing his eyes again. This time I risk a fall into the recliner and give him a hug. "I'll see you later, buddy."

I WAS there on that day back in 1976, along with close to a thousand students, faculty, and administrators. But I wasn't involved. I swear! You could call me a well-informed spectator, but now, over 40 years later, it was time to do some investigating. The word "on the street" was that Paul (Wally) Sugnet knew quite a bit.

I text him: Do you know the details about the "Smoke Bomb Incident?"

A few minutes later he texts back: Yes! Since he and I planned it … his fucked up idea … I have started a list of our adventures, will expand on today and you can pick and choose which ones you want.

This is great. I have a source for the details.

A few days later I receive an email from Wally. It's two pages of bullet points listing the highlights and *lowlights* of their crazy times together. And I'm pretty sure these are the ones where the statute of limitations have expired. I hope he doesn't expect me to get to all of them. If he does, I'll have to tell him, as Rick Ohler would remind me, "Wally, I think you have to write your own damn book."

SEVERAL MONTHS later, Wally and I connect. He sits at the kitchen counter as Chris circles the island, following his invisible stepping stones. I go to Chris first and give him a hug, "Hey, buddy. How're you doing?" He laughs and walks away, down the hallway stepping stones. "Hey, Paul. Great to see you." We shake hands. Wally and I catch up on what's been going on in each other's lives. It's been quite a while. His voice is strained; it sounds funny as he pushes the words from his throat, as if through a thin straw, or a peanut is lodged in his windpipe. I want to ask what's up with his voice, but I think better of it.

"Wow, that was quite a list you put together of the things you and Chris did. Oh, my God, I was laughing my ass off when I read it. I could see it so clearly. You guys were insane."

Wally laughs, "We did a lot of shit together."

"I want to hear more about the Smoke Bomb Incident."

"Maybe we can talk about it at lunch. It doesn't look like hiking weather."

We head into town, deciding on Pasquale's. Wally and I sit down while Chris wanders around the restaurant.

The waitress picks up the other place settings, "There's going to be two of you today?"

"No. There are three of us." Wally nods to Chris walking between two tables near the back of the restaurant. "Our friend will be joining us in a bit."

"Oh." The waitress looks confused. I want to explain, but before I have the chance she asks if we want anything other than water to drink and lets us know about the daily specials.

When she leaves, I ask Wally, "Is he okay to be wandering around like that?"

"Hell yeah, it'll be okay. He'll join us in a little while." It's evident this is now standard operating procedure when out to lunch with Chris. I hope he doesn't grab an onion ring off someone's plate.

Chris sits down as the waitress comes back. He surveys the restaurant like he's watching an invasion of bees overhead. The waitress takes our order and looks at us when she asks, "Is your friend having anything today?"

Wally asks Chris, "Merle, you want anything?"

Chris shakes his head no. I worry about his eating. His legs are so much thinner these days.

After the waitress leaves I ask, "So whose idea was it anyway? You know, for the smoke bombs."

"His, of course!" He looks at Chris. Chris laughs, but I don't think he knows what we're talking about. We carry on as if he's not listening to what we're saying.

"By the way, you might have noticed this thing with my voice. I think it's allergies."

Noticed? How the hell could I have not noticed?

"At first I was thinking it was something with my cholesterol pills, but that wasn't it. We're still trying to figure it out."

How sad it's come to this, talking about cholesterol pills.

I start with the most obvious question, "So how did Chris get the idea in the first place?"

Wally draws a breath. "He was looking through a magazine—I think it was *Outdoor Life* or something like that—and he found an advertisement for military-grade smoke bombs. You know from one of those ... oh, what do you call them ... you know those places that used to have excess stuff."

"Army Surplus?"

Wally points a finger at me. "Yeah, that's it."

"Anyway, I think we might have been at his house drinking Golden Goebels and he showed me the ad. I remember him looking at me, you know, with that look of his, and he told me, 'We *have* to smoke bomb the high school.'"

"And what did you say?"

"I said, 'Okay.'"

Wally looks at me like I'd asked him a very stupid question, something like, if Chris had asked you to jump off a covered bridge into the Battenkill River with him, would you have done it? "So then what did you guys do?"

"We ordered the smoke bombs—six of them."

"I remember the actual incident was around June, but when did you start planning for it? And how long did it take to get the smoke bombs?"

Wally thinks, letting the memories rise to the surface. He appears to be enjoying this. With a smile he answers, "I guess it must have been late April." He doesn't say what year. He assumes I know that much. None of us could forget the year. It was our senior year, 1976. "It took quite a while for us to get them. No internet back in those days, no Amazon. Good old mail order. I think it was like three or four weeks before we got them."

Chris laughs as the waitress sets our food on the table. I can't tell if it's the sight of the food that makes him laugh or hearing Wally talk about the Smoke Bomb Incident. It might be neither.

"We planned the thing for weeks, recruiting at the Ice House (a bar on Elm

Street a short walk from Wallenwein's). I remember we had at least two meetings there."

I assume those recruited were of legal drinking age for those times, making it a prerequisite of the smoke bomb team. *Sure they were.*

"I can't remember who all joined us, but I could find out if you want."

A week after our lunch I received a text from Wally. I read it, anxious to find out once and for all who the other culprits were. I didn't want to incriminate, or in some minds, pay tribute to the wrong person or persons. Unfortunately, there was no further clarity on that point.

From Wally: Got nothing more from Patrick, other than it was Mr. Martina that caught them after they had hidden out in one of the media center side rooms. He was wearing his usual lab coat.

Another text comes minutes later: And Ed Bob said to contact Caz ... who I don't recall participating, but doesn't mean he didn't!

Later I check with Caz and he pleads the Fifth. I don't press it further. I don't think it's something he'd like Mary to find out about, even now, 40 years later.

Wally explains, "I didn't know it at the time, but while we were at the Ice House someone overheard us planning. It might have been Sue Wilson; you know her father was the police chief or something like that. So apparently the coppers knew something was afoot. I doubt that part of the story, but Merle (Chris) swore that's what he was told while being interrogated."

Wally is getting ahead of the story. I ask, "What did they look like? The smoke bombs." I had a picture in my mind of a super-sized cherry bomb. It wasn't as if someone had never lit a rotten egg smoke bomb inside a school bathroom before. That wasn't good enough for Chris; he had to ratchet things up a few levels.

"They were like sticks of dynamite ... with wicks on both ends!" Wally laughs, and stops eating. He extends an index finger of each hand, holding them over his plate to show me the length of a stick of dynamite, as if I needed a visual. *I get the picture, Wally. Jeeesus!* And then he tells me, "They were green," like this was an important detail.

I picture young Chris, holding the package from Army Surplus, ripping plain brown wrapping paper from a sturdy cardboard box, and prying open the flaps to get his first glimpse of the smoke bombs. Like a young boy getting a train set for Christmas. In this case, Chris would be using his "train set" like Gomez Adams, excitement building on his face as two engines hurtled down the tracks at full speed towards a bridge, pushing the plunger with perfect timing as the rest of us looked on in disbelief.

> *"You meant to blow them up?"*
> *"Of course. Why else would a grown man play with trains?"*

"Did you guys, at any point in time, think that maybe this wasn't such a good idea?"

"Hell no!"

Yeah, I figured. "What did you do once you had the smoke bombs?

"We planned who was going to light the smoke bombs and where. I had the library. I think the others were Dickie, George, Ed Bob, and Swapy."

"Wasn't there something with Silly String? I think that might have been the first time I ever saw the stuff."

"Yeah. That was Phase II of the attack. Patrick and Thad volunteered for that. There might have been others. I can't remember. The plan was for them to go in and Silly String the hell out of the halls after we lit off the smoke bombs." *What creativity! An artistic touch to the mayhem foisted upon EAHS.* "I was in the library and here's the thing—after all those weeks of planning, I hadn't given a thought to how I was going to attach the smoke bomb in place while I lit it."

"What do you mean?"

"I was in one of those cubicles we'd sit in and listen to music and stuff. I was supposed to light it off under one of those, but I had nothing to attach it with. So I went up to the librarian with the smoke bomb under my shirt and borrowed some scotch tape. Problem was—it was too heavy for the tape. They were like a couple of pounds apiece. I was fumbling with it when Wags (math teacher and our soccer coach, Don Wagner) tapped me on the shoulder. He told me, 'Cease and desist and come with me.' The jig was up. That was when the alarm went off!"

"I remember that. It was third period. The Geek and I were in Rozler's math class in one of those big rooms—Large Group B. We saw the smoke through the little window in the door. It was filling the hall!" We both laugh. On our cue, Chris joins in. "So what happened with Wags? Did he haul you down to Lawson's office?"

"No. When the alarm sounded he told me, 'Get out of here. I'll deal with you later.' So I took off down the hall exiting the building with everyone else. I think only two of the smoke bombs actually got lit. Whoever did the auditorium—it might have been Dickie—put it on a plastic chair which melted and caused most of the damage. Mr. Martina, seeing all the smoke, probably thought there was a fire and went into the auditorium to rescue whoever might have been in there. He was overcome with the smoke. That's my biggest regret."

Mr. Martina was the physics teacher. Most of us didn't like the difficulty of physics, but we liked Mr. Martina. He'd worked on the Manhattan Project. It was sad that he'd endured the risks inherent in building an atomic bomb, only to be temporarily taken down by Chris's Smoke Bomb Incident. I hadn't known anything about the internal madness these guys had created. My memories were limited to watching the smoke billow from opened roof vents as I sat outside on the berm along Center Road. It was a gloriously warm sunny day—a good day to be outside. However, now hearing about Mr. Martina, I think about how bad this could have been.

"They caught Thad and Patrick. They were the ones shooting Silly String."

"Yeah. I remember the cop car parked in the circle by the flagpole." We all watched as they shoved a couple of our classmates into the back seat. I was too far away to tell who it was at the time, but I figured one of them had to be Chris (it wasn't).

Wally remembers, "When they paraded Thad outside to the waiting cop car, he had his shirt up near his head and then everyone started chanting 'Attica,' which really wasn't funny. I mean we probably thought it was cool back then, but we were so stupid."

"Attica" referred to a prison revolt in 1971. Inmates in New York's maximum-security Attica Correctional Facility seized control of the prison and took members of the prison staff hostage to demand improved living conditions. After four days of negotiations with the inmates, state police officers stormed the prison, killing 29 inmates and 10 of the captive correctional staff members.

Recently I spoke with Thad about his role in the Smoke Bomb Incident. It's remarkable how much we all remember from that day, 40 years ago. The first thing he brought up was the Attica chant and then told me, "Do you remember? The students surrounded the cop car and started shaking it. And when they wouldn't stop, the cops inside told us, 'If they don't stop shaking the car and back off, we're going to have to blast them with fire hoses."

"So what happened?"

"They couldn't get everyone out of the way so they took us back into the school. I remember DJ (Principal Donald J. Lawson) saying that he was going to throw the book at us and then when he was done with us he said, 'Get them out of my sight!'"

Good Lord, and Thad was just one of the silly string guys!

What was wrong with us? I don't remember joining in on the "Attica" chant, but that doesn't mean I didn't.

Wally and I continue our conversation. "I thought I might have a chance to get away with it until I heard my name over the loudspeaker, 'Paul Sugnet, report to the principal's office—immediately."

"So then what?"

"I went to DJ's office. I was at a conference table with Lawson and Officer Wilson. They wanted me to give them names, telling me, 'You don't want to take the full rap for this, do you?' Hell, no. I confessed immediately, like a pussy. I gave them all the names."

"Did Chris know you gave them his name?"

"Yeah."

"He must have been so pissed!"

"No not really. He said they knew anyway. He let me off the hook."

That was Wally's story. I'd heard from others that Chris didn't take it well. Years later when he'd talk about that day he'd say, "Wally, that fucker! He gave them all our names." And I'd heard Chris took the offensive when they'd told him that he could be arrested. I could picture it. His body of work with authority figures over the years was consistent—he didn't ask permission, *or* beg for forgiveness. But the more I thought about it, I believe Chris's words were bluster. He wasn't one to shirk his comeuppance, not that he often thought his actions were deserving of a consequence, but in this case, there wasn't a doubt. He wouldn't have allowed others to be the only ones to take the rap for something that was his idea. Or maybe—he didn't want them getting all the credit. We'll never know for sure.

After listening to Wally talk about it from his vantage point I ask him, "Do you know where Chris was supposed to light his smoke bomb and if it went off?"

"You know—I can't remember. I can check with Dickie. He might remember."

I tell Wally to check it out, but it's not that important. By now I think we can all imagine a clear picture of Chris grinning ear to ear as he lit one end of the two-pound military-grade smoke bomb, and then the other, before pitching it into the boys' shower, or wherever his plan called for him to be.

"So what ended up happening to you guys after you got caught? Were you arrested?"

"No. We had to do community service. It was just Chris and me. I think we had to mow the high school lawn for a week and maybe had to paint the bleachers. We didn't really have much supervision."

I couldn't help but wonder who the idiots were, back then, that made decisions on discipline at EAHS. Letting those two miscreants on the grounds of our high school with little supervision was just asking for more trouble. The word Brent had used, blowback, conjures up ramifications, but in the end, trying to stop Chris from doing anything with simple blowback was futile.

There was never any criminal or malicious intent. He did what he did to push the limits, to do the unthinkable, to see what he could get away with, and to do what no one else would. Some people channel their creativity into painting, singing, or writing; for Chris, the Smoke Bomb Incident was his painting.

CHRIS AND Wally leave the restaurant as I settle up with the waitress. I explain things to her, "Our friend has Pick's disease. It's a type of dementia."

"I'm so sorry." Her smile disappears, replaced by an extended puffed lower lip. She looks toward the front door. "He looks so young."

We leave Pasquale's and drive to the Knox polo field parking lot. The rain has stopped and we'll try to get our hike in. As we walk, I ask Wally, "So Paul, let me ask you something. And before you answer, give it some thought, okay?"

"Shoot."

"Do you wish you would have known sooner about Chris? You know, that he had Pick's disease?"

He doesn't think about it. He answers me with authority, "Hell yeah!"

"I'm glad you said that. I was starting to think I was the only one that thought that way."

He tells me, "I feel like I was one of the last to know. Shit, if everyone had known, there might have been more understanding. I heard some bridges were burned. You know, because of Chris's crazy behavior."

There were so many incidents of his unhinged conduct. Like his uninvited visits to the offices of 42 North Brewing Company, where he sat at the owner's desk eating pizza meant for the employees, or the time he pilfered pizza and three Cokes while trespassing through his former employer's private box at the Buffalo Bandits indoor lacrosse game. I heard he'd sauntered into a friend's house, unannounced, during his family's Easter dinner, and had attempted to enter another friend's house, peered through windows, and scared the shit out of his girlfriend's young daughter. Thankfully the doors were locked. And I can't confirm this, but I understand there was an incident, involving the EAPD, with a former Buffalo Sabre who lived in Chris's neighborhood. It's only now, years later, that we've come to realize what was happening to Chris. His inappropriate behavior caused collateral damage, that, in some cases, was irreparable. We were hurt, ran for cover, scoffed, steered clear, laughed, because we didn't know what else to do, and we were left in disbelief. Those of us that were willing to forgive, to understand that it was the disease, came back.

I don't share any of this with Wally; instead I simply reply, "Yeah, there were a few incidents."

"That's too bad, man."

When we come to the buildings near the main entrance, Chris prepares to take a leak on the side of the administrative building. I holler over, "Hey Chris, do you have to go to the bathroom? They're right over there, why don't you go over there." I point to the building labeled "Milk House." Before it became a visitors' center, many decades ago, milk from the dairy barn was brought here to a foot-operated milk churn that separated the milk from the cream. Eggs were also boxed here, some being shipped south on trains. Today we'll just be using the bathrooms.

Chris goes in and shuts the door. He's in there for a while before Wally knocks on the door, "Chris, you almost done?"

"Yeah."

While we wait I ask Wally about his and Chris's nickname, "Why Wally? Why Merle?"

"One day we were just sitting around and decided we needed some nicknames. So I became Wally, you know like Pauly Wally and Chris became Merle."

"That's it?" I'm disappointed in his answer. "Why Merle? Is it for Merle Haggard?" Wasn't Chris a big fan?

"Yeah, I guess. That was probably it."

It's my turn to roust Chris from the throne, "Hey, Chris. You okay, buddy? You almost done in there?"

"Yeah."

Wally tries the bathroom door. It's locked. Chris has been in there for 45 minutes.

"Chris, unlock the door," I tell him without conviction. We hear laughter from behind the door.

Wally looks around. There's no panic as he runs his fingers along the top of the doorframe to find the little pin thing that will open the door, but there's nothing there. He walks over to the bulletin board where long push pins hold park information in place. He pulls one out and goes to work on the lock. Voilà, in a matter of seconds Wally has the lock picked. He opens the door and we're treated to Chris sitting on the toilet, pants around his ankles, first smiling at us and then, when Wally tells him to get moving, he laughs at us.

"Do you need a few more minutes?" Wally asks.

"Yeah," he laughs again and we close the door.

"It looks like you've had some practice picking locks."

"Hell yeah!"

We discuss sketchier times from his past when he'd acquired that skill and I tell Wally, "No wonder I steered clear of you guys in high school."

"Those were some crazy times." He thinks for a minute before reminding me, as if it's of critical importance that I remember, "You know—I was one of the original EAHS streakers."

"Yeah, I guess I kind of remember that."

I listen as he recounts the story. Surprisingly, Chris isn't involved, but it's a funny story. It's a story about taking responsibility for your own stupidity and turning it into something fun. *I'm sure Chris was very proud of you, Wally.*

"We were at Bwana's house. You know, on South Grove, near the Roycroft."

"Yeah, I remember!" Bwana was a social studies teacher at East Aurora High School and our class advisor. His house provided a 24-hour location for drinking and gambling for those so inclined. *Not good.* On most nights five or six students would gather at his dinky kitchen table, help themselves to a beer from the refrigerator and sit down for a game of low-stakes poker.

"He had a brand new car; I think it was an Audi. And he let me, Jeff Spring, Doug Hagen, and, oh, who else was in the car ... oh, yeah, John Fattey; he let us borrow the fucker. We were flying up Center Road to the high school to set up some stuff for Homecoming or something like that and my hat flew out the window. I jumped out of the car to get it and left the door open. I think Jeff was driving, and he backed the car up so I wouldn't have so far to walk once I retrieved my hat. I guess he didn't realize I'd left the door open, and while driving in reverse it caught on a telephone pole. It destroyed the fuck out of the rear door on Bwana's brand-new car."

"I never heard about that one," I say wondering what the hell this all has to do with streaking. "What did you guys do?"

"We streaked."

"Huh?"

"Yeah. The four of us raised money from the students, you know, like a couple of bucks each to get us to run naked down the hallways. Some of the teachers contributed, too. We raised over $1,000 to fix Bwana's car. I remember running down the halls and everyone was watching; some were slapping us on the ass."

"Yeah, I remember that now. So that's what that was all about."

Wally adds, "Later, when we got older, I called it strolling."

We both laugh. I don't tell him I missed his last naked appearance, but I'd heard about it from classmates. He'd strolled through our 25th year high school reunion at the South Wales Community Center. Despite being Chris's side-kick and "branching" out on his own, Wally has done quite well for himself in adulthood. He's been married for over 35 years (to the same woman), is a father of three children, and retired early from a very important-sounding job as a vice president heading up the industrial, science, and high-tech business segments for a well-known development company.

We turn our attention back to the closed bathroom door.

It doesn't look like Chris is coming out anytime soon. "Hey, Paul, I've got to get back to my house by 4:00."

"You stay with him. I'll run back and get the car."

I check in on Chris every so often. There's been no movement toward getting his pants pulled up. When I try to help he swats me away, so I wait for Wally. He returns in twenty minutes, opens the bathroom door, slams it closed, and in a few minutes they're both outside the door—Chris's pants pulled up and belted. He laughs.

I wait for it, wanting Chris to tell both of us it's all been a fantastic joke, like the Smoke Bomb Incident, that there's nothing wrong with him, he's been goofing us the whole time. But it's not a joke. We ride back to his house, not saying much as Chris finds the beat on his thighs. *Rat-ta-tat-tat-rat-ta-tat-tat.*

Me wearing "The Original" rabbit fur hat and Chris at Emery Park - 2019

Life is Short

So what do you think Chris? You know, about your stories? Did you like them? I know there are a lot more, but out of respect for the way you like such things, I've done my best to condense a lifetime of your "epic" adventures, hoping these will be enough to give people an idea of the kind of guy you are. I told your stories the way they happened, although you might have noticed I occasionally combined our many rides, hikes, floats, and crashes into composites for better storytelling.

Composites! Jeesus, Jack. Just tell them how we came up with the name, Angry Tuna.

I hear you Chris, but it's been suggested I leave that one between you, me, the Geek, and Caz.

Who told you that? That's bullshit. Put it in!

Chris, I'm not doing it. You're never going to stop are you?

Stop what?

Aggravating the shit out of me.

No.

So you didn't answer me. What do you think about your stories?

Chris? Did you hear me?

Yeah. I was just thinking about hiking up to Grace Camp.

Which time?

All of them. And how you never dragged the toboggan filled with beers. You were always too busy taking fucking pictures. And now you're fucking writing about it. Jeeesus.

I'm sorry Chris. There are people that want to hear your stories. And they want to better understand what you are going through now.

Who the hell would want to know about any of that shit?

Lots of people.

Like who?

People that know you. When they hear that I'm writing about you they tell me their own "Chris" stories, some of which I'd never heard. They'll say, "Hey, remember when Chris came up with that idea for … or what about the time Chris and I … Did you tell that story?" What do you want me to say to them if I left that one out of the book? Should I encourage them to tell their own Chris Kelley stories? There's probably enough for a Book II.

Jack, stop writing about all this shit and get out and do something.

I know, I know. I hear you. Just be patient with me. Okay? I have a few more things to say.

Chris, I gotta ask. Did you know you had this disease? I mean Jen said you never wanted to talk about it. And I remember you telling me, "I'm in the worst shape of my life." There were ample warning signs. Your penchant for repeating, the go-to stories, your new found craving for sweets, your willingness to argue about the most trivial topics (I suppose you always did that), and the obliteration of your filters. I'm sorry for the times that I didn't understand, for the times I was mad at you, and didn't want to be around you. I wish I had known, but I was too focused on trying to keep up with you, anxiously preparing for what was up next on your list of "epic" things to do. It's okay if you don't answer. I understand now. And I'm certain, even if you did know about the shit fermenting in your brain, you wouldn't have wanted to waste a bunch of time talking about it.

Jack, we don't have time for this bullshit.

There was riding to do, winds to tame, pranks to play, mountains to snowshoe, and always at the end … you say it Chris. I like when you say it.

Come on Jack, let's go. There's cold beer waiting.

I like how you took your "action figures" out of the box. It wasn't about preserving the value of material keepsakes. It was about living in the moment with us, your friends and family.

Action figures? Jack, what the fuck are you talking about?

It's a metaphor Chris. It makes the words more interesting. Just let me finish, okay? It makes me sad to see your "action figures" sitting motionless in your garage. Your mountain bike leans against the wall, caked in dried mud from a last ride; dull-edged skis hang between the studs, never tuned despite me badgering the shit out of you to get them sharpened; backpacks lie in a pile preserved with the musty smell of past expeditions; and footwear of all kinds litter the back entrance. Thankfully your original omnipresent rabbit fur hat, manky as ever, has been preserved.

Omnipresent?

Yeah. Omnipresent, it means you were always wearing it.

I know what it means, Jack. But why don't you just say I wore it a lot?

It sounds better that way.

Jeeesus.

You remember when I had Jennifer pull it out a couple of months ago? I wanted to take a picture of it, to safeguard its memory before it disintegrated to bits of soiled cloth and fur. Remember? That was the day we hiked Emery with Brent and I wore *your* hat. I paraded through the park like Babe Ruth had lent me his baseball cap.

I'm telling everyone your stories to remind them as you always reminded us. Say it Chris.

Life is short.

Yeah. That's it. You got me to do a lot of stuff with that little phrase. I say it now, too.

I like how you'd remind us in your "patient way" to get away from the TV, stop wasting time on stupid bullshit, put down our "fucking phones," that there's a bunch of cool stuff to *actually do* out there in the world instead of punching out texts and tweets (even though I doubted you knew what a tweet was), posing for fake-smile selfies, and living in virtual reality all "fucking day." You never let us forget. You never danced around what you said to us. It was always direct, and if you couldn't get through to us, you'd take a step back and charge us with a "battering ram" of your philosophy.

Jack, what are you talking about? Finish this fucking book and get out there!

I get it Chris. I know. Just give me a few more minutes. Let me just say it my way, in my words, okay?

Jeeesus.

I think what you are trying to say is: don't waste a minute, visit a long-lost friend, go to a distant relative's memorial service, reacquaint yourself with someone you've lost track of, take a hike in the woods (or a new neighborhood if you don't have a woods handy), play catch with your son. Do stuff. Know that your friends, your relatives, the people in your life aren't perfect. And if they were, they probably wouldn't be hanging out with you. See the good in people, soak up the essence of their company, and let the rest, the not so good, drain like silt through the bottom of a gold prospector's pan. Spend your premium time with these people, face-to-face; we remember how to do that, don't we? You just never know when the final buzzer will sound; there won't be any more tick-tocks to get your kicker on the field for a last second field goal attempt. The game is over my friend, my brother, my sister, Mom, Dad; I'll see you on the other side. How does that sound Chris?

Yeah, I guess. You kind of dragged it on a bit. I like the way I said it better.

Chris, I count it as a blessing that you're my friend, someone who's pushed me, someone I wanted to scream at for getting me into "this," someone who had so much passion for life that he raised me to places I couldn't get to on my own.

I'll say it again, my good friend. You were so right. Life *is* short!

There were times I was angry with you, embarrassed by you, times when I had to explain to those that didn't know you well, "That's just Chris being Chris. You just have to get to know him better. He means well and all. It's just sometimes he says things that ... well, you know ..." And sometimes they'd come back for another round while others asked, "Hey, how's the crazy friend of yours? You know the one we did that insane ride with down at ..."

And I answer, "You mean Chris?" as if there was any doubt.

"Yeah, Chris," they answer, "Man, that guy was crazy."

"Yeah, that's him," I reply, proudly smiling because I have a friend like you. And then I continue. "He's not doing so well."

"No?"

"No. He's got this disease. You've probably never heard of it. It's called Pick's." Then I'll explain the symptoms and wait for their response.

Why the hell do you tell them about the disease, Jack?

Because they want to know how you are doing. There are quite a few people that really care about you, you know.

What do they say when you tell them?

They might start out by saying, "That's a real bummer. I'm so sorry man." But mainly they have a cool story to tell about you.

"Yeah, it's not good," I'll answer. And then when I'm alone, I'll think about all the times we've had together, and the times we are having now, your family and friends coming to your assistance, just the way *you* would have if the circumstances were reversed. I see the blessing in the time we have now. You're still impacting others, bringing us together to rally around our fearless leader.

So are you almost done writing all this shit down?

Just about. You know, maybe I'm writing this stuff down for the same reason I drank Coronas with a lime in your presence. Because I want to and because I know it pisses you off.

The big laugh.

I've been a witness to your incredible family uniting to help their husband, their father, their brother-in-law, their uncle. I've seen Jennifer, a rock of stability, doing the things she does without complaint, keeping her sense of humor, being strong, and through it all, maintaining her responsibilities as a mom, a grandmother, a wife, and working Monday through Friday caring for others in her position as a program coordinator at Baker Victory Services. I've cherished being around your family that included me in so many of your special occasions; graduations, weddings, birthday celebrations, holiday hors d'oeuvres parties where Mar and I felt honored as the only non-family members. Do you remember what you said to Mar at one of those parties?

Nooo.

You told her, "Do you see why I love this family?" Mar was very taken by how much fun all of you were having and the love you have for each other. It stuck with her. Do you remember telling her, Chris?

Yeah. I have a great family.

And now, there is something else, a tragedy. But that same family is doing what you would have wanted, not wasting time feeling sorry for you, helping beyond expectations, and still getting out there and doing stuff, despite the current limitations.

A special place is being reserved in the great beyond for your brother, Brent.

Fucking Brent.

I know, I know. You guys didn't always get along, but how cool that we get out hiking with him almost every Tuesday.

Fucking Brent.

Remember that time at Chestnut Ridge when he hollered at you not to walk up the slope that leads to the big rock with the plaque honoring the park's land donor? Remember? And you did it anyway. You always get "stuck" up there, like a cat up a tree. You know what Brent told me when we were looking up at you? "Chris is teaching me patience. Who would have ever guessed?" The irony isn't lost on me.

Fucking Brent.

Admit it Chris. He's a great brother. I've seen how much he cares about you. You're pretty damn lucky he does what he does to help you out.

Yeah, you're right. Good deal. Thanks a bunch, Brent.

Rick helped me with your stories.

Rick?

Yeah. Rick Ohler.

Rick's a great guy.

And he's a damn good writer. I'm not worthy to hold his writing pencil.

I remember the time we walked to see Paul Fick in the "lockup" during a winter travel ban.

I told them Chris. Didn't you read that part?

Yeah, yeah, that was great.

Without Rick, you wouldn't be reading these words. We spent many hours sitting at the front window of Taste in East Aurora and at the back table of Spot Coffee in Hamburg, where Rick would ask me, "Are you sure you want to write that? Do you want to own those words?" He'd leave the question hanging, not seeming to care how I answered it. He knew what was right. It was up to me to figure it out. I told him during one of our times together that I wished I'd known sooner about your condition. I would have done things differently.

Like what, Jack? What would you have done? You couldn't have changed anything.

Yeah. That's what Rick said. I wonder if Wally and I are the only ones that wish we'd known sooner. I'll tell you what, Chris. I certainly would have been more understanding during those times that I didn't want to be around you. When you said something or did something that embarrassed the shit out of me, offended friends of mine you'd just met, and made me want to say, "Enough already." I would have understood that wasn't really you. And I would have been quicker to get you the hell out of the house for our hikes and give Jennifer a little break. We could have had a talk. I could have told you how much I cared about you, an actual two-way conversation. You've been a great friend. I just wish somehow there was an answer, something to reverse this horrible thing.

Jeeesus, Jack. It's not like you're going to fucking discover the cure. I'll just deal with it. Now quit your whining.

I miss those days that we got out there, did things, exciting things, sometimes dangerous things, ill-advised things. Unearthing what the day had to offer. You'd remind me, remind all of us: to do two fun things (sometimes three) in one day, to realize everything can't be solved with a spreadsheet or by looking it up on your phone, to not let our ski tips cross, to never look where we don't want to go, not to sweat the small stuff, to maximize angle and velocity, to laugh hysterically at anything, to crank our music to 38, and to salute each other with the toast, "Beers up, beers in."

For those times you led us, showing us what life has to offer, you were my best friend. It's because of you that my life is filled with stories worth telling, a friendship that endures, and memories that make me wish I could press rewind. Thanks, Chris. I love you like a brother. And one more thing, let's promise each other to keep hiking the trails.

Yeah, yeah. Good deal. Thanks a bunch, Jack.

It's a lot like fun—only different.

Chris and Brent at Chestnut Ridge Park -2019

Epilogue

It's a damp, rainy day in late October of 2020. We've finally resumed our Tuesday hikes we'd put on hold while COVID-19 savaged the world.

At some point I made a decision to follow scientific guidance and get back together with my friend. We're back on the trails, six-feet apart, following social-distance guidance. And I've masked-up on the few occasions I visited Chris at his house. It may seem like a small thing to others that have lost so much during the pandemic, and maybe it is, but I sorely missed my friend and our hikes together.

I try to think of something remarkable that happened during today's hike with Chris and Brent, but I can't come up with anything. We didn't even hike in the woods, opting to take the paved park roads to avoid the soupy trail conditions. Old Chris wouldn't have stood for such nonsense, but current Chris walked in front of us and didn't seem to mind at all. It's not that he told us with words. He had none for us today, but I could tell. We've been around each other long enough to know such a thing. He had good stamina going up Heart Attack Hill and laughed at everything I said when we'd stop for a break. It was a good day with friends.

Author's Note

THE PROCESS OF writing about my friend Chris took me on a wild ride. There were times when I enthusiastically pecked at my keyboard, remembering our times together, or in some cases recounted the memories of his family and friends. And there were times when I wanted to let my head slam solid against that same keyboard, frustrated by my struggle to give Chris's stories the words they deserved. And which stories made the cut? There were so many. I had to figure it out. I had to finish the book. After all, this was Chris I was writing about. He didn't quit anything.

What fueled me when I needed a boost were the interactions with close friends, friends from the past, Chris's family, and those whom I only knew through Chris. Everyone had a story to share with me. I'm thankful for Chris's mom who took the time to put her memories of Sandra Lee on paper. I'm thankful for Thad Rice sharing a conversation, from 45 years ago, he had with Chris after his stepfather died. I'm thankful for Paul Sugnet filling in the colorful details of the Smoke Bomb Incident. I'm thankful for Brent Kelley sharing his hurtful memories of the young Kelley boys' (short-lived, thankfully) abduction by their father. And I'm thankful for those I only knew because Chris was my friend. I wrote about Sam the Chinaman in the book and told you that I never knew his full name. I'm happy to tell you that, recently, I tracked Sam down. In the process of getting his approval to use his image in the book, I now know his name, Shaohai Yu. We talked for a half an hour. Sam is married with an eleven-year-old son. He's a peaceful man. I will leave you with Sam's words about Chris:

> Though I was usually left far behind during the ride, at least I kept riding with the team. Unfortunately, I did not get much chance to ride the mountain bike after leaving Buffalo, even though I bought a more expensive bike in Salt Lake City. The team is not there.
>
> Chris is wonderful not only because he was active, like riding a mountain bike or sailing his boat in Lake Erie, but also because he was a sincere person,

very frank but also very considerate, and had the spirit of exploring and taking risks. Besides doing fun stuff in his free time, he was a great worker and also a good boss. He always encouraged the people he worked with, always had enthusiasm in the job he was doing, and never shied away from giving his honest opinion. I never met another boss that compared to Chris after leaving Buffalo. He is unique. The more I work and live, the more I realize the inner soul is more important than any other skills or knowledge. I miss the days in Buffalo, the time with Chris and your guys.

Appendix 1

Menu:
- Home
- Class Standings
- Team Search
- Rider Search
- Fastest Laps

RealTime Race Timing System

Granny Gear Productions

2004 24 Hours of Snowshoe

Sat. Jun 26 &
Sun. Jun 27, 2004

Class Standings: ALL

1   display standings

Angry Tuna
team number: **140**
class: **Men's Masters**

18 laps completed
Elevation Gain: 23346 ft
Class place: 5
Overall place: 55

Rider	Laps Completed:
Dave Norton	5
Jack Livingston	5
Christopher Kelley	6
Mike Lazickas	2

2004 24 Hours of Snowshoe

Team: Angry Tuna
#140
From: Buffalo, NY USA
Class: Men's Masters (45+)
Team Theme Song:

Christopher Kelley
(Team Captain)
T-shirt size: large
Race Age: 46

Dave Norton
T-shirt size: large
Race Age: 46

Jack Livingston
T-shirt size: large
Race Age: 46

Mike Lazickas
T-shirt size: large
Race Age: 46

Lap #	Rider	Start	Finish	Lap Time
1	Christopher Kelley	Sat 12:00:00 PM	Sat 1:13:13 PM	1:13:13
2	Dave Norton	Sat 1:13:13 PM	Sat 2:32:59 PM	1:19:47
3	Jack Livingston	Sat 2:32:59 PM	Sat 3:49:44 PM	1:16:44
4	Mike Lazickas	Sat 3:49:44 PM	Sat 5:10:56 PM	1:21:12
5	Christopher Kelley	Sat 5:10:56 PM	Sat 6:20:44 PM	1:09:48
6	Dave Norton	Sat 6:20:44 PM	Sat 7:38:10 PM	1:17:26
7	Jack Livingston	Sat 7:38:10 PM	Sat 8:56:14 PM	1:18:04
8	Mike Lazickas	Sat 8:56:14 PM	Sat 10:34:01 PM	1:37:47
9	Christopher Kelley	Sat 10:34:01 PM	Sat 11:47:45 PM	1:13:45
10	Dave Norton	Sat 11:47:45 PM	Sun 1:21:45 AM	1:33:59
11	Jack Livingston	Sun 1:21:45 AM	Sun 2:47:08 AM	1:25:24
12	Christopher Kelley	Sun 2:47:08 AM	Sun 4:02:05 AM	1:14:57
13	Dave Norton	Sun 4:02:05 AM	Sun 5:35:29 AM	1:33:24
14	Jack Livingston	Sun 5:35:29 AM	Sun 7:06:52 AM	1:31:23
15	Christopher Kelley	Sun 7:06:52 AM	Sun 8:18:12 AM	1:11:21
16	Dave Norton	Sun 8:18:12 AM	Sun 9:43:02 AM	1:24:50
17	Jack Livingston	Sun 9:43:02 AM	Sun 11:09:12 AM	1:26:10
18	Christopher Kelley	Sun 11:09:12 AM	Sun 12:18:11 PM	1:08:59

Appendix 2

Published in the East Aurora Advertiser
February 6, 1975

The East Aurora Village Board grants a special permit to raise a pig in the village to Chris Kelly [sic] of Buffalo Road, citing precedent set by a previous decision by the board to grant special permission to a village resident to own a goat within village limits. Board member Charles Lamb is quoted as saying, "I think we ought to be as fair to pigs as we are to goats."

Made in the USA
Middletown, DE
18 March 2021